Sir Paul Lever was British ambassador to Germany from 1997 to 2003. During his earlier diplomatic career he specialised in European political, economic and security issues. His postings included service in NATO, in the European Commission, as chairman of the Joint Intelligence Committee and as EU and economic director in the Foreign Office. From 2004 to 2010 he was chairman of the Royal United Services Institute.

'In this cool, shrewd and richly detailed account of Germany in Europe, a former British ambassador analyses Berlin's rise to dominance. Without panic or illusion, Paul Lever is mercilessly clear about the decline of French influence in the EU, leaving Mrs Merkel's Germany effectively in control of a Union whose structures closely reflect Germany's own. "The EU is Germany writ large." But Paul Lever, confident in German democracy, thinks that this power will not be misused, not least because Germany has no clear idea of how the EU should develop. Europe suits Mrs Merkel as it is, and Lever – contrary to current pessimism and alarm – predicts that in 20 years the European Union will not be radically different.'

Neal Ascherson

'Timely and enlightening, Paul Lever's insightful book tells us why Germany is vital to Europe and why Europe is so essential to Germany.'

Peter Mandelson

'Paul Lever has had a long and close relationship with Germany, and knows it and its leaders well. His book is required reading in Britain, where we are astonishingly ill-informed about the country that will matter most to us as we negotiate our exit from the European Union.'

Lord Jay of Ewelme

'Few people can claim that their views on the EU's future, the UK's decision to leave and the priorities of the key player in the coming negotiations, i.e., Germany were formed on the basis of a long diplomatic career. Having been "our man" in Berlin at a time when British German relations were closer than they had ever been, Paul Lever can make that claim and his insights cannot be ignored by the politicians, diplomats and negotiators who will be charged with charting our, as well as the EU's, future in the next few years. Germany has succeeded in shaping the EU in its own image. Economic advantage and minimising competition trumps grander visions of military or diplomatic influence on the world stage. What will matter in the years to come is who will be in the EU and the single currency and what the EU decides to do as well as what it decides not to do. Germany is the key player in all these decisions.'

Gisela Stuart MP

'Paul Lever's readable and dispassionate account of modern Germany and what informs and drives its politics and foreign policy should be required reading for UK policy makers as they try to work out what Brexit means for us and our future relations with Europe as well as anyone who would like to understand Europe's most important nation better.'

Ben Bradshaw MP

EUROPE
AND THE
GERMAN WAY

BERLIN RULES

PAUL LEVER

Published in 2017 by
I.B.Tauris & Co. Ltd
London • New York
Reprinted twice 2017
www.ibtauris.com

References to websites were correct at the time of writing.

ISBN: 978 1 78453 929 0
eISBN: 978 1 78672 181 5
ePDF: 978 1 78673 181 4

A full CIP record for this book is available from the British Library
A full CIP record is available from the Library of Congress

Library of Congress Catalog Card Number: available

Typeset by JCS Publishing Services Ltd, jcs-publishing.co.uk
Printed and bound by CPI Group (UK) Ltd, Croydon, CR0 4YY

Contents

For Patricia

Preface

Following the referendum of 23 June 2016, the principal pre-occupation of the British government for the next ten years or so will be to secure a satisfactory withdrawal from the European Union and to find a new place in the wider world outside it.

When we in the United Kingdom applied for membership of the European Economic Community (as it then was) in 1961, it was France that decided whether, and if so on what terms, we should be allowed to join. President de Gaulle's initial '*Non*' was accepted without demur by the five other member states. So too was President Pompidou's subsequent willingness to open negotiations.

During those negotiations it was French concerns and interests which set the agenda. The European Commission was responsible for the talks themselves and for the technical preparatory work. But it operated on the basis of a mandate which was shaped largely by the French government.

Now that we are leaving, it is Germany that is in charge. The 27 other member states will agree the framework within which the negotiations will take place. But it is Germany whose voice will be decisive. The German government will effectively determine what sort of trade agreement Britain will be able to conclude with the entity which accounts for just under 50 per cent of its exports. This element of our economic fate will be in German hands.

There have been occasions in the recent past when Germany has exercised power in a way which was, to put it mildly, not appreciated by the British government of the day. Chancellor Helmut Kohl's agreement with Soviet president Mikhail Gorbachev in 1990 about the terms for German reunification dismayed British prime minister Margaret Thatcher, who was at the time determined to try to stop it. The German government's refusal in 1992 to intervene when Britain was forced to leave the European Exchange Rate Mechanism irritated Thatcher's successor John Major. But on the whole Germany has hitherto been an ally and a partner with whom we share many interests and instincts.

For the British ministers and officials in charge of our withdrawal from the EU, dealing with Germany as an adversary (for the negotiations will be largely adversarial in character) will be a novel experience. We will face directly the reality of German power in Europe.

We will face it in other ways as well. Germany not only dominates economic policy making in the EU, it also increasingly takes the lead on international issues. How the EU deals in the future with, for example, Russia and Turkey will be decided essentially in Berlin. For the United States, Germany will be the European power of prime interest and importance, as it will for China, India and Brazil.

Britain outside the EU will have to adjust to this new reality. We will still be a significant player in the world. Our permanent membership of the Security Council, our relationships with other English-speaking countries, our role in NATO and our military capabilities will remain important assets. But we will not have the authority or be able to exercise the leadership that Germany will have.

Not only will Germany's voice be decisive in shaping the terms of Britain's divorce from the EU. Germany will also determine how the EU itself will develop after we leave. Its membership, its powers and its policies will reflect the choices and priorities of the German government; and these in turn will be a product of Germany's history, its social and political structures and, above all, of its economic interests. Any forecast of how the EU may look in 20 or so years' time needs to be rooted in an awareness of these interests; as well as in an understanding not just of what German politicians say about Europe, but of how they behave within it.

Preface

*   *   *

The United Kingdom's relations with Europe, in both the political and economic fields, dominated much of my professional life. I was in Brussels when we signed the Treaty of Accession on 22 January 1972 – as was my future wife, whose job it was to mop off the ink which an irate British woman, a proto-UKIP-er perhaps, had thrown over the British Prime Minister's suit for his (as the woman saw it) surrender of national sovereignty. I served in the 1980s in the European Commission. In the 1990s I was the senior Foreign Office official dealing with the EU. From 1997 to 2003 I was the British ambassador to Germany.

Throughout this time I watched Germany's power grow, and overall I have admired the way senior German politicians have used it. Some, like Willy Brandt, Helmut Schmidt and Helmut Kohl, have been towering personalities. Others, like Angela Merkel, have more modest virtues. But nearly all of them have been people of substance and of distinction.

I enjoyed too nearly 40 years of dealing with German officials. Cheerful, open and competent, they were the best of colleagues with whom to try to tackle a common problem and the best of company outside the office. Many of them have become personal friends.

I am sorry that, as Britain and Germany will in the future have less to talk about together, my successors in the Foreign Office will probably not enjoy the same easy relationship with their German counterparts.

German power is unique in that it is not based on military might and is not something which Germany's own leaders take pride in or celebrate. It is nonetheless the underlying reality of Europe today. I hope that this book is a small contribution to understanding it.

𝍢 ONE 𝍢

Now We're Speaking German

In November 2011 a German politician, little known outside his home country, achieved his Andy Warhol ration of 15 minutes of fame by boasting in a speech that '*Jetzt auf einmal wird in Europa deutsch gesprochen*' ('Now suddenly Europe is speaking German').

Volker Kauder, the leader of the parliamentary group of the Christian Democratic Union (CDU) party, made clear that he was speaking figuratively not literally. He was not referring to the use of the German language: rather he meant that the German government's view on how to achieve economic stability within the eurozone – namely by eliminating budget deficits, raising taxes and reducing public expenditure – was now shared by all other European governments.

He was right on both counts. A survey published a few weeks after his speech showed that in the five previous years the number of pupils at European schools studying German as a foreign language had declined dramatically. In the Netherlands, for example, they had decreased from 86 per cent to 44 per cent. (In Britain the figures are even lower – to the point where some head teachers have begun talking about the likely extinction of German as a subject taught in British schools.) In the same month, at the height of the eurozone financial crisis, the decision was taken at a European Council meeting to begin negotiations for the so-called Treaty of Fiscal Union. The rules set out in the treaty were precisely those which the German government had long been advocating: binding legal commitments to balanced national budgets and to strict limits on the size of national debt and national deficits. There was speculation that once the treaty was in force Germany might be more open to other ideas for dealing with the crisis, such as eurobonds or more intervention by the European Central Bank. But no commitment of this kind was given by the German government. The message from the decision was clear: if the euro needed to be saved, it would be saved on German terms.

The treaty was eventually signed in March 2012 (by all the members of the EU except the United Kingdom and the Czech Republic). It established in legally binding form the context within which members of the eurozone have to implement their fiscal and budgetary policies, and it provided for supervision and sanctions if they fail to respect its rules. It reflects a view, not unique to Germany but prominently championed by successive German governments, of how national economies should be organised. Henceforth this view will govern the whole of the eurozone. No deviation from it will be allowed.

Since 2012 Germany's domination of policy making in the EU has increased still further. In the succession of crises which have hit Europe – Greece's bankruptcy, Ukraine, the refugee influx – it is Germany which has provided the solutions (such as they are) and Germany which has taken the lead in getting them implemented. It was Germany too which set the rules for the renegotiation of the terms of Britain's membership, and Germany's will be the determining voice in deciding what sort of deal the EU will offer now that Britain has decided to leave.

This is, for Germany, a golden age of power. It coincides, as it happens, with German success in the field which Europe's citizens care most about, namely football. In 2013 two German teams, Bayern Munich and Borussia Dortmund, contested the final of the Champions League at Wembley. In 2014 Germany won the World Cup in Rio de Janeiro. It was the semi-final of that World Cup, where Germany played the hosts, Brazil, which perhaps encapsulated the new era. Both teams were unbeaten and the match was expected to be close, with Brazil the favourites. Instead it was a rout. Germany scored four goals in six minutes, were 5–0 up at half-time and eventually won 7–1. The German team, modest and generous in victory, became national heroes. It really did seem somehow as though Germany ruled the world.

Ever since the establishment of the European Union (initially the European Economic Community – EEC) in 1957, Germany has been, along with France, one of its two most important members. The EU emerged from Franco-German reconciliation and developed through Franco-German leadership. Understandings, often implicit rather than explicit, between Germany and France underpinned many of the EEC's key decisions. The original combination of free trade and support for agriculture was one example of such an implicit understanding. The endorsement of German reunification and the commitment to a single currency was another.

For the first 40 years or so of the EU's existence the French and German economies were comparable in size. Though the German economy performed better in terms of growth and GDP per head, the difference was not such as to call into question the credibility of France as an equal partner in the management of Europe. Reunification of Germany in 1990 changed the numbers. Germany acquired 20 million more citizens and a third more territory. Still, even during the first two decades after reunification, the appearance of equality of status between France and Germany was retained. The proposal for a Fiscal Union Treaty was made jointly by the chancellor of Germany, Angela Merkel, and the French president, Nicolas Sarkozy. The term 'Merkozy' acquired a temporary vogue as a denominator of Europe's source of power.

In reality it was Germany which was by then calling the shots. The relationship between Germany and France had become that of senior and junior partner. French ideas and initiatives were listened to and, to the extent that they were compatible with German interests, the German government sought to accommodate them. But France could not push through EU policies to which the German government was opposed.

The election of François Hollande as president of France in April 2012 made this clear. Hollande did not challenge the Fiscal Treaty as such, even though he had criticised it during his presidential election campaign. Rather, he sought to complement it with measures to foster growth. Among these he included some form of common responsibility by the eurozone as a whole for individual members' national debts. He even, at the European Council in June 2012, lined up with the prime ministers of Italy and Spain to put pressure on the German Chancellor to go down this road (something which no previous French president would ever have done in such a public way). For a time there were articles in the German press about Angela Merkel being outmanoeuvred or isolated.

There was indeed some softening of the German government's position. The European Central Bank was allowed to pursue a more activist policy on the bond markets and the scope of the European Stability Mechanism, the fund set up in 2012 to provide financial assistance to eurozone members in temporary financial difficulty, was expanded. But these were essentially measures to deal with short-term problems. Even within Germany there was recognition that, if a collapse of the euro was to be avoided, steps needed to be taken which would involve exposing Germany to further financial risk. What did not change was Germany's determination to ensure that, once the short-term problems had been managed, no member of the euro would ever again be able to behave irresponsibly. Whatever concessions the German government may be prepared to make in order to deal with the legacy of others' past mismanagement have made it even more insistent on the need for rectitude in the future.

The relationship with France has been a casualty of this determination. President Hollande's reluctance, to put it mildly, to buy into the mantra of austerity, and the stagnation of the French economy, mean that France is no longer Germany's natural partner of choice in discussions about European economic governance. From time to time German politicians muse publicly over the need to revitalise the Franco-German relationship but there seem now to be few areas in which the two countries share genuine interests or instincts.

This is likely to become evident in the discussions about how to negotiate with Britain over the terms of its withdrawal from the EU. The German government sees it as a major blow for Europe but will want to come to some agreement on trade relations which will preserve access for Germany's manufacturing exports to the British market (though its main priority will be to preserve the integrity of the EU's fundamental principles, including the rules on free movement). The French, while professing regret, see Britain's departure more as an opportunity to obtain political and economic advantage.

There had been hopes in some quarters in Europe that the federal German election in September 2013 might produce a change in the German approach to the eurozone. Some commentators optimistically forecast that Chancellor Merkel's insistence on budgetary rigour had been maintained for reasons of domestic politics and that once the election was out of the way she, or her successor, would soften Germany's stance.

The election did indeed change the German political landscape. Angela Merkel's party, the Christian Democratic Union, and its Bavarian sister party, the Christian Social Union (CSU), achieved an impressive 42 per cent of the popular vote, their highest total since the post-reunification election of 1990. With 311 seats in the Bundestag they were only five short of an absolute majority. It was for Mrs Merkel a huge personal triumph.

But it left her with no obvious political allies with whom to form a government. The Free Democrat Party (FDP), with which the CDU/CSU had previously been in coalition, failed to reach the threshold of 5 per cent of the vote needed to qualify for representation in the Bundestag. Hence the choice was between the Green Party and the Social Democrats (SPD); after preliminary negotiations with both, Mrs Merkel opted for a so-called Grand Coalition with the SPD, thus repeating the model she had experienced as chancellor between 2005 and 2009.

The negotiations for the Grand Coalition's government programme lasted for over two months. The SPD was able to secure the inclusion of a number of commitments to which it was wedded, notably the introduction for the first time in Germany of a national minimum wage. The strength of the SPD's position in the negotiations did not reflect a particularly successful election result on its part. With 25.7 per cent of the vote and 193 seats, it improved only marginally on its dismal performance of 2009. But it was able to point to the fact that overall there was in the Bundestag a 'Red/Red/Green' majority. The SPD, the Greens and Die Linke (the party of the far left) had between them 320 seats. But neither the SPD nor the Greens were willing to share power with a party which, in the eyes of most Germans, is the direct successor of the communist party of the former German Democratic Republic.

But though on domestic issues the Grand Coalition's government programme had a social democrat tinge to it, on European policy there was little change. The German government would continue to oppose any pooling of EU member states' debts and would press for binding legal commitments obliging them to respect the eurozone's budgetary rules. In this field the Iron Chancellor, as Angela Merkel is sometimes described (in homage to Bismarck), maintained her policy, and also retained in office the finance minister, Wolfgang Schäuble, who was directly associated with it. It is a policy which reflects the mainstream of German public opinion. There are no calls in Germany for a more generous approach to those EU countries which have got themselves into financial difficulties (just as there are no calls for a generous treatment of Britain following its decision to withdraw from the EU). Indeed, the public mood is if anything tougher than that of the government.

* * *

Germany's formal position under the European treaties is no different to that of any other member state – it is in theory up to the European Commission to make proposals and for the European Council and the European Parliament to take decisions. But in practice it is Germany's view which is sought by the Commission before it acts, and by other governments before they decide.

Without Germany's support it is now virtually impossible to secure change in Europe of any significant kind. This became apparent in the discussions over who should succeed José Manuel Barroso as president of the Commission at the end of 2014. The procedure for appointing a new Commission president is set out in the EU Treaty in ambiguous terms. In the past it was the European Council – that is, the heads of government of the member states – who made the choice by consensus among themselves. But, according to the most recent revision of the treaty, the version signed at Lisbon in 2007, the Council, acting by qualified majority, makes a nomination 'taking account of the results of the European elections', which then has to be agreed, or rejected, by a simple majority of the European Parliament.

In the run-up to the 2014 European elections, the German president of the Parliament, Martin Schulz, sought to force the Council's hand. He persuaded the members of the Socialist group in the Parliament, of which he had himself previously been the leader, to select him as the *Spitzenkandidat* (top candidate) of the group, meaning that he was the group's choice to be the next president of the Commission.

This is, of course, exactly what happens in elections in Germany. Each party, or at any rate each of the main parties, identifies in the six months or so before an election the individual whom they propose as federal chancellor or, in the case of a *Land* (province) election, minister president. Everyone knows therefore for whom they are voting.

At the time when Schulz launched his initiative the Socialists appeared to be doing well in the polls in many European countries and it seemed likely that they would be the largest group in the European Parliament. But it was not just the prospect of personal advancement which motivated him. He wanted to establish the principle that it was the European Parliament, not the Council, which should determine the choice of Commission president. He regards the European Parliament, not the parliaments or governments of the member states, as the source of democratic legitimacy in the EU.

The other big group in the European Parliament, the European People's Party (EPP), soon followed suit and nominated the former long-serving prime minister of Luxembourg, Jean-Claude Juncker, as its candidate. The EPP is a collection of Christian Democrat and right-of-centre parties which, like its socialist counterpart, traditionally favours more integration within the EU, with the eventual goal of creating a federal European state.

The other feature which the two groups have in common is that they are both dominated by their German members. In both of them the German parties usually form the largest national contingent (although in the 2014 election the Italian Socialists, who performed particularly well, obtained more seats than their German colleagues), and they regularly provide the leadership of the group. This happened again in 2014. Both the EPP and the Socialists elected Germans as their leaders. And they agreed, as their predecessors had on previous occasions, that they would share the presidency of the Parliament between them for the next five years.

Angela Merkel did not particularly care for Jean-Claude Juncker. She had supported his selection as the *Spitzenkandidat* of the EPP mainly in order to frustrate the candidature of his rival, the former French commissioner and foreign minister Michel Barnier. Barnier, though a conservative, might have had views on the euro which reflected a French perspective. Juncker, on the other hand, was a Luxembourger and thus more sensitive to German concerns and more biddable.

Nonetheless, when it turned out that the EPP had secured the highest number of votes (although fewer than at the previous election and well short of a majority), Angela Merkel clearly did not regard Juncker as having any automatic right to the job. Both before the election and afterwards she made a point of recalling that, though the Parliament had the last word, it was for the Council to make the initial nomination. On 27 May, five days after the election, she said that she wanted a 'broad tableau' of candidates from which the European Council might choose.

Other heads of government also had their doubts about Juncker and about the procedure which the European Parliament had adopted. Indeed, it was hard to find a single one of them who was prepared to argue that on the grounds of personal merit Juncker was the best man for the job.

The prime minister of the United Kingdom, David Cameron, was the most vociferous in his criticism – though he was tactically inept in focusing on the individual rather than on the substance of the changes he thought were required in EU policies (playing the man rather than the ball, as a former permanent secretary of the Foreign Office put it) and in appearing to threaten that selecting Juncker would make it harder for Britain to remain an EU member. But several others, for example the prime ministers of the Netherlands, Sweden and Hungary, said publicly that they did not think Juncker was the right choice, and others were alleged to have shared such doubts privately. So for a time it looked as though the Council might consider other names.

Then Angela Merkel changed her mind. She came under pressure both from senior members of her own party and from the Social Democrats. In both cases the motive was not any particular regard for Juncker himself. It was a determination to ensure that the primacy of the European Parliament in making the appointment was established. The Social Democrats preferred to support the *Spitzenkandidat* from the opposing group rather than explore options which might have involved another Socialist.

Juncker also received, unexpectedly, the support of *Bild*, the newspaper with the largest circulation in Europe. The editorial demanding that he be appointed in the interests of democracy was written not by the paper's editor but by the chief executive of the Axel Springer group, the paper's owner. This led to allegations, never substantiated, that Juncker had privately given assurances that he would be sympathetic to the complaints which the Axel Springer group were making on competition grounds about the dominance of Google in certain fields.

It seemed to matter little that Juncker's name and face had not featured at all in the campaign literature published in Germany and that few Germans knew who he was. Nor that his rival *Spitzenkandidat* had run in Germany a purely nationalist campaign under the slogan '*Nur wenn Sie Martin Schulz und die SPD wählen, kann ein Deutscher Präsident der EU Kommission werden*' (Only if you vote for Martin Schulz and the SPD can a German become president of the European Commission). The issue in Germany had become one of euro-ideology.

It was an issue of internal party politics too. The two parties in the governing coalition negotiated not only about who should be the president of the Commission, but about who should become the president of the European Parliament. They seemed to take it for granted that whatever they agreed between themselves would indeed determine the outcome. The other 27 member states could, given Germany's dominant influence in both the European Council and the Parliament, be expected to fall in line with whatever was decided in Berlin.

Once it became clear that the German government was, after all, going to support Juncker and was not interested in discussing any other possible candidate, opposition to him melted away. Some countries, such as France and Italy, which had previously sat on the fence, tried to secure private deals over the interpretation of the Fiscal Treaty as the price for their support. Others, like Sweden and the Netherlands, which had expressed opposition, indicated that they would now go with the flow, hoping perhaps that this might help secure them a more important post for their commissioner. Only the British and Hungarian prime ministers maintained their position and voted against.

The outcome was widely, and rightly, characterised as a humiliating defeat for David Cameron and for the United Kingdom. A president of the Commission took office for whom not a single person in Britain had voted, whose candidacy was opposed not only by the British government but by all the main political parties and who did not, as far as is known, receive the support of a single British member of the European Parliament. A significant transfer of power from the member states to the Parliament happened without the member states being prepared to oppose it.

It was also a demonstration of the power which Germany, and Germany's Chancellor, now exercises within the EU. So long as the position of the German government remains open, discussion and argument can thrive. But once that position is decided, it is usually the end of the matter. No one, it seems, has any appetite for challenging the German government once it has made up its mind.

It is unlikely that the appointment of Jean-Claude Juncker featured prominently in the thinking of the voters who opted for 'Leave' in the British referendum on membership of the EU. They were more focused on domestic concerns, principally immigration. But it did illustrate the underlying dilemma of Britain's position in the EU before the decision to leave was taken: completely without influence in the European Parliament and with no ability to persuade its fellow Council members to resist the Parliament's grab for power.

*   *   *

Since his appointment, Juncker has done nothing to dispel the impression of sensitivity, if not subservience, to German interests. He selected an ambitious and abrasive German, Martin Selmayr, to be his chief of staff, and in his reorganisation of senior official posts in the Commission, six Germans were appointed to be directors general, more than any other nationality. In addition, many other commissioners followed Juncker's example by appointing Germans to key positions in their private offices. The Commission services, originally French in their culture and later containing a cadre of impressive British officials, are now firmly under German influence. So too are the policies and initiatives which the Commission gener-ates – particularly in relation to the two issues which dominated the EU agenda during the first part of its term of office, namely the handling of Greece's relationship with the euro and the response to the refugee crisis in the Mediterranean.

The Greek sovereign debt crisis began in late 2009. It was one of five such phenomena in Europe, but by far the most serious. In the years between then and 2015, Greece received two injections of emergency financial aid from the European Stability Mechanism and its forerunner. As a condition of these bail-outs Greece was obliged to accept a range of measures limiting its public expenditure, raising its tax revenue and reforming its economy. The two main political parties, the socialist PASOK and the conservative New Democracy, had accepted, albeit reluctantly, the conditions involved.

But in January 2015 the parliamentary election in Greece was won by Syriza, a party which had campaigned against the austerity measures. Its slogans and election manifesto had a particularly anti-German tinge. They demanded, among other things, that Greece in 2015 should have its debts cancelled in the way that Germany's debts had been cancelled in 1953, and/or that Germany should pay reparations for the damage to the Greek economy in World War II. Once in government Syriza modified its anti-German rhetoric, but still demanded substantial changes to the bail-out conditions. It argued that unless the Greek economy was given more scope to grow, the country would be unable to pay back its debts.

The sight of the young tieless new Greek ministers arguing fluently for a different approach to the eurozone's problems was at one level quite refreshing. It was not their party which had got Greece into the mess it was in. Their condemnation of the corruption which had been endemic in Greek political and economic life for decades was undoubtedly sincere. Their argument that Greece could only repay its debts if its economy was allowed to grow was one which many economists endorsed.

It found only a limited echo elsewhere in the eurozone. The Italian prime minister, Matteo Renzi, sounded sympathetic and indicated his support for extending the period within which the debt had to be repaid. The French President spoke of the need for compromise and implied that France might have a key role to play in the search for one.

But nobody endorsed the idea of a debt write-off. And nobody made any specific proposal for how to respond to the new Greek government's demands until Angela Merkel had spoken.

As so often, she took her time. But from the outset she and the German finance minister, Wolfgang Schäuble, indicated her priorities. She emphasised the need for Greece to stick to the programme of internal reform to which it was committed. She ruled out any cancellation of Greece's debts. She did indicate, though, her willingness to consider a third bail-out package to help re-capitalise Greek banks. The parameters of any new agreement were thus made implicitly clear by the German government. Any further financial support for Greece would be dependent on reforms to Greece's economy which would ensure that in future its budgets would be balanced and its statistics reliable.

None of the other member states of the eurozone criticised the German position. None of them offered anything other than muted sympathy of a general kind for the position of the Greek electorate. Their position seemed to be that it was up to the German government to decide what, if anything, was to be offered.

Given that German taxpayers would have to bear the financial brunt of any changes to the terms of Greece's debt repayment, such reticence was understandable. And there were good objective reasons for not letting Greece off the hook: others might then ask for similar treatment, the Greek economy could only survive in the eurozone if reforms to its competitiveness were implemented, and member states should not be allowed unilaterally to renege on their commitments.

Nevertheless, both President Hollande of France and Prime Minister Renzi of Italy – as well as Pierre Moscovici, the (French) commissioner for economic affairs – had previously been critical of the terms of the Fiscal Treaty. Hence, their acquiescence in an approach which offered no more than minimal concessions to a country that was undergoing a clear economic catastrophe was striking.

As the Greek crisis deepened, and the negotiating atmosphere worsened, German control of the terms of any deal became more apparent. If the Greeks thought that by going to the brink they could get Germany's position to soften, or get other eurozone members to argue publicly for a less harsh line, they miscalculated. Their

Prime Minister's ploy of calling a referendum on the terms offered by Greece's creditors backfired. The German government remained unmoved and indicated that it was ready if necessary to walk away from the negotiating table. Wolfgang Schäuble tabled a document which, for the first time, identified a temporary Greek exit from the euro as one option to be considered.

Meanwhile, Greek citizens were unable to withdraw more than 60 euros a day from their accounts and it looked as though some Greek banks would have to declare themselves insolvent. The French government was desperate for Greece to remain in the euro and sent a team of experts to Athens to offer advice. But the advice was about what Greece would have to do to satisfy German demands. It was probably not what the Greek government wanted to hear.

The result was a capitulation. At an acrimonious meeting of eurozone heads of government on 11–12 July 2015 – described by some participants as the most brutal which the EU had ever experienced – the Greek government was forced to choose either to leave the euro or to accept austerity measures much more stringent than those which its citizens had rejected in a referendum only a week previously. The Greek Prime Minister opted bitterly for the latter.

The humiliation of Greece was rubbed in by the sequencing of the implementation of the deal. The Greek parliament was obliged to enact the key pieces of legislation incorporating the reforms demanded of it within three days, before any negotiations on the size and nature of the bail-out could start. There was no mention of the other Greek demand, namely for some element of long-term debt relief.

The Greek government's negotiating tactics had annoyed all its partners. Christine Lagarde, the head of the International Monetary Fund, at one point memorably remarked that the discussions would not make any more progress until there were adults in the room. But it was the German Finance Minister who was most critical of them. He made no secret of the fact that he did not trust the Greek government to do what it had promised: hence the need for the legislation to be in place first.

President Hollande of France emphasised throughout his determination that Greece should stay in the euro. He sought in private to persuade Chancellor Merkel to soften somewhat her stance. They certainly spent a lot of time together before and during the summit meeting. They conducted many joint meetings with the Greek Prime Minister. But there was little sign that France's views had much effect. The French position was that Greece had to be kept in the euro at all costs. For the German government, Greece's membership had, by the time of the meeting on 11–12 July, become of questionable value. The Germans did not seek to force the Greeks out but they made it clear that if the Greeks chose to leave, Germany would not try to stop them, and that if they wanted to stay it would have to be on the terms which Germany laid down.

Tellingly, President Hollande never made any public criticism of Germany's position, nor were there any last-minute French proposals for resolving the deadlock. Whatever his personal misgivings, President Hollande seems to have concluded that it was better to go along with whatever Germany demanded than to risk a political rebuff. The same was true of others, such as the Prime Minister of Italy, from whom Greece might have hoped for more understanding. They realised that if the German position was firm, neither they nor anyone else was going to change it.

The negotiations with the Greek government were conducted by the eurogroup, the eurozone's finance ministers under the chairmanship of Jeroen Dijsselbloem from the Netherlands, with the participation of the European Central Bank and the International Monetary Fund. Dijsselbloem's instincts were similar to those of the German government, and his frustrations over the performance of Greek ministers just as strong. But at the key moments it was Wolfgang Schäuble, his German counterpart, whose voice was authoritative.

The Commission, by contrast, played no serious role at all. Jean-Claude Juncker made a few general statements about the need to find a solution but he made no specific proposals for what the solution should be. He indicated, by such omission, that this was something for the German government to decide. When his chief of staff commented on Twitter that a response from the Greek government was encouraging, he was promptly, and publicly, slapped down by Schäuble and told to shut up.

As federal chancellor, Angela Merkel had the decisive voice in deciding Germany's policy towards Greece. Her party, and above all her Finance Minister, would have preferred an even tougher approach. As the crisis progressed, Schäuble's ratings in the opinion polls recording the popularity of German politicians overtook Angela Merkel's for the first time. When it came to the vote in the Bundestag authorising the opening of negotiations with Greece for a third bailout package over 50 members of her party voted against.

* * *

In her attitude towards Greece, Angela Merkel represented the mainstream of German public opinion and was consistent in her approach. In dealing with the refugee crisis in the summer of 2015 her touch was much less sure. But, once she had announced what she wanted the EU to do, the Commission made the corresponding proposal and, despite bitter opposition from four countries in Central and Eastern Europe, the Germans got their way.

Illegal migration across the Mediterranean into countries of the EU – principally Greece, Italy and Spain – had been a problem for many years, but in the early summer of 2015 it reached unprecedented proportions. Hundreds of thousands of refugees, exploited by people-smugglers and crammed into small boats, risked their lives to get to Europe. Thousands of them drowned on the way.

The administrative arrangements previously agreed within the EU for dealing with the refugees quickly became inadequate and overrun. Under the so-called Dublin Regulation of 2003 it was the responsibility of the first EU state on whose territory the refugees appeared to register and fingerprint them and to process any appeal for asylum. But the numbers were such that Greece and Italy simply could not cope. And the refugees themselves did not want to stay there, so they headed north. Many of them ended up in Germany. A lot of them came from war-torn countries such as Syria, Iraq, Afghanistan or Eritrea and might therefore qualify for asylum. Others were economic migrants just seeking a better life. Most of these were fit young men; nearly all of them had, before entering the EU, been living in places of relative safety, such as Turkey, Lebanon or Jordan.

The EU's border protection agency, FRONTEX, had been set up in 2004 to help control the borders of the Schengen Area within which anyone, whether EU citizen or not, could move freely. FRONTEX was a mainly advisory body and lacked the resources to patrol the Mediterranean. An ad hoc naval operation was set up to provide assistance, but all it could do was to rescue the migrants at sea and transport them to safety on EU territory.

There was shock all over Europe at what was happening. One photograph of a dead child being lifted ashore by a Turkish policeman was especially poignant. In Germany there was a widespread feeling of sympathy for the refugees' predicament. It was inspired partly by simple humanitarian concern; partly, probably, by memories of the 12–15 million Germans who were forced to flee their homes elsewhere in Europe in the aftermath of World War II.

By June of 2015, 400,000 refugees had arrived in Germany and the government warned that the total for the year would probably reach 800,000. Not all the new arrivals came from countries afflicted by war or oppression. Nearly half came from the western Balkans – Albania, Kosovo, Bosnia, Macedonia or Serbia – countries which aspire to EU membership and whose citizens would be unlikely to qualify for asylum. It was Germany's failure to winnow out these economic migrants that made the German refugee figures so high. But far from looking for ways of reducing the flow, Angela Merkel unexpectedly announced that since the Dublin Regulation was not working, Germany would automatically grant entry to anyone from Syria.

The decision was welcomed by the humanitarian organisations but it caused consternation among Germany's EU partners, particularly those over whose territory the refugees heading for Germany would have to pass. It was seen as encouraging even more to put themselves in the hands of people-smugglers and as simply compounding the problem. Within Germany public reaction to the announcement was mixed. There were many private initiatives to welcome the refugees (as well as a few isolated incidents of hostility). But there was disquiet at the extent to which it would expose Germany to even bigger numbers of migrants. There was also some criticism that the government had taken a decision of this kind without apparently any co-ordination with its EU partners.

Outside Germany chaos reigned. Hungary built a fence along its borders with Serbia and Croatia to keep the refugees out. Other Balkan countries bussed them as quickly as possible through their territory in the direction of Austria and Germany. A number of countries, including eventually Germany itself, introduced border controls. The Schengen regime looked as if it might be beginning to collapse.

As a result, there was within a few weeks a change of policy. The German interior minister, Thomas de Maizière, now demanded that all EU member states should play their part in accommodating the refugees and suggested that there should be a system of compulsory quotas forcing them to do so. He added that any state which refused to take part in the scheme should suffer (unspecified) financial penalties.

The Commission promptly made a proposal of the kind for which Germany had asked (albeit without the financial penalties). It envisaged that all member states (other than those which, like Britain, had an opt-out from the EU's asylum policy) should accept a fixed number of refugees from among those who had already arrived in Greece or Italy. The total involved was 120,000 – a huge number, but a drop in the ocean compared with the size of the problem.

The countries of Central and Eastern Europe argued forcefully against the proposal. They pointed out that they had no experience of having to absorb people of a different culture and religion and had no facilities for doing so. They characterised the issue as a German, not a

European, problem. They used strong language. The Hungarian prime minister, Viktor Orbán, accused Germany of 'moral imperialism'. His Slovak counterpart, Robert Fico, talked of a 'Berlin/Brussels diktat' and threatened to refuse to implement the decision. It was to no avail. Under the EU's rules, decisions on asylum issues can be taken by qualified majority. And the Luxembourg presidency, under German pressure, called for a vote. Hungary, the Czech Republic, Slovakia and Romania voted against; Finland abstained; but everyone else voted in favour. The Polish government, which had previously joined its Central European partners in opposing the proposal, explained limply that since it could not prevent the adoption of the policy, they might as well go along with it. The German Interior Minister specifically thanked them for their about-turn.

Then the mood in Germany changed. As more and more migrants poured over the border from Austria it became increasingly difficult to find accommodation for them. The arguments within the EU about how the burden should be shared were replicated in Germany itself. Individual *Länder* (provinces) threatened to impose quotas on the number which they should each take. Bavaria, which bore the brunt of the initial impact and whose governing CSU traditionally takes a hard line against immigration, was particularly vociferous. Its minister president, Horst Seehofer, was scathing in his criticism of the policy of the federal government.

Much of the criticism was directed against Angela Merkel personally. She was perceived as having misjudged public opinion and as having been swayed, uncharacteristically, by emotion. As a result her popularity rating which stood at 73 per cent in 2014, the highest ever for a German chancellor, declined in the summer of 2015 to below 50 per cent. Since then, though, it has recovered: by the end of 2016 it was back up to nearly 60 per cent. Germans remained unhappy with her policy on immigration but they seemed to respect her for it.

*   *   *

Britain felt directly the reality of German power in the EU during David Cameron's attempt to renegotiate the terms of its membership. It was a chastening experience. Before the talks started, several months of soundings took place in which ideas were floated for how British concerns, particularly about immigration, might be met. But when it came to anything which meant actual limitations on numbers – for example through some kind of emergency brake mechanism – the German reaction was negative. Angela Merkel herself consistently made clear that she would not agree to anything which called into question the principle of free movement. In the end David Cameron had to settle for some minor change to social security entitlements. It was widely, and rightly, seen as a defeat.

Angela Merkel in effect set the terms of Britain's renegotiation in advance. Only by establishing what was and what was not acceptable to her could a British government hope to persuade the rest of its EU partners. The same will be true in the negotiations on the trading relationship between Britain and the EU following the British referendum on EU membership. They will be conducted on the EU side by the Commission but the decisive voice in deciding what the EU offers or how it responds to British requests will be Germany's.

* * *

Angela Merkel is the dominant figure in German politics, as well as, according to *Forbes* magazine, the most important woman in the world. She has been in office since 2005, but she shows no sign of becoming weary of the job. In December 2016 she was adopted as the CDU's candidate for the chancellorship in the federal election of 2017 and was reappointed to the chairmanship of the party, a post she has held since 2002. There were no rival candidates. Before she announced her decision to stand, there had been rumours in the press that the CDU's Bavarian sister party, the CSU, was reluctant to endorse her. But once she made her intentions known it rallied behind her.

It is not certain that she will remain chancellor after the election. Until early 2017 she had a commanding lead in the polls but the selection of Martin Schulz as the SPD's candidate for chancellor caused its dramatic erosion. If she is re-elected and serves a full fourth term she will have been in office for 16 years, the same length of time as Helmut Kohl, who first appointed her as a minister. At 66 she would still be seven years younger than Konrad Adenauer was when he first became chancellor.

Since World War II no German chancellor has left office voluntarily. Some, like Adenauer and Willy Brandt, have been forced out by scandal. Some, like Ludwig Erhard and Helmut Schmidt, have lost votes of confidence in the Bundestag. Others, like Kurt Georg Kiesinger, Helmut Kohl and Gerhard Schröder, have been voted out by the electorate. It could be that Angela Merkel will be the first one to decide for herself when to step down.

Until then she will continue to make the weather in both her own country and in the EU, where she has achieved, without ever seeming to have strived for it, a level of power which no leader has ever before come near to. As the diplomatic editor of *The Times* put it in June 2014: 'The First Iron Law of Europe is simple enough to be learned by rote. Europe proposes. Angela Merkel disposes.'

* * *

Of all Germany's recent chancellors, Angela Merkel had the least direct experience of the EU before she came to power. Born in 1954, she grew up under communism in East Germany. It was only as an adult that she was able to travel in Western Europe. Having been born after World War II, she was not brought up, as were her predecessors, to see the EU as a factor in ensuring peace.

The first time she had any contact with any EU institution was in the mid-1990s when, as a cabinet minister, she had occasionally to attend EU Environment Council meetings. This was also the first occasion on which she met any British politician. Her British counterpart at the time was John Gummer, with whom she got on rather well. He invited her to visit his constituency in Suffolk, where she was struck by the hostility to the EU shown by most of the people she met.

Her attitude to Europe does not therefore reflect the ingrained assumptions of most West German politicians. She has not been brainwashed into thinking that the EU and the euro are good for Germany. She has reached that conclusion through her own pragmatic judgement. It is a judgement of the head rather than of the heart.

Angela Merkel is sometimes accused of having no vision. Her critics allege that she simply responds to events, waits a long time before making up her mind and never sets out any long-term goals. It is true that she often takes a while to reach a decision. There is a story of her as a young girl being ordered during a swimming lesson to dive from a high board into a cold pool. She is said to have stood on the board in silence for half an hour before diving in just before the bell for the end of the lesson sounded. It is true also that she is essentially pragmatic in her outlook. There is no Merkelism to compare with Thatcherism, no ideological reference point to which she alludes, no doctrinal tag which can be attached to her. She makes no grand speeches about the future: she simply addresses the issues of today.

And she tends to hide her personality. In private she is good company: funny and self-deprecating with piercing blue eyes, a ready smile and an infectious laugh. She is happily married (to a physicist with a world-class reputation) and she has a wide range of interests – cooking, opera, walking. If her political career suddenly came to an end, she would continue to enjoy life to the full.

But in public she suppresses much of her human side. She does not tell jokes, she does not show emotion, she always wears trouser suits. She is in a sense the personification of the stereotype of the country she leads: efficient, organised and successful, but just a little bit dour.

(Her penchant for trouser suits does not mean that she is oblivious to fashion. I once, before she was chancellor, found myself standing next to her at the opening night of the Wagner Opera Festival in Bayreuth. As we were chatting I complimented her on her rather striking long dress: though simple in style it was extremely elegant. She was obviously pleased that someone had noticed it and happily discussed where she had bought it and why it had appealed to her. The incident reminded me of an occasion in 1979 when Margaret Thatcher, as a newly elected prime minister, was attending her first European Council meeting in Strasbourg. As she emerged from her hotel room to attend the formal dinner, the officials in the adjoining office, of whom I was one, stood up and her Private Secretary quite spontaneously said, 'Gosh, Prime Minster, you do look nice.' Indeed she did: she had obviously taken trouble over her appearance and was clearly happy that this had been recognised.)

In the past Angela Merkel showed herself able to act with a degree of ruthlessness. The German political landscape is littered with the bodies of those, usually middle-aged men, who underestimated her in her early years. She came to power in her party, as did Margaret Thatcher, by challenging an incumbent leader when other, more traditional, potential successors held back from doing so. Having obtained power, she has been astute and tenacious in consolidating her position.

She does not, however, enjoy domestic political confrontation, and she can sometimes give in quickly to short-term pressure without assessing the long-term consequences. She did so over the appointment of Jean-Claude Juncker and in the migrant crisis. She had previously shown the same tendency in other areas: over the UN Security Council Resolution on Libya in 2011, when she authorised a German abstention, and in the aftermath of the Fukushima nuclear accident the same year when she abruptly altered Germany's policy on nuclear power and decreed that all the country's nuclear plants would have to close 20 years earlier than previously planned. In both cases the prospect of having to campaign against the flow of public opinion caused her to take decisions which many in Germany considered misconceived. She may be slow to make up her mind but she can be swift in changing it.

* * *

Angela Merkel's European policies have not made Germany loved. In many of the countries where EU bail-outs have been agreed (Ireland is perhaps the exception) there has been much public resentment at the conditions which the EU, at German insistence, has imposed. Posters of her with a Hitler moustache abounded in the streets of Athens in 2014 and 2015. But being popular outside Germany is not something which Angela Merkel particularly cares about. Saving the euro is her priority.

Her policy for saving it is the one which all the EU's member states endorsed when the single currency was conceived and introduced. The criteria for entry into the euro were set out at the European Council in Maastricht in 1991. The rules on budgetary discipline were agreed by finance ministers in May 1998. It was the responsibility of individual member states to stick to them; there was never any suggestion that they might benefit from loans or resource transfers from others in order to cope with the consequences of not doing so.

In pressing for a fiscal treaty and for legally binding contracts on debt and deficits, Germany was not asking for anything new. Nor, in rejecting proposals for eurobonds or for other forms of debt pooling, was Germany reneging on any promises. Quite the contrary: German politicians in all positions on the spectrum had consistently made clear that the EU must not become, in their words, a transfer union.

Nonetheless the rigidity of the German position seems to have come as something of a shock to many of its eurozone partners. Perhaps they interpreted the siren song of 'more Europe' so often heard from the mouths of German politicians as meaning that Germany would accept responsibility for the failings of others. Perhaps they thought that Germany's own economists would question the intellectual case for austerity in a time of recession. Whatever the reason, they have been disappointed. The coalition agreement of December 2013 offered no prospect that German policy would change. The German response to Greece's demand for a renegotiation of its bail-out terms showed that it had not moved.

German pre-eminence in matters of economic governance is now an accepted fact of EU life. The Commission, which is in any case historically imbued with a culture of economic thinking based on that of Germany, does not make proposals to which Germany is opposed. And the other member states, despite occasional grumbles from the southern ones, have recognised that they have to take the medicine which Germany prescribes.

The German approach to Europe does not envisage any special leadership role for Germany itself. What Germany argues for, in the economic field at least, is a bigger role for the institutions of the EU. Provided that the EU's overall economic framework is established on a legally binding basis to reflect the German model, the Germans are willing to allow the European Commission, the European Parliament and the European Court to exercise authority on a scale that most people in Britain would find unacceptable. But this authority will have its limits, and these limits, though commonly agreed, have been set by Germany.

* * *

For nearly half of the last millennium a central aim of British foreign policy was to prevent the emergence in Continental Europe of any single dominant state. The alliances which Britain entered into and the wars which Britain fought were mainly linked to this goal. Maintaining the so-called balance of power in Europe was what successive kings and prime ministers sought to do – overall with great success. Britain's thousand years of freedom from occupation, something which no other European country has enjoyed, attests to it.

Of course the power which concerned Britain for all those years was military power. Germany today does not wield power of this kind. Its armed forces are substantial and their capabilities serious but they do not dwarf those of Britain or France, and no country in Europe sees Germany as any kind of military threat. Where other European countries have worries about German military capabilities, it is not over their size but over the German government's reluctance to use them.

Although Germany's dominance in Europe is in soft, rather than hard, power, it is no less real. In time it will extend beyond the field of internal EU policy making. Throughout the crisis in Ukraine it has been Germany which has taken the lead in seeking to bring about a political solution: both in the immediate aftermath of the demonstrations in Kiev in 2012 and in response to the outbreak of war in Eastern Ukraine in 2014 and 2015.

It was Angela Merkel who was the driving force in the negotiation of the Minsk Agreement of 12 February 2015 providing for a ceasefire and the de-escalation of the conflict. She was accompanied in her various visits and in the negotiations at Minsk itself by President Hollande of France, but it was clearly she who was in the lead. In one week of diplomacy she travelled 12,500 miles, visiting Kiev, Moscow, Washington, Ottawa, Munich (where a high-level transatlantic security conference was taking place) and Brussels as well as Minsk itself. She has spent more time on the telephone to both President Putin and President Obama than any other world leader. She has provided the answer to Henry Kissinger's apocryphal question: 'Who do I call if I want to speak to Europe?' Clausewitz observed in 1832 that war is the continuation of politics by other means. Modern Germany has shown that politics can achieve what used to require war.

German leadership of Europe may be benign, but former generations of British statesmen would see its emergence as a failure of British foreign policy. Now that we are leaving the EU we are powerless to influence it.

* * *

Germany is, in the words of Professor William Paterson, Britain's leading academic expert on the country, a 'reluctant hegemon'. Power of the kind that Germany now wields in Europe is not something which German governments have consciously sought, nor indeed is it welcome to German public opinion. No German politician would dream of using the sort of phrases (born to lead, manifest destiny, the city on the hill) which trip so easily off American tongues when discussing their role in the world. The idea put forward by Nicholas Ridley in 1990, which brought about his resignation from the British government, that

Economic and Monetary Union was a 'German racket designed to take over the whole of Europe', is as absurd now as it was then.

It is not Germany which has set out to lead; it is others who have chosen to follow.

And they have chosen to follow an admirable country. Germany is a liberal democracy with high standards of decency, integrity and freedom in public life, coupled with an efficient system of public administration and services. It is a country with a remarkable intellectual and cultural tradition which is open to the wider world. It has recovered, by its own efforts, from economic and political catastrophe and has come to terms with its own past in a way which no other country has. Its response to the refugee crisis may have been clumsy, but it was based on a widespread and enviable mood of public compassion. To live in today's Germany, as I was fortunate to do for over five years, is to experience to the full the virtues of European, and Western, civilisation.

Even from outside the EU, Britain will be profoundly affected by how the EU develops, so it is perhaps worth examining why Germany has acquired such a dominant position in Europe, and, more importantly, what aims Germany is seeking to achieve. Like any country, Germany has its own national interests which distinguish it from its friends and neighbours. These interests are well served by the EU in its present form – not surprisingly since the EU has been largely shaped by Germany itself. But is there anything more to Germany's leadership of the EU than a simple wish to get results which are good for Germany?

German politicians like to pretend that there is. They pontificate regularly about the need for a so-called 'political union' in Europe, albeit without ever spelling out what such a union would look like and how it would differ from the present arrangements. The one thing they all seem to be agreed on is that this union should not involve any more expenditure of German taxpayers' money.

They also tend to profess a certain disdain for those who justify the EU solely on the basis of what it does for their own prosperity.

In Germany it would be considered, at best, poor form to emphasise how much the German economy benefits from the internal market, the common trade policy, the competition rules and, above all, the common currency. Not because it is not true. But because in German political discourse the EU is portrayed as something greater, something almost more noble, than a mere transmission mechanism for Germany's economic success.

The slogan of an ever-closer union has helped sustain the notion that the EU is on a constant journey of self-improvement. Germany's partners, apart from Britain, have hitherto been prepared to undertake this journey without asking any awkward questions about the eventual destination. There has always been the prospect of a new intergovernmental conference or a new initiative to keep the show on the road and to offer the hope of changes to come.

This prospectus is looking increasingly shaky. Even following Britain's decision to leave, there are no plans for any fundamental revision of what the EU does or how it works. True, there is talk of a need for new rules for the eurozone, but there is no agreement on the form which these new rules might take. Should they, as Germany advocates, involve more binding legal commitments to budgetary discipline and surveillance, together with some harmonisation of taxes? Or should they, as others would like, provide for more pooling of eurozone countries' debts and for a recourse to common borrowing?

So long as such basic questions are unresolved the EU will just drift along in its present form. Any new treaty would require referenda in several of its member states. The experience of the United Kingdom's referendum will deter most governments from taking that risk.

Meanwhile, the EU is gradually losing the confidence of its citizens. A survey carried out in June 2016 by the Pew Research Center showed that in France only 37 per cent and in Spain only 47 per cent of respondents had a positive view of the EU. In Germany the figure was 50 per cent. These are big decreases from ten or even five years ago. Eurosceptic parties are on the rise in many member states. There seems nothing in prospect to halt this trend.

So, as German power in the EU increases, it is Germany whose political leaders will come under pressure to explain how they see the way forward. The countries who have, at German insistence, adopted deflationary policies and budgetary austerity in order to stay within the euro will want to know what their reward will be for their sacrifice. Electorates not only in Greece, but in Spain, Italy and France as well are becoming increasingly disillusioned. They will look to Germany to explain how things will improve.

They will, on present form, receive no answers. No political party in Germany has any plans to improve the economic situation of any of Germany's EU partners. No German politician has advocated the need for any change of course in the EU's overall approach. There is no vision for the future. The status quo suits Germany well.

The Europe which is emerging from the recent economic crisis is not the one which its founding fathers envisaged. It is a German Europe. Not because the leaders of Germany have sought to impose their rule, but because their partners have chosen to be governed in this way. They admire and envy what Germany has achieved. They hope that under German leadership some of the success may rub off on them.

They may hope in vain. Germany certainly exercises power in Europe and provides the impetus for all the EU's decisions, but there is no goal which these decisions are intended to serve, no light at the end of any tunnel, no crock of gold at the end of any rainbow.

It is, to coin a phrase, power without purpose.

♔ TWO ♔

It's the Economy, Stupid

The underlying reason for Germany's pre-eminence in Europe is self-evident. As Bill Clinton so convincingly demonstrated in winning the 1992 American presidential election against George Bush, it is the economy which really matters.

Germany's economy is the largest in Europe. Its gross domestic product, at 2.5 trillion euros, is around 25 per cent higher than those of France or the United Kingdom. So too, at around 80 million, is Germany's population. Out of the EU's total GDP of 12.3 trillion euros, Germany's represents just over 20 per cent. Although it is the largest single economy, it does not dwarf all others. Nor, in terms of GDP per head, is Germany's performance exceptional. Several other EU member states, Denmark, the Netherlands, Austria and even at one point Ireland, have performed better in this respect in the recent past.

What is different about Germany's economy is not just its size but its nature. Four characteristics make it unique:

- The German economy is based on manufacturing. Germany produces goods which people want to buy; they buy them because of their quality, reliability and technical innovation, not just because of their price.
- Germany is particularly successful at exporting, including to the emerging powers such as China, India, Russia and Brazil.
- Germany's public finances are in good order. Its trade surplus is high, its deficits and debt levels low.
- Germany's economic success has been complemented by a high level of social solidarity and security.

To most other countries in the EU this is an attractive and enviable record. And they are willing therefore to take lessons from the leaders of the country which has achieved it.

The German economic model has sometimes been called, at any rate by outsiders, 'Rhineland capitalism'. The Germans themselves have long used the term 'social market economy'. Among academics 'ordo-liberalism' seems currently to be the vogue name. It has many features in common with other models. It shares with the United States a commitment to the primacy of markets; with France a significant role for the state; with the Nordic countries high levels of social protection. But it is unique and has not, so far at any rate, been replicated elsewhere.

Its principles are:

- Economic activity is undertaken by the so-called social partners, that is to say the people who own enterprises and the people who work in them, acting together. The government does not interfere with their decisions.
- An independent body, the Bundeskartellamt (Federal Anti-Trust Office), ensures that this activity takes place in the optimum conditions of competition.
- An independent central bank – previously the Bundesbank, now the European Central Bank – maintains low inflation and monetary stability.
- The federal government controls national revenues and expenditure to ensure that they are in balance or near to it, and it maintains a system of education, training and research which provides enterprises with the workforce, skills and basic scientific innovations which they need.

A key element of the model is the importance which is attached to the safeguarding of competition. The Bundeskartellamt is, along with the Bundesbank and the Bundesverfassungsgericht (Federal Constitutional Court), one of the most respected institutions in

Germany. All three of them are independent of both government and parliament. As if to emphasise this, none of them is located in Berlin: the Bundeskartellamt is in Bonn, the Bundesbank in Frankfurt and the Constitutional Court in Karlsruhe – cities which are not even capitals of a *Land*.

The model is based on a wide degree of political consensus and has long-standing intellectual roots. German academic economists have traditionally looked to Hayek rather than to Keynes for their inspiration.

* * *

Why and how, under this model, has Germany developed the way it has?

Germany has few natural resources (coal is the only significant one). Historically it has depended on the education and skills of its workforce and on the dynamism and commercial acumen of its business community. The industrial revolution began somewhat later in Germany than in the United Kingdom, but already by the end of the nineteenth century German industrial production had outstripped Britain's. Germany developed on the basis of a combination of big manufacturers, many of whose names have survived for over a century as global icons (Siemens, Bosch, Mercedes Benz, ThyssenKrupp) and of small and medium-sized enterprises, often family owned – the so-called *Mittelstand* – able to find niches in the market and to exploit them successfully. This combination remains a key feature of the German economy today.

So too does another element in Germany's success, namely the commitment to training and technical skill. This applies both to shop-floor workers and to senior managers. The availability of a pool of well-trained young workers able to adapt to the demands of increasingly sophisticated equipment has always been one of the requirements of the large German companies. In contrast to their British counterparts, they have accepted part of the responsibility for delivering it. They expect the state to educate children well in secondary school, but from the age of 16 onwards there is in Germany, for those who do not go on to higher education, a unique system of industrial apprenticeship. Young boys and girls receive a combination of classroom training and practical experience to equip them with the skills necessary in key areas of engineering and other forms of technology.

This training is provided by the companies themselves, who are under pressure from the government to offer as many such apprenticeships each year as there are applicants. (They do not always quite achieve this, but the companies accept that they have a duty under the terms of the social market to try to do so.) Apprentices are paid, albeit at a modest rate, and, having completed their apprenticeship, they are virtually guaranteed a permanent job for life with the company which has trained them. Many apprentices go on to receive a higher education paid for by their company and achieve senior managerial positions. Jürgen Schrempp, who became CEO of Daimler-Benz and one of the best-known German industrialists of his day, began his 43-year career with the company as an apprentice at a Mercedes plant in Offenburg. The system ensures not only that German industrial workers are probably the most technically competent in the world, but also that they acquire and retain a particular commitment and loyalty to their employer.

To this competence and commitment has to be added the other long-standing German virtue of *Fleiss* (hard work). It is rash to generalise about national characteristics and there are plenty of stories in the German press about skivers and sickies, just as there are in Britain. But there has never been in Germany any phenomenon comparable to the 'Friday car' of 1970s Britain or to the closed-shop practices of the British print industry which lasted until Rupert Murdoch faced the unions down in the 1980s. The willingness to work hard and efficiently has always been a feature of the German industrial landscape.

It is not just the workforce in Germany which is well trained. So too are their managers. By and large the big German companies are run by people who understand the technology of whatever it is that their company makes. Of course they have senior staff who are accountants or marketing experts, but when the time comes to choose the next chief executive it is not usually those staff who are in the frame: rather it will be someone with experience in the fields of production or quality control.

I once had lunch at BMW's headquarters in Munich with the Chief Executive and some of his team. We discussed the composition of the company's main board. Out of, I think, 11 members, seven had doctorates in mechanical engineering and three also had part-time posts as associate professors at Munich Technical University. My impression was that if you wanted to run BMW you needed to be able to assemble a car yourself. I doubt if any British manufacturing company has ever had a senior management team with this level of expertise.

The headquarters of these companies are located at their main centres of production: Volkswagen in Wolfsburg, Mercedes and Bosch in Stuttgart, Siemens and BMW in Munich, ThyssenKrupp in Essen. This is where their chief executives and senior management are to be found: not, like so many of their counterparts in France or Britain, in an executive ghetto in the national capital.

Curiously for a country with so many successful large enterprises, Germany has no internationally known business school, and few senior managers in Germany have attended one. This may partly be because university education in Germany in the past took so long that people tended to graduate at the age of around 27, at which point few were attracted by the idea of another couple of years doing an MBA. But the main reason is that general managerial skills have traditionally been less prized in Germany than knowledge of a particular industrial sector.

The people who work for the big-name German companies are the country's elite. What the brightest and best of Germany's young university graduates aspire to is a place on the board of a company like Volkswagen, not a career in the civil service or a job as a lawyer or a banker. There has never been in Germany any of the disdain so prevalent among past Oxbridge generations in Britain for manufacturing or for the private sector. Quite the contrary: the senior executives of Germany's manufacturing industries are revered public figures. They are, like the bond dealers in Tom Wolfe's *Bonfire of the Vanities*, the masters of the universe.

They achieve their positions on merit, but their world, once they enter it, is closed and clannish. There is no tradition in Germany of interchange between the public and private sectors of the kind which is common in France or America and no institution such as the École Nationale d'Administration which provides a common educational platform for both government officials and industrial managers in France. Nor, as in Britain, are the boards of German companies populated by retired ministers or civil servants.

The big German companies are international in their outlook, and their senior managers often have experience of working abroad. They all speak English fluently and are at ease conducting meetings in it. But, with the exception of the occasional Austrian or Swiss, no non-German is likely ever to run, or even occupy a senior executive level position in, a German manufacturing company. The subsidiaries of German companies in other countries are also usually led by Germans.

The emphasis on skills and training is one of the defining features of the German industrial landscape. Another is the practice of co-determination (*Mitbestimmung*). This has two elements, the micro and the macro.

At the micro level, companies in Germany are required by law to establish at each individual production facility a works council (*Betriebsrat*) as a forum at which decisions about local terms and conditions of employment are taken jointly by workers' and management representatives.

At the macro level, German companies are run by two boards: a main board (*Vorstand*), consisting of senior managers and chaired by the chief executive, which is responsible for day-to-day business;

and a supervisory board (*Aufsichtsrat*), which takes the big strategic decisions and appoints the members of the main board. The supervisory board is composed, in equal numbers, of representatives of employees and shareholders, chaired by a shareholder representative who has a casting vote. The employee representatives are a mixture of members of the company's own works councils and senior national officials from the big unions. The shareholder representatives are either individuals who own, or represent the owners of, a significant equity in the company, or outsiders who have relevant business or specialist expertise.

It was until recently an incestuous system, with the same names appearing in different contexts. Gerhard Cromme, for example, has served as chairman of the supervisory boards of both Siemens and ThyssenKrupp (simultaneously) and has been a member of the boards of Allianz, Germany's biggest insurance company, of Axel Springer, the country's biggest newspaper publisher, of Lufthansa, the national airline, and of E.ON, the biggest energy company. Berthold Huber, the chairman of IG Metall, the immensely powerful metal workers' union, was deputy chairman of both Siemens and Volkswagen.

The degree of overlap in board membership is now somewhat less than it used to be, and the composition on the shareholder side is more varied: the occasional foreign name crops up, as does the occasional woman. But it is still a fairly closed world. Many chairmen of supervisory boards are former chief executives of the company concerned. When looking to replace fellow board members they turn naturally to people like themselves.

Co-determination is popular in Germany. Even employer organisations support it. They argue that it gives all employees a sense of belonging to – and therefore wanting to see prosper – the enterprise in which they work; that it allows managers better to exploit the creativity of their own workforce; and that it reduces the likelihood of strikes or other forms of industrial action because unions are involved in decision making and are aware of the financial background to wage negotiations.

I once visited a car factory in Bavaria where a new production line had recently been installed. Everything seemed automated, robots went merrily about their business, the whole site was spotlessly clean, and the cars eased their way relentlessly towards completion. I expressed admiration to the manager who was showing me around and commented that it was presumably because of the company's investment in all this technology that it was able to maintain its competitive edge. To my surprise he denied that this was the key factor. All car plants in Europe, indeed in the world, would probably now look pretty similar, he said. What was important was to be able to motivate the workforce to operate the line more efficiently. For this he was reliant on the workers themselves coming up with ideas. Co-determination gave them the incentive, and the opportunity, to do so.

It is a labour market model which works well and which has proved more adaptable than its critics expected. In the late 1990s and early 2000s it seemed to be past its sell-by date and to be too tainted by conflicts of interest to survive. A case in point came in 2003 when the newly formed Verdi union, an amalgamation of three trade unions in the public sector, called for a strike at Lufthansa in protest at changes which the company was seeking to bring in, relating to the terms of employment of certain members of their staff. The management argued that in order to cope with increased competition, particularly from low-cost airlines, they needed to have more flexibility over staff costs; without this flexibility the company's long-term interests would be critically damaged. Verdi objected and called its members out. But the national chairman of Verdi continued to sit on the Lufthansa supervisory board.

The idea of someone with a fiduciary duty to a company organising a strike against it is difficult to reconcile with British or American corporate governance, but in Germany it is not considered anomalous. This is because the concept of co-determination is based on the notion that companies do not exist simply for the benefit of their shareholders: the interests of the company's employees have to be considered as well.

Not the interests of all of them, however. Most big German companies have production facilities all over the world – two-thirds of the Siemens workforce, for example, is employed outside Germany. But the employee representatives on their supervisory boards are exclusively German. This hardly encourages objective decision making when the issue at stake is, for example, at which plant a new car model should be produced or a new facility established. And it of course constitutes discrimination within the European Union between German and non-German employees of the same enterprise. Why, if a supervisory board is to choose whether to invest in Bremen or Bratislava, should the workers in Bremen have a say in the decision but the workers in Bratislava do not?

Two decisions taken by German companies over their investments in Britain illustrate this. In 1997 Siemens opened a computer chip manufacturing plant in north-east England. It was a brand-new, state-of-the-art facility on a green-field site and was lauded by British ministers as a symbol of the sort of foreign investment which a Britain open for business could attract. The productivity of the plant's workforce was high and there were no problems with the quality of its output. But after less than two years it was closed down. Siemens concluded that the economic realities of competition from low-cost Asian manufacturers meant that there was no way the plant could ever be viable. Similarly in 2000 BMW sold off Rover, the car manufacturer which it had bought six years earlier. Rover was haemorrhaging money and the BMW supervisory board decided that, with the exception of the Mini brand (which they kept and which has subsequently prospered), they preferred to cut their losses and get rid of it.

Both these decisions were taken for valid commercial reasons, but they were taken rapidly and without any consultation with the work-forces involved. If the plants concerned had been located in Germany, things would have been very different. Because under German employment law it is much more expensive to make workers redundant than in Britain, the economic case for closure might have been less compelling. Even if the management had favoured closing a plant down or selling it off, it would have had to agree the terms in the supervisory board, of which half the members would be trade unionists.

It is puzzling that this difference in the way EU workers of different nationalities are treated under German co-determination law has not attracted the attention of the European Commission and the European Court. It is on the face of it incompatible with the principles of the EU. The Commission has been prepared in the past to act against other aspects of German industrial tradition, such as the *Reinheitsgebot*, a protectionist law which prevented the import into Germany of foreign brands of beer which did not conform to Germany's arcane beer production rules.

Maybe challenging such a fundamental principle of German corporate governance as the composition of supervisory boards would be a step too far. To do so would certainly provoke a major row in Germany. Despite their professed commitment to the ideals of the single market in Europe, successive German governments have consistently rejected any change to their own national employment legislation. When the idea of a European Company Statute was under discussion in the EU's legislative machinery – its aim was to give companies which operated in more than one member state the option of selecting a single corporate identity – the German government, under pressure from the trade union movement, fought tooth and nail to ensure that this did not mean that a company in Germany might be able to escape the requirements of German co-determination laws by becoming European.

* * *

Most of the major German industrial companies started as family enterprises. Not one of them is today. The descendants of Robert Bosch still have interests in the firm which he founded in 1886 as a small electrical workshop and which is now a major producer of domestic appliances. The Quandt family owns a significant share of the car manufacturer BMW, as do the Piech/Porsche family in Volkswagen. But the big names of German industry are now public companies, subject – like any in the world – to the demands of shareholders who are increasingly prepared to use their power on supervisory boards. In the past, many of their big shareholders were the German banks, and the banks saw themselves as long-term investors, willing to take a long view of their interests. They were not obsessed by day-to-day variations in the share price and were more interested in how it might develop over the coming decade than over the coming year.

This has changed somewhat in recent times. The banks themselves have come under pressure from international competition to deliver more value for their own shareholders, and a change in the laws about the taxation of asset disposals introduced in 2003 made it less costly for them to get rid of underperforming shareholdings. Banks were expected to facilitate mergers and acquisitions and the like but not themselves to become long-term dominant part-owners of private companies. As the shareholder base of the big German companies became more widely distributed and more international, it seemed likely that they would become more susceptible to short-term pressures.

In the event the change has been less dramatic than some commentators predicted. Some big German companies found other institutional investors prepared to take a long-term view – the biggest single shareholder in Volkswagen, for example, is the Qatari sovereign wealth fund. Others adjusted to demands, or potential demands, for better share price performance by disposing of less efficient units (though not usually units in Germany). BMW got rid of Rover, and Daimler-Benz sold off both Chrysler and Mitsubishi. In each case the companies accepted big losses and a reversal of earlier expansionist dreams. But their core operations remained intact, and they have retained their independence.

Unlike their equivalents in Britain the managers of publicly quoted companies in Germany do not live in fear of hostile or unwelcome takeovers. Not because they enjoy special legal protection against those approaches (though Volkswagen does through the golden share which belongs to the *Land* government of Lower Saxony), but because of the extreme unlikelihood that their supervisory boards would make such a recommendation and the difficulty of obtaining shareholder support against the advice of the supervisory board. In recent times there has been only one successful hostile takeover in Germany – that of Mannesmann by Vodafone in 2000. The circumstances in this case were unusual. Mannesmann had, by German standards, an exceptionally loosely distributed shareholder base and it had diversified out of its traditional manufacturing activities into the telecommunications field. The late 1990s saw a huge wave of consolidation, mergers, takeovers and disposals in the European telecommunications sector. Mannesmann, which owned the D2 mobile telephone network in Germany, had itself benefited from this by acquiring Orange, a direct competitor to Vodafone in the United Kingdom.

For Vodafone, Mannesmann's D2 network represented the only realistic opportunity of access to the German market and it was willing therefore to pay a high price to buy the company. Chris Gent, Vodafone's chief executive at the time and one of the most skilful deal-makers in the world, put together a package which the Mannesmann shareholders, particularly the Hong Kong-based Hutchison Whampoa, eventually found impossible to refuse.

The takeover was hugely controversial in Germany and dominated the headlines in the economic and business press for weeks. For many people it was incredible that a company like Mannesmann, founded in 1890 and one of the great names of the German industrial landscape, could be acquired against the wishes of its management by an unknown upstart from Newbury. Not only incredible but somehow morally wrong: there were calls for the rights of shareholders to be curtailed so that they could not go against the advice of the company's management or for the government to intervene in some way to ensure that Mannesmann stayed in German hands. Even the federal chancellor, Gerhard Schröder, initially spoke out against the deal. It did not seem to bother him that as minister president of Lower Saxony he had been a member of the supervisory board of Volkswagen when Volkswagen had acquired Rolls-Royce and Bentley, two of the iconic names of British car manufacturing.

This was one rare occasion when Schröder's political instincts proved faulty. None of the big names of the German business community joined in the campaign against the deal. When asked their views they said that it was a matter for the Mannesmann shareholders to decide and that the government should keep out of the affair. By and large the editorials in the business press also followed this line. Big business in Germany may be less than wholly enthusiastic about the short-term aspects of shareholder value, but they are even more allergic to government intervention.

*   *   *

It is not only the big names of German manufacturing which have survived from the nineteenth century to the twenty-first. A surprising number of small and medium-sized companies have done so as well. They have prospered for the same reasons as their larger counterparts – by concentrating on technical innovation and by seeking global markets for their products.

Many of them are still family owned and family run. It is not unusual in Germany for a firm to trace its origins back through four or five generations of the same name. The pattern of ownership disposal once so common in Britain, whereby grandfather establishes a successful company, son installs a manager and lives off the profits and grandson sells it off, has not on the whole been the German way. Of course there are mergers and takeovers. But most German *Mittelstand* firms take pride in their independence and their history. Their owners want to expand the business and hand it on in better shape to the next generation, not to extract the capital value for themselves.

I once sat next to someone at dinner who described himself as the manager of a typical German *Mittelstand* engineering company. It turned out to have a turnover of over 1 billion pounds and around 10,000 employees and to manufacture a range of products from clocks to missiles. I asked him what he thought of the concept of shareholder value, which was then much in vogue. 'We're all in favour of it,' he replied. 'We have regular shareholder meetings: every month my brothers and I take our father out to lunch.' I commented that this sounded rather unusual; my impression had been that most *Mittelstand* companies had a long-term relationship with a bank which took an equity stake in return for loaning them money. 'Why should we need money?' he asked. 'In the 120-year history of our company we have never borrowed a pfennig. All our investments have come from retained profits.'

I went on to ask about succession planning. After four generations of family management, what would happen next? It would depend, he replied, on competence. If a family member was up to the job, then fine. But if not, they would unsentimentally appoint an outsider. It later emerged that his son, having completed a doctorate in engineering at a German university, was currently doing an MBA at Wharton Business School in the United States. It sounded as though the family would be in charge for a few more years.

My dinner companion's firm was something of an exception. Like the bigger enterprises, most *Mittelstand* enterprises also benefited in the past from a close relationship with a local bank. But for many of them, that bank has been in the public rather than the private sector. Most of the German *Länder* established their own *Landesbank*, whose original function was to provide support for small and medium-sized local firms. Over time these banks expanded their operations to the point where some of them are indistinguishable from commercial banks. Several *Landesbanken* were among the casualties of the banking crisis of 2008, having displayed the same levels of irresponsibility in exposing themselves to the American real estate market as their private sector counterparts, but they still perform their basic function as lenders to local firms. You do not often hear small German companies complain about difficulties in gaining access to capital.

Nor do they expect the government to help them find markets. There is no department of the German government responsible for the promotion of exports, nor do German embassies abroad have commercial departments (the same is true for Japan). All German firms are members of their local chamber of commerce and the German Chambers of Commerce Association maintains offices all over the world to provide them with information and advice. The service is paid for out of membership subscriptions and is extremely effective.

The *Mittelstand* companies are also assiduous attenders at industrial fairs, where they keep track of technological developments in their field and make contact with potential customers. Fortunately for them, many of the top such fairs take place in Germany. Every big German city has its own *Messegelände* (commercial fairground) and most of them are municipally owned in part or full. They are on a scale which dwarfs anything in the United Kingdom. (Birmingham's National Exhibition Centre, the biggest British commercial exhibition space, is smaller than the top five German *Messegeländer*). In many industrial sectors it is the annual or biennial fair in Germany which is the biggest or most prestigious international event of its kind: the Frankfurt Motor Show and Book Fair, the CEBIT information technology fair in Hannover and even the toy fair in Nuremberg (Germany is home to Steiff, the world's most famous producer of teddy bears). At these fairs manufacturers, designers, importers and wholesalers from all over the world converge. German companies, small and large, are there in abundance.

* * *

The German economy is not solely based on the manufacturing of goods. SAP, the world's largest producer of business management software, is German. So too is Bertelsmann, among the biggest publishers of books in the English language, and Allianz, one of the world's leading insurance companies. The second biggest supermarket chain in the world (after Walmart) is German-based Aldi.

Still, it is things, rather than services, which are the backbone of Germany's success. German firms are less strong in the creative industries. Germany has produced many good films in recent years – and has in Babelsberg outside Berlin a film studio with a long and distinguished movie history. But the quality of German television is mediocre and that of its advertising dire. The stereotype of the German national character – disciplined, efficient but unimaginative – finds some echo in the structure of the modern German economy. But it is an economy which is highly resilient and which has shown a remarkable ability to adapt.

Modern Germany was built from the ashes (literally) of World War II. The year 1945 was *Stunde Null* (zero hour). The country was in a state of complete physical and psychological collapse and under foreign occupation. For a time the most powerful of the occupying powers, the Americans, toyed with the idea of implementing the Morgenthau Plan, under which Germany would have been deprived of all its industrial facilities and reduced to the role of a village-based agricultural producer. That did not happen, largely because of fears by the Americans that too weak a Germany would fall under Soviet influence. Instead, the Germans were allowed, indeed encouraged, to rebuild both their cities and their factories. And they did so with grit and determination.

German women played a key role. There was an acute shortage of men in Germany after 1945. Over 5 million had been killed in the war and 3 million were still prisoners of war, mainly in the Soviet Union. So it was women, the so-called *Trümmerfrauen*, who had to clear the rubble and provide the labour force for the rebuilding of the destroyed urban landscapes. Many of them had themselves recently experienced extreme physical and sexual violence. Over 100,000 women in Berlin, and over 1.5 million elsewhere in East Germany, between the ages of 10 and 80 were raped by Soviet soldiers in the first six months of 1945, in many cases on a multiple and continuing basis. They did not talk about it; there was no counselling. They just carried on as best they could.

So too did the 12 million Germans who were forcibly expelled from their homes in East Prussia, Poland, Czechoslovakia and elsewhere in Eastern Europe in the biggest example of ethnic cleansing the world has ever seen. Between 0.5 million and 2 million of them (estimates vary) died or were killed on the way. Those who made it back to Germany itself had to begin their lives again with nothing.

When gradually children grew up and the prisoners of war returned, the demographics became more normal and Germany had a more balanced workforce. The returned prisoners did not talk much about the war – neither what had been done to them in Soviet camps nor what they had themselves done to the civilian populations they had conquered, brutalised and murdered.

What followed in the 1950s and 1960s in the western part of the country was the so-called *Wirtschaftswunder* (economic miracle). Germany regained its status as Europe's leading industrial economy and its people began to enjoy the prosperity which this brought. Along with most of the rest of Western Europe, Germany benefited from Marshall Aid. This was important in the late 1940s for kick-starting the process of national recovery. But the *Wirtschaftswunder* of the following decades was achieved through the efforts of the Germans themselves. They are understandably proud of it, even if it is not their style to be publicly triumphalist. But it makes them sceptical of the claims by others in Europe that the EU can only succeed if the Germans now share their resources. It makes them particularly reluctant to hand over money to countries whose citizens do not seem to share the German commitment to hard work.

* * *

The reconstruction of Germany after 1945 was a homegrown success. So too were the two other big economic challenges which the Germans have faced, and overcome, since then: reunification in 1990 and a loss of international competitiveness ten years or so later.

The reunification of Germany was one of the most difficult political, economic and social undertakings with which any government in the modern world has been confronted. It required courage and imagination on the part of the political leadership in both East and West Germany, and a huge commitment of solidarity and sacrifice by West Germans. It was something for which no plan existed before it happened. The division of Germany had seemed a permanent phenomenon. There were some who anticipated, or at least hoped, that conditions in the East might improve and that travel, communication and contact might be easier. But no one expected that the German Democratic Republic (GDR) would actually disappear.

Reunification up until 1989 was a theoretical aspiration. To have advocated it in the GDR would have meant imprisonment. To do so in the Federal Republic of Germany (FRG) would have been interpreted at best as showing a lack of political realism or at worst right-wing revanchism. So no practical preparations were made. (There was a rumour that someone in the office responsible for allocating car licence plates in the early days of the Federal Republic had kept back L and P so that they could one day be used for Leipzig and Potsdam, whereas all the other single letters were assigned to West German cities, but this is no doubt legend.) Given that historically Germans have been better known for their qualities of planning, rather than improvisation, reunification was a massive challenge.

German civil servants in the former West Germany were asked to volunteer to help set up the new institutions in the East. A former colleague of mine did so. She described arriving in a dreary, freezing Portakabin building near Potsdam with the task of establishing from scratch a provincial tax administration for the new *Land* of Brandenburg (no such body had existed in the former GDR). There was no heating, no records of income or economic activity, no expertise, no data and a sullen workforce who all assumed that they were going to be fired. Within a few years, though, the system was working.

Reunification was not a merger, still less a merger of equals. It was an agreed takeover. The German Democratic Republic voted to dissolve itself and to join the Federal Republic of Germany, which expanded in size and acquired six new *Länder*. The institutions of the FRG continued in existence unchanged. Those of the GDR disappeared. Nothing, but nothing, of the former East Germany was preserved as part of any common heritage. No achievement of it is commemorated, no personality revered, no tradition maintained. It is as if the country never existed.

The result has overall been an enormous success. A prosperous functioning social market of 60 million people has absorbed, and given almost overnight the same economic and social rights to, 20 million citizens of a run-down and demoralised command economy dictatorship. The Germany which emerged in November 1990 remains a liberal, tolerant, free market democracy. Those, like Margaret Thatcher, who feared that following reunification Germany would somehow break free from the Western world and its institutions and be susceptible to right-wing extremism, have been proved emphatically wrong (it was Britain, not Germany, which in 2009 elected two fascist members of the European Parliament).

The political success of reunification came at an economic and social cost. The decision to expose East German industry virtually overnight to Western market forces at a Deutschmark/Ostmark exchange rate of 1:1 was catastrophic for firms in the former GDR. Many simply went bust. Others, in a drive to compete with their Western counterparts, shed labour on a massive scale. On one cold day in the early 1990s Jenoptik (formerly Carl Zeiss in Jena and supposedly the jewel in the East German technological crown) dismissed 18,000 workers – probably the biggest single layoff in world history. By 1997 East Germany had lost 70 per cent of its pre-1990 industrial capacity.

Opinions differ about whether the economic transformation could have been better, or at any rate more humanely, handled. The argument for a 1:1 conversion ratio was that, as the East Germans put it, 'either the Deutschmark comes to us or we go to the Deutschmark', i.e. if East Germans were not given equivalent spending power in East Germany, they would simply migrate westwards and, as German citizens, claim social security benefits in the old Federal Republic.

Critics argue that although some migration of this kind might have occurred, it would nonetheless have been better to allow the East German economy a cushion of currency competitiveness of the kind enjoyed by Poland, the Czech Republic and Hungary. Or at any rate that East German industry should have been given much greater freedom to compete with lower wage levels (wages in East Germany have remained somewhat lower than in the West and there is more labour market flexibility, but the differences are relatively minor).

Reunification involved massive painful adjustments for the former citizens of the GDR. There were also massive sacrifices by their fellow citizens in the West. For 20 years after 1990 West Germans had to pay a special solidarity tax on their income to cover the reconstruction and social costs of the former GDR. They did so with the occasional grumble about the East Germans' ingratitude and fecklessness, just as the East Germans complained about West German arrogance and condescension. But on the whole the West Germans paid willingly. They were, after all, a single nation.

The experience of reunification, for which the term *Wende* (turning point) is commonly used, has had a huge psychological impact on Germany. For East Germans it meant freedom, but for many of those who were already middle-aged in 1990 it has also meant exclusion from the job market and the abandonment of the solidarity of former times. For West Germans it has meant financial sacrifice, but also pride: a sense that at last the country has become whole and normal again. As Willy Brandt put it: *'Jetzt wächst zusammen was zusammen gehört'* (Now what belongs together is growing together).

It has also been crucial in influencing German attitudes to the euro. The former GDR was exposed to a strong currency and had to cope with the consequent loss of competitiveness. It took a decade at least for the pain to subside. But it was what East Germans wanted. Reunification was, like the euro, a political project driven through at high economic cost. If the East Germans were able to bear the brunt of it, so too, in German eyes, should the Greeks, Irish and Portuguese, who also chose, deliberately and knowingly, to give up their old currencies.

It can of course be argued that precisely because of their experience of reunification, and the scale of inner German resource transfers which were necessary to make it work, the Germans should have been more cautious about allowing so many relatively weak southern European economies to join the euro in 1999. Many Germans would agree and criticise their own government for not being more forward in pointing out the risks. But the leitmotif of German policy towards the single currency, that it should not involve the creation of a 'transfer union', is also born out of the reunification experience. Germans were willing to make economic sacrifices for their own countrymen. They are not prepared to do so, or at any rate not on anything like the same scale, for foreigners.

* * *

The other occasion on which the German economy showed its inherent resilience was much less dramatic than either the recovery from World War II or the achievement of reunification, but it was also important in sustaining Germany's pre-eminence in Europe and in influencing German attitudes to the euro. By the end of the 1990s the German economy seemed to be in the doldrums. Its growth had slowed down (to the point where in some years it was lower than Britain's), unemployment rose to 4.8 million (9.4 per cent of the workforce) and the country seemed to be struggling to cope with the newly identified phenomenon of globalisation. The phrase 'sick man of Europe' was bandied around, only this time it was targeted at Germany, rather than Britain.

The malaise coincided with the end of the 18-year chancellorship of Helmut Kohl, a towering figure in German, and European, history who had risen magnificently to the political challenge of German reunification but who had never taken much interest in economics. His prophecy that the absorption of the GDR into the FRG would be straightforward and would soon result in *Blühende Landschaften* (blooming landscapes) turned out to be wildly optimistic. By 1997–98 there was a general consensus on the part of the German establishment that a fundamental change was needed if Germany was to remain internationally competitive. As the then president Roman Herzog put it in a speech (making speeches is just about all that German presidents are allowed to do) in 1997 which caught the prevailing mood, the country needed a '*Ruck*' (a jolt).

There was widespread agreement on the reasons for Germany's apparent decline: the cost of reunification; the catastrophic state of industry in the former GDR; excessively high wage levels and the lack of flexibility in wage negotiation arrangements; the crippling burden of non-wage costs which employers had to carry; the difficulty and expense of making anyone redundant and the consequent reluctance of employers to recruit; stifling bureaucracy and over-regulation; and a refusal to encourage the development of a low-wage sector to help create jobs in services. The problem was that Chancellor Helmut Kohl had been unable, or unwilling, to persuade Germany's blue-collar workers and their unions that change was needed.

Kohl's successor, Gerhard Schröder, made the effort. He promulgated a new vision of the social market which he called the '*Neue Mitte*' (the New Centre) and which for a time he ran in tandem with Tony Blair's Third Way. The underlying philosophy was that the role of the state was to act as a trampoline to help people who lost their jobs bounce back into work, rather than a mattress on which they could comfortably repose. He established a commission, under the chairmanship of Peter Hartz, the personnel director of Volkswagen, to review the workings of the labour market.

Hartz had good relations with the unions from his time at Volkswagen (indeed, they turned out to have been rather too good as he subsequently had to resign over a scandal involving the provision of Brazilian call-girls at away meetings of the Volkswagen Works Council), and he succeeded in keeping them broadly onside. The reforms which his commission proposed were backed by the Schröder government and were passed by the Bundestag in four stages from 2001 to 2005.

The reforms did not call into question the fundamentals of the German social market model, but they introduced greater elements of flexibility for small enterprises and start-ups, a simplification and rationalisation of welfare entitlements and stricter conditions for their disbursement. In parallel with the work of his commission, Hartz succeeded in getting the Volkswagen unions to accept some measures of part-time and temporary contract working. As Volkswagen is something of a bellwether for the German motor industry as a whole, these changes were influential in encouraging similar flexibility elsewhere.

Schröder has never been given, either inside or outside Germany, the credit he deserves for pushing through these labour market reforms. Many of them did not actually come into effect until he had left office in 2005, and his wider reputation was by then tarnished by his defence of Russia's Vladimir Putin and by his assumption of the chairmanship of the Gazprom-led consortium responsible for the construction of a gas pipeline from Russian to Germany across the Baltic. But, just as his government showed political courage in deploying the German armed forces on NATO operations in Kosovo and Afghanistan (something which most observers would previously have regarded as unthinkable and which involved a vote of confidence in the Bundestag), so too did he personally – for it was his own commitment to the changes which was decisive – in modernising Germany's social model.

Germany still has, at any rate compared to Britain, generous standards of social provision and high levels of regulation in many areas of its economy. The public mood favours security of existing employment, rather than flexibility in the creation of new jobs. The Germans, including the German trade unions, have not set their faces against change, however. They have been willing to accept reforms when persuaded of their necessity, and they have negotiated these reforms for themselves. Unsurprisingly they do not see why Greeks and Italians, who benefit in some cases from even more comfortable entitlements, should not do the same.

*   *   *

Technology-based exports are one key reason for German's economic success. Sound public finances are the other. This means: a healthy balance of trade surplus; a small current account deficit; low levels of borrowing; steady growth; and, above all, low inflation. Virtually all shades of political opinion in Germany agree that these should be the goals of economic policy. By and large, most German governments in the last 50 years have achieved them – or at least have made a better fist of it than other European countries.

They have done so partly through deliberate policy choice and partly as a result of patterns of public behaviour. Until 1999 inflation was kept low by the actions of the Bundesbank, whose mandate required it to give low inflation an absolute priority, and thereafter by those of the European Central Bank, whose terms of reference were, at the insistence of the German government, cast in similar terms. It is noticeable that the German members of the board of the European Central Bank and the bank's German permanent officials are the most stringent in their interpretation of the institution's anti-inflationary mission and the most hawkish in arguing against any policy measures which, in their view, might threaten to dilute it.

It is sometimes asserted by commentators that the German aversion to inflation dates back to the experiences of the Weimar Republic of the 1920s and folk memories of million-mark banknotes and prices which changed on an hourly basis. There is some truth in this, but for the modern generation of Germans it is the period between 1945 and 1948 (the year of the currency reform which introduced the Deutschmark) which is probably more influential. In any case, it is not just the historical recollections of old people which are relevant. The idea of inflation as evil is firmly embedded in German popular thinking.

So too is a reluctance to borrow. Germans are enthusiastic consumers but they consume within their means. They are not used to the idea of having substantial personal debts. Credit cards came late to Germany and even today cash is used for a surprisingly large number of transactions: the scandals over political party funding in the CDU which brought Angela Merkel to power as its chairman in 2002 involved the handing over of brown envelopes filled with euros rather than the writing of cheques. Nor did Germans ever have the attachment to hire purchase agreements, or the never-never, that have been a feature of the British commercial landscape.

There is very little advertising of credit arrangements at all. German householders are not bombarded with letters urging them to take out new cards; German billboard hoardings do not feature loan schemes. This is not because of regulations against them: rather it seems to reflect a common feeling among both financial institutions and customers that this is not a field where the dark arts of advertising ought to be in play.

A British *Financial Times* correspondent posted to Berlin in the early 2000s recalled his experience of obtaining a credit card from his German bank. The bank checked that he had a regular source of income from his employer and readily gave him the card. He emphasised that he did not want a card which would allow him to get into debt: he wanted one which involved the payment by direct debit each month of any expenditure incurred. No problem, was the bank's response: it's the only sort we do.

Nor do many Germans have big mortgages. The proportion of the population who own, rather than rent, their homes is much lower than in Britain. Those who choose to buy do so for reasons of convenience and for the freedom to decorate or make changes to the property, not in the expectation of making a capital profit. House prices in Germany have historically been relatively stable and there is usually no clear financial benefit in buying rather than renting. Those who do buy tend to take out a mortgage of only around 10 years or so.

For many years any propensity towards excessive consumer expenditure was also discouraged by the country's draconian laws on shop opening hours. Until the late 1990s German shops closed at 18.00 on weekdays and at 12.00 on Saturdays – and that was it. On Sundays bakers were allowed to open in the morning, and food (and alcohol) could be bought at railway and petrol stations, but everything else, including, for example, garden centres, remained shut.

There were other restrictions too. The opening of factory outlet shops was discouraged, partly by the imposition of discriminatory planning laws and partly by claims that consumers might be 'confused' if they were offered something which was from a previous year's collection. The same argument, that consumers might be 'confused', was used to prevent a mail-order firm from doing business in Germany because it offered an unconditional returns policy on its goods. The government argued that though such a policy was more beneficial to customers than the minimum standard required by German law, it was nonetheless wrong because it involved the introduction of a different level of consumer protection. Sales too were limited to specific times of the year.

Gradually these restrictions have disappeared or been mitigated, though Sunday opening is still taboo. Shopping in Germany is now an experience more like that in other European countries. Public pressure for change, assisted no doubt in border areas by the ability simply to pop over to another country to buy what was not available at home, gradually overcame the resistance of the trade unions and other groups.

It was perhaps illustrative that in the years-long public debate over shop opening hours, one argument which featured in the similar, but much earlier, argument in Britain was completely lacking. No one, whether small shopkeeper or libertarian, asked the question: 'What right does the state have to stop me plying my trade when I want to?' Perhaps the fact that so many of Germany's corner-shop owners are Turkish in origin made them reluctant to enter the debate. Perhaps it is also the case that questioning the role of the state in regulating public behaviour does not come naturally to the German population.

German governments argue that their country's huge balance of trade surplus is the result of choices made by individual consumers in Germany and elsewhere. Fundamentally they are right. If German exports are successful it is because customers in other countries decide to buy German products. If imports into Germany are lower than they might otherwise be, it is because German consumers prefer to save rather than to spend.

The German model is not one which can be replicated throughout the European Union or the eurozone. This is the impression that German governments tend to give when challenged as to how the peripheral or highly indebted European countries should put their economic houses in order. Be more like us, is the message. Improve your competitiveness. Stand on your own feet. Don't expect others to bail you out.

Critics reply that one country's surplus is another's deficit; that it is statistically impossible for all the EU's member states to have surpluses with each other; if Germany wants to maintain its balance of trade position it needs to take some responsibility for the consequences for others. Hence the regular calls on the German government to do something to encourage imports from other EU countries or at least to stimulate demand generally. German governments have consistently resisted this on the grounds that, as Angela Merkel put it, 'Germany is an over-indebted, export-oriented economy with an ageing population. It cannot boost consumption at the expense of exports.'

It is in any case not easy to see what action a German government could take. It could hardly put a tax on German exports to make them less competitive in other European countries. It is the European Central Bank which sets interest rates and is responsible for monetary policy. The German market is open; if German consumers choose on the whole to buy German products, this is not because of artificial trade barriers or protectionist measures. Non-German companies which export to Germany do not complain of discrimination or of difficulty in finding outlets or distributors. On the contrary, many of them are highly successful in penetrating the German market. It is just that, overall, German exporters are more successful still.

* * *

Although balance of trade patterns reflect the behaviour of individuals, deficits and debt reflect the decisions of governments. Here Germany's performance, though still better than that of most other European countries, has been more ambiguous.

The Treaty of Maastricht, signed in 1992, established the basic criteria for membership of a European single currency. All its member states should have a track record of being able to maintain low inflation, their deficits at less than 3 per cent of their GDP and their national debt at less than 60 per cent of it. These figures were then enshrined in the Growth and Stability Pact agreed in 1997 as the rules of the currency itself. They reflected the requirements of Germany for giving up the Deutschmark. Keeping inflation low was the *raison d'être* of the Bundesbank, and successive German finance ministers had imposed rigorous control on debt and deficit levels. In the negotiations leading up to the establishment of the single currency the German finance minister, Theo Waigel, was determined to ensure that the euro should maintain the reputation of the Deutschmark as a strong and stable currency. The Growth and Stability Pact was very much his creation.

The omens for strict adherence to the criteria were never good. As far as deficits were concerned the EU average was indeed by 1997 below 3 per cent, down from the 5.5 per cent of five years earlier, but the target had only recently been achieved. Germany itself had a deficit of over 3 per cent in 1994, 1995 and 1996. And the debt criterion of 60 per cent was never taken seriously. Only a minority of EU countries were in compliance when the euro was introduced. Germany was one of them, but Germany subsequently failed to meet it in every year from 2003 onwards.

Waigel was especially concerned, during the negotiations for the Growth and Stability Pact, to ensure that there were no provisions in it for bail-outs or for further resource transfers through the EU budget. In this he was successful. The single currency was created without any stipulation as to what should happen in the case of so-called asymmetric shocks (situations in which one or more member states are subjected to particular economic difficulties which do not affect

57

the majority). And the analysis of the Werner and MacDougall reports of the 1980s, which had suggested that a single currency could only be viable if there was an EU central budget of around 3 per cent of total EU GDP, was ignored.

Waigel's critical failure was not to include in the Pact any provisions for what should happen if a member state failed to abide by the rules. When challenged about this he replied simply that peer pressure would be so compelling that no finance minister would dare appear before his colleagues in the Council if his country was in breach. The Commission was given the authority to open proceedings against a member state which was running in its view an excessive deficit, but the procedure was complex and the fine which that member state might eventually have to pay was no more than symbolic.

Maybe Waigel assumed that the only participants in the single currency, at least initially, would be the traditional pillars of financial rectitude and prudence from northern Europe. Right up until the publication of the Commission's report in 1998 it was widely expected that the euro would begin with a membership limited to perhaps Germany, France, Benelux, Austria and Finland. But the Commission, basing itself on figures of doubtful reliability, recommended that Italy, Spain, Portugal and Ireland should qualify as well. So the euro was set up in 1999 with 11 members (Greece was admitted a year later on the basis of even more contrived data). Germany, which could have insisted on a narrower euro, chose to go along and take the risk.

Predictably the consequence was that adherence to the Stability Pact criteria became a matter of aspiration, rather than an absolute requirement. By 2001 Portugal was in breach of the deficit limit and the Commission duly opened proceedings against it. The following year both Germany and France failed to comply and the Commission concluded that rather than enforce the criteria it should re-interpret them. The proceedings against Portugal were dropped and discussions began about how the criteria might be softened. In 2005 it was agreed that the deficit limit should be calculated on the basis of an economic cycle rather than of a single year and that importance should be attached to trends as well as to absolute value (i.e. if a country seemed to be going in the right direction it did not matter so much whether it had actually arrived).

There are indeed good economic reasons for interpreting data on deficits and debt in this way. But the precedent set was unfortunate. Germany had insisted initially on strict rules, then found itself unable to stick to them and had connived at getting the rules changed. By refusing again in 2005 to address the question of what would happen if a euro member found itself simply unable to cope with the discipline of the Growth and Stability Pact, Germany merely postponed the eventual day of reckoning.

This is of course a comment with hindsight. Until the banking and sovereign debt crises which emerged from 2008 onwards, the euro seemed to be in pretty good shape. The European public had accepted it with enthusiasm, the European Central Bank had succeeded in its primary mission of controlling inflation, and the currency itself had recovered from its initial weakness to become a strong international adjunct to the US dollar. The EU as a whole seemed to be embarked on a virtuous circle of steady, sustainable growth. Those member states who needed to borrow had no trouble in doing so. What was there to worry about?

Although Germany may have been out of line with the Stability and Growth Pact criteria on a strict interpretation, it is still a model of prudence by comparison with most others. Since the introduction of the euro the worst that Germany's deficit has been was in 2003 when it narrowly exceeded 4 per cent, and its debt has peaked at around 80 per cent. Its triple-A credit rating has never been called into question and the interest it pays on its bonds is the lowest in Europe.

No other economy in Europe can match this performance. No wonder that Germany is seen as a model to follow.

* * *

The competitiveness of German enterprises is reflected in their success in penetrating markets all over the world: they are as adept at selling outside the EU as inside it. But the existence of the EU and of the euro has been of enormous benefit to Germany and has helped accentuate this competitiveness. From the outset the EU has offered Germany a large tariff-free market for its industrial goods and a degree of tariff protection against competitors from the wider world. Already by 1957, the year of the signature of the Treaty of Rome, German companies were confident of their ability to outperform those of other European countries. In the decades that followed they proceeded to do so. They treated the EU as their domestic market and they thrived.

In the early years, when international tariffs were relatively high, they also benefited from the fact that the EU was a customs union. This meant that German firms were shielded from competition from outside the EU – for example, from the United States or Japan – not only in Germany itself but in all other member states as well. They do not need such protection today; successive German governments have pushed the EU to pursue a free trade agenda both in the World Trade Organisation and in bilateral agreements. But initially the EU was, for Germany, both an internal opportunity and an external defence.

This is even more true of the euro. Once locked into a single currency, the other eurozone members no longer had the ability to enhance their competitiveness through the devaluation of their national currencies. They could only survive and prosper by increasing the efficiency of their enterprises and/or by reducing their wage costs. Unsurprisingly this has been monumentally difficult for some of them.

The euro has proved to be a stable currency (it still is despite the turmoil within the eurozone's economies) and the European Central Bank has kept as tight a lid on inflation as did the Bundesbank before it. Though its value against the dollar, and against other key currencies, fell in the years immediately after its introduction, it subsequently recovered, albeit not to the previous levels of the Deutschmark. If Germany had retained its own national currency, that currency would have appreciated to the point where German goods would, despite their quality, have become too expensive for many markets. Switzerland is facing this problem, but since its economy is less dependent on the manufacturing sector it can cope. For Germany it would be much more of a challenge.

Germany is by far the biggest beneficiary of the euro, just as it is of the EU's internal market. This is no coincidence. It has been German policy to ensure that the structures and rules of the EU and of the euro were cast in a German image. They have succeeded in doing so.

The other member states of the EU have admired the German model and have consciously adopted it as the EU's template. It is not Germany's fault if they have been unable to live up to the discipline which it involves. If Germany's EU partners had invested more and consumed less, had given their enterprises access to finance on a long-term basis, had encouraged innovation and fostered technological skills, then they might look more like Germany today. As countries like Finland and Korea have shown, it is not necessary to have centuries of industrial tradition to become a high-performing modern economy.

Similarly, if all the countries of the eurozone had managed their public finances in the way that Germany has, they would have had less need to borrow and fewer problems in doing so. Now they have no choice. The Fiscal Treaty agreed in March 2012 obliges them to follow Germany's example, whatever the cost to their public services or social security systems.

There is, however, still an inherent dilemma. Germany's economic model depends on outperforming its European partners. But this in turn means that many of these partners will be uncompetitive within a single currency area. They will therefore inevitably struggle to generate the growth needed to sustain the fiscal discipline to which they are now, at Germany's insistence, committed.

In effect, therefore, Germany's position is similar to the comment attributed to Gore Vidal about his own literary reputation: 'It is not enough that I succeed. Others must fail.'

☷ THREE ☷

Proud of the F Word

Margaret Thatcher's speech to the House of Commons on 30 October 1990 provoked Geoffrey Howe's resignation from her government and ultimately her own fall from office. In that speech she responded with the words 'No, no, no' to three proposals which she attributed to Jacques Delors, the president of the European Commission. The proposals were that the European Parliament should be the democratic body of the European Community, that the Commission should be its executive and that the Council of Ministers should be the senate.

This was indeed Delors' vision of the future of Europe. But, more importantly, it is that of successive German governments as well; it corresponds precisely to how Germany itself is governed. Germany is a federal state. The federal nature of its constitution and its politics is one of the country's defining peculiarities, one which is especially difficult for those who are not familiar with it to understand. It affects not only the way Germans think about their own country, but also how they think about Europe.

As with so much about modern Germany, history is partly responsible. Germany only became a state in 1871 as a result of the exertions of Chancellor Bismarck and Field Marshal von Moltke. Before then it had been a patchwork of units, small and large, whose inhabitants spoke German and felt a certain sense of kinship with one another but who had not been brought up to think of themselves as a single nation. Goethe, the most celebrated writer in the German language, who lived from 1749 to 1832, would have described himself as a citizen of Saxe-Weimar-Eisenach. Being German before 1871 was to possess a cultural identity, not a political one. Even after 1871 the sense of national unity was still relatively weak in Germany, certainly in comparison to France and Britain. It was only in 1934 that the term 'German' was used to describe nationality in German passports. Until then passport holders were described as Prussian, Bavarian, Saxon, and so on.

As a result many Germans still feel a residual affinity with the entity – kingdom, princely state, Hanseatic city or whatever – which previously constituted the sovereign layer of government in their region. The extent of this affinity varies. The inhabitants of Hamburg are immensely proud of their city, with its traditions of free trade and tolerance. Bavarians are proud, in a different way, of their distinctive history and their more relaxed attitude to life.

Bavaria is also unique in having a political party of its own. The Christian Democratic Union, unlike the Social Democrat Party, the other big national party, does not put forward candidates for elections in Bavaria. Instead it operates an alliance with the Christian Social Union, a purely Bavarian party which broadly shares its political agenda but has its own profile on a number of issues – for example, social policy and agriculture, on both of which it is extremely conservative.

Curiously, of all the former components of what in 1871 became Germany, the one which has disappeared from the political map is the one which was the largest, namely Prussia. In the eighteenth century Prussia, under Frederick the Great, had been one of the dominant powers of Europe; though it had been previously defeated and humiliated by Napoleon it was Blücher's Prussians who saved the day at the battle of Waterloo. In the nineteenth century Prussia gradually won back its influence, initially through the creation of the North German Federation and finally by the settlement of 1871 in which in effect it took over the remaining German states to form the new German Reich. The Hohenzollern kings of Prussia became the emperors of Germany.

Even though Prussia constituted 60 per cent of the population of the new Germany in 1871, no one today describes themselves as Prussian.

This is partly because of the overtones of militarism and hegemony which are associated with the Prussian name, partly because so much of the territory of the former Prussia is now in Poland, the Baltic states or, in the case of the former Königsberg, in Russia. It also perhaps reflects the fact that Prussia itself subsumed a number of more local identities and so had less of an identity of its own.

The Hohenzollerns, whose surviving members lead quiet and reclusive lives in Berlin, are not the only German royal family. The Wittelsbach kings of Bavaria, the Wettin kings of Saxony and the Welf princes of Hannover all have descendants who feature from time to time in the gossip columns of German newspapers. They are not public figures in any political sense but they serve to remind Germans of a time when their ancestors' loyalty was to a different country.

None of this means that there are in Germany any secessionist tendencies or any nostalgia for a different political order. Quite the opposite: Germany is today the most homogeneous of all the large countries in Europe, and the miracle – as it seems still to most Germans – of reunification is what dominates their thinking about their country. Rather, their history means that they find it less difficult to adjust to the idea of multiple political affiliations. Feeling both Bavarian and German makes it easier to feel both German and European.

Regional affiliations are not just a relic of Germany's past. They are also, and more significantly, inherent in the country's modern governance. When the victorious Western Allies set about the political reconstruction of their part of Germany after World War II, they deliberately encouraged a structure which diffused power and which was not based on too strong a central government. This coincided with the instincts of those German politicians who were directly involved in the drafting of the new constitution, notably the then mayor of Cologne, Konrad Adenauer, who later became the country's first chancellor.

As a result the Germany which emerged in 1949 was, and still is, a federal republic. Its constituting entities are the *Länder* (provinces). It was their representatives who signed and ratified the constitution, and it is by decisions of the *Länder* that Germany exists as a sovereign state.

The word *Land* has the connotation of country as well as province. And the governmental structures of the *Länder* – and the terminology used to describe them – are similar to those of sovereign countries. Each *Land* has its *Landtag* (parliament), whose members choose a *Land* government headed by a minister president with a full panoply of ministers. They are thus similar to the governments of Scotland, Wales and Northern Ireland, rather than the administrations of English county councils.

Initially there were 11 *Länder*. But in 1952 three combined to form the *Land* of Baden-Württemberg, so for the next 38 years of the Federal Republic there were nine. Curiously, Bavaria, one of the founding *Länder*, never ratified the constitution. The reasons for this failure, which seems to have had no practical consequences, are obscure; it is unclear, following German reunification, what criteria remain to be fulfilled to persuade Bavaria to change its mind.

The GDR, when it voted to annexe itself to the Federal Republic, had to accommodate itself to this structure. It had by then no real equivalent of *Länder* of its own (the ones which had previously existed were abolished in the 1950s in favour of smaller local administrative units, but these had little real power), so there were no *Land* governments to sign the constitution in the way that the original West German *Länder* had done. But, following the decision to reunify, six East German *Länder* – Brandenburg, Mecklenburg-Vorpommern, Sachsen, Sachsen Anhalt and Thüringen – were created. With Berlin itself becoming a *Land*, rather than a city subject to special four-power status, Germany now had 16 *Länder*, but the constitution itself, and the form of governance which it prescribes, remained unchanged.

This constitution (in German the 'Grundgesetz', which literally translated means Basic Law) ascribes certain powers to the Bund (the central government). All powers not so ascribed remain within the competence of the *Länder*. The guiding principle in assigning competences was the extent to which citizens were directly affected as individuals. Where they are – for example, in such areas as health, education, culture and policing – the *Länder* have the competence. Where the effect is more indirect, such as in foreign and defence policy, control of borders, immigration and general economic and fiscal policy, the competence lies with the federal government.

Even in areas where the federal government has responsibility, the actual administration often lies with officials who work for *Land* governments. Tax collection is one example. Germany has national rates of income tax and other taxes but there is no equivalent of the UK's Inland Revenue (i.e. a national body responsible for tax collection). Instead, taxes are collected by the individual *Länder*, who have their own tax services for the purpose, and the money is transferred from them to the national exchequer. The Federal Ministry of Finance has a very small taxation department which deals with policy issues but has no administrative power.

In theory the separation of competences between the federal government and the *Länder* should have meant that legislation was either a matter for the Bundestag, the national parliament, or for individual *Länder* in their own *Landtags*. But the constitution also provides that in instances where the interests of the *Länder*, particularly their financial interests, are affected by decisions at the federal level, the Bundesrat, the council of the *Länder*, has to approve the legislation in question. This has profound effects on how politics in Germany work. In order to get its legislation into force, a German government needs in most cases to secure not only the approval of the Bundestag, in which it has by definition a majority, but also of the Bundesrat, whose political composition may be different.

* * *

The Bundesrat is not a body to which anyone is directly elected or appointed. It is a council whose members are the representatives of the governments of the 16 *Länder*. It is up to each *Land* to decide whom to send to any Bundesrat meeting. In practice it is usually the minister president who attends for anything important, but he or she is accompanied by whichever *Land* minister is responsible for the subject under discussion.

The Bundesrat's composition, and its political balance, is subject to change every time there is a *Land* election. The *Länder* hold their elections at different times but, given that there are 16 *Länder* and that the term of office of their parliaments is usually four years, there are on average four such elections a year.

Votes in the Bundesrat are weighted. The *Länder* with the largest populations have more; the smaller ones have fewer. But the weightings are not arithmetically proportionate to size. There are only four categories, with a maximum vote entitlement of six and a minimum of three. Thus North Rhine Westphalia with 18 million inhabitants has six votes. Bremen with 663,000 inhabitants has three. It is an odd model. Logic might suggest that either all *Länder* are equal, in which case they should all have equal votes, just as all American states, large or small, elect two senators; or that all citizens are equal, in which case voting weights should correspond directly to demographics.

It is, however, an oddity with which most Germans seem to be comfortable. Though there are many arguments in Germany about constitutional issues, changing the voting system in the Bundesrat is not one of them. It also perhaps explains why Germany has never argued in favour of voting rights in the EU Council of Ministers which directly reflect the population sizes of the member states.

For a draft bill to become law it needs to secure 35 positive Bundesrat votes out of a total of 69. An abstention therefore has the same effect as a negative vote. How each *Land* votes on any issue is a matter for decision by the government of that *Land*. In cases where a *Land* government is a coalition of representatives of different political parties – and most of them are coalitions – the agreement to which the parties subscribe when they decide to form the coalition usually stipulates what is to happen when the members of the coalition cannot agree on how to vote in the Bundesrat. In most cases this means that the *Land* abstains. Thus, getting a positive decision out of the Bundesrat for anything which is controversial is never easy.

Just as American presidents do not often have the good fortune of a Congress with a political majority in their favour, so too in Germany it is unusual for the majority in the Bundestag to be similar to that in the Bundesrat. Federal governments therefore frequently face a challenge in securing the passage of their legislation. Their ability to do so can sometimes require political skills of a kind which resemble those of the horse-trading and pork-barrelling of Washington.

Some chancellors are more adept at this than others. In the summer of 2000 the federal government led by Gerhard Schröder had, as a result of a series of defeats in *Land* elections, lost its majority in the Bundesrat. But it was committed to the adoption of a tax reform law which was the first step along the painful road of bringing order to Germany's public finances and improving the competitiveness of the economy. The main opposition party, the Christian Democrats, had opposed the draft bill in the Bundestag and it was widely assumed that because they had the votes to defeat it in the Bundesrat they could prevent it from becoming law.

However, in the 48 hours before the crucial meeting at which the Bundesrat was due to vote, Schröder made a series of telephone calls to the coalition leaders of the key swing vote *Länder* and – literally – bought them off. He only needed to secure the support of three or four of the smaller ones, all of which were in the poorer parts of Germany. Schröder picked them off one by one by offering financial support from the federal budget for projects on their territories which they would not otherwise have been able to afford. When the vote came to be taken, all four of them, to the amazement of the political commentators and the chagrin of the national leadership of the Christian Democrats, voted in favour of the bill. It was a remarkable, and perfectly legal, political tour de force.

I asked Schröder afterwards how sure he had been that they would vote his way. He chuckled and said that he had been pretty confident.

He knew them all from his own time in the Bundesrat as minister president in Lower Saxony and he understood exactly what mattered to them back home. A successful political manoeuvre of this kind is rare. Normally the *Länder* vote not on the basis of specific issues which affect them individually, but in accordance with the national positions of the political parties which make up their governments. This can often mean deadlock between Bundestag and Bundesrat. In the final years of the government of Helmut Kohl the *Länder* led by the SPD, which at the time had a majority in the Bundesrat, adopted a so-called 'blockade policy'. They systematically voted down all attempts (admittedly rather tentative ones) by the federal government to reform the welfare state. They did this under pressure from the national leadership of the SPD, and in particular its then chairman, Oskar Lafontaine, who wanted to portray the Kohl government as malign and impotent and the SPD as the defender of the hard-won rights of the working class. The tactic did great damage to Germany's long-term economic interests but probably helped the SPD to win the Bundestag election of 1998. Lafontaine was able to maintain discipline over the Bundesrat in large part because he was, as minister president of Saarland, one of its members. This in turn is illustrative of where political power in Germany really lies.

* * *

In theory the German constitution allows for significant differences between the *Länder*. In the areas for which they have responsibility, it is open to each *Land* to organise its affairs and its policies according to its own choices. In practice they do not do so. They all organise their administrations and deliver their services in pretty much the same way. Germany is, despite its federal constitution, a homogeneous country.

Even in the field of education, the biggest policy area within the competence of the *Länder*, the differences are smaller than they might appear. The federal government has no responsibility for education. There is no federal German ministry of education. Each *Land* is free to develop its own educational system, with its own arrangements for admission to schools and universities.

As a result there are types of school which are prevalent in one *Land*, but rare, or non-existent, in another. Bavaria, for example, favours *Gymnasia* (grammar schools) based on academic selection, while other *Länder* do not. But in all *Länder* pupils are at some stage separated into those who will go on to secondary education and those who receive vocational training, the quality of which is high. Though the description and nomenclature of schools vary, the nature of the education received is broadly the same.

This is the result of deliberate choice by the *Länder*. They have set up a body called the Kultusministerkonferenz (Conference of Education and Culture Ministers), a standing body which co-ordinates their policies. The conference is supposed simply to guarantee a minimum of compatibility in the educational systems of *Länder* in order to facilitate mobility between one *Land* and another. In reality it has brought about a very high level of similarity and conformity. Thus Germany has a single set of school examinations, culminating in the *Abitur*, the school-leaving exam taken at age 18 or so, to which all pupils in every *Land* are subjected. And though universities receive financing from their individual *Länder*, they offer entry on equal terms to anyone from anywhere in the country.

Universities too organise their affairs on a collective basis. Other than in the very tiny number of private colleges, they teach the same type of courses in the same way, with lecturers and professors paid on the same basis, throughout the country. It is almost as if, having been offered the prospect of diversity, the Germans have decided to forgo it.

*   *   *

If Edmund Stoiber, the candidate of the Christian Democrats, had succeeded, as he nearly did, in becoming federal chancellor in 2002, he would for the first time in his career also have become a member of the Bundestag. The same would have been true if Frank-Walter

Steinmeier, the SPD candidate, had succeeded in 2009 or Peer Steinbrück, also the SPD candidate, in 2013.

To anyone brought up in the British political tradition the idea of becoming prime minister without ever having previously been a member of the House of Commons is (Alec Douglas-Home notwithstanding) bizarre. But to Germans there is nothing odd about it. It is just a trivial detail, like being left-handed. This is because, unlike the House of Commons, the Bundestag is not the dominant centre of German political life.

Until the advent of Angela Merkel, all German chancellors had been minister presidents of a *Land* or at any rate had served as prominent local politicians. Konrad Adenauer had been mayor of Cologne, Ludwig Erhard had been economics minister in Bavaria, Kurt Georg Kiesinger had been minister president of Baden-Württemberg, Willy Brandt had been governing mayor of Berlin, Helmut Schmidt had been interior minister in Hamburg, Helmut Kohl had been minister president of Rheinland Pfalz, and Gerhard Schröder had been minister president of Lower Saxony.

Only three of them – Erhard, Brandt and Schmidt – had also served as ministers in a federal government. It was as local politicians that they began their careers and made the critical breakthrough to success and recognition. It was by virtue of being locally known that they became nationally known.

Similarly with would-be chancellors. Stoiber in 2002 was the minister president of Bavaria, and before Gerhard Schröder succeeded in 1998 the three previous candidates whom the SPD had put up to challenge Helmut Kohl had all been minister presidents: Johannes Rau from North Rhine Westphalia in 1987, Oskar Lafontaine from Saarland in 1990 and Rudolf Scharping from Rheinland Pfalz in 1994. In this respect German politics are similar to those of the United States. Far more American presidents have been former state governors than former senators or congressmen.

Service as a minister president is not just a potential springboard to the chancellorship. It is also a path to senior ministerial office at the federal level. Among the 25 or so cabinet ministers who served under Gerhard Schröder, seven were former minister presidents. By contrast, only one or two of his other ministers were long-standing members of the Bundestag who had achieved political prominence by virtue of their performance there. Things are different under Angela Merkel. She is not herself a former minister president, nor has she ever served in a *Land* government. And there are no former minister presidents in her cabinet.

Angela Merkel is an unusual chancellor in many respects. Not just because she is a woman and an '*Ossi*' (an East German). She is also Protestant, divorced and a physicist, a unique combination for the leader of a party previously run by Catholic lawyers or historians with traditional family backgrounds. At 51 she was the youngest chancellor ever. Above all, she is unusual in the way she became leader of her party.

She did so in the same way that Margaret Thatcher did: by challenging the incumbent when her rivals lacked the courage to do so. Mrs Thatcher (like Angela Merkel also something of an outsider in that she was a Nonconformist, married to a divorced man and a chemistry graduate) stood against Edward Heath for the leadership of the Conservative Party in 1976 when her colleagues felt constrained by loyalty, or inertia, not to do so. She had been a minister for education but had never held one of the big offices of state. She was not especially popular within her party and there were many men in suits, like Willie Whitelaw, who were seen as more natural candidates for the post. But by seizing the initiative in the way that she did Mrs Thatcher was able to see them off.

Angela Merkel too had been a cabinet minister, minister for the environment, under Helmut Kohl, who patronisingly referred to her as '*das Mädchen*' (the girl), but she was seen as a competent performer, rather than a political star. In 2000 she became secretary general of the CDU, an important organisational post but not one which had traditionally been a natural springboard to the top.

But in 2002 she seized her moment. The party was beset by financial scandals involving cash contributions in brown envelopes from anonymous donors. Angela Merkel spoke out forcefully against the system which had tolerated such behaviour and called for change. This led to the resignation of Wolfgang Schäuble, who had succeeded Kohl as party chairman and who had himself accepted one of the envelopes.

Angela Merkel put herself forward as his replacement and was elected without opposition at a special party conference. She had caught the popular mood, and the regional party barons – Germany's equivalent of the men in suits – who might have thought themselves more suitable for the job, were left floundering. More than a decade later some of them still cannot quite believe that she is the party leader. She does not have the characteristic of *Stallgeruch* (the smell of the stable), the long years of intimate involvement in party affairs and familiarity with party quirks and foibles, which most CDU and SPD party leaders are expected to have and which Helmut Kohl exemplified.

I had lunch with her not long after she became party leader. She was remarkably candid in acknowledging how different she was from her predecessors and what a shock her election had been to the traditionalists in the party. But she noted that for many of them it was her background in the GDR and her Protestant religious upbringing which were more troubling than her gender.

She was also impressive in her curiosity. She asked me a lot of questions about the workings of the British political system, about how much time British ministers spent in their constituencies, about the relationship between the prime minister and the backbench MPs. I sensed that she was preparing herself for the international role which the post of party leader involved and was happy to use the lunch, which she ate with gusto, to gain some information of her own.

To say that the Bundestag is not the dominant centre of German political life is not to downgrade its role or importance. German governments and German chancellors take, and remain in, office only on the basis of the Bundestag's support. The Bundesrat plays no role in this.

It is not, however, the only route to political power. Ministers in the federal German government do not have to be Bundestag members.

Nor indeed does the federal chancellor. It is customary before a federal election for the main parties to announce who is their candidate for the chancellorship and for that candidate to stand for election to the Bundestag. But if, for whatever reason, a new chancellor needs to be appointed between elections, then it is possible for someone from outside the Bundestag to be proposed. Kurt Georg Kiesinger was elected chancellor in this way in 1966 when he was minister president of Baden-Württemberg.

Each ministry in the federal government has at least one parliamentary state secretary – a junior minister, who is an elected Bundestag member. Otherwise it is up to the parties who form the coalition to appoint whoever they choose. Ministers with no previous political experience whatever are rare (though not unknown), but such political experience can be gained as effectively via service in a *Land* government or parliament, or even at other levels of civic administration, as in the Bundestag.

So, if you are a politically ambitious young German with dreams of one day becoming the leader of your country, you do not automatically think of standing for your national parliament. You are more likely to look to a career in local politics first and to try to build up a power base there.

* * *

Even within the world of national politics, regional interests are still important. This is illustrated in the way the Bundestag functions. Its activities follow something of a set pattern. It meets usually for one week in the month. Politicians who are not government ministers are normally therefore only to be found in Berlin during such a *Sitzungswoche*. The rest of the time they are in their constituencies or regions. They arrive in town on the Monday. On Monday evenings, at least as far as the two big parties are concerned, the *Landesgruppen*, the groups of Bundestag members from individual *Länder*, meet to discuss the issues coming up in the forthcoming week's session. On Tuesdays the full *Fraktions* (parliamentary groups) meet. These are often the key meetings of the week and government ministers take the meetings of their own *Fraktion* very seriously. On Wednesday it is the turn of the Bundestag committees, who offer recommendations on draft legislation and discuss whatever other matters they have chosen to put on their agendas. Only on Thursday does the Bundestag meet in full plenary session. By Friday midday that session is usually over and it is time for members to return to their constituencies.

Of course there are often exceptions to this routine and there are sometimes emergency sessions to discuss something of burning importance. But to convene such an emergency session requires two days' notice. The Bundestag is thus not a body which sees itself as having a finger continually on the pulse of the public mood or as one to which ministers are expected to report regularly on their doings.

There is, for example, no equivalent of the UK's Prime Minister's Questions, or indeed of ministerial questions generally, in the form in which they take place in the House of Commons. This absence of direct parliamentary challenge also reflects the fact that Germany has no position, either formal or informal, of leader of the opposition. Parties only decide in the run-up to a federal election who are their candidates for the chancellorship.

For a governing party the choice has hitherto been a formality. No German chancellor has not stood for re-election, and no party has sought to get rid of an incumbent chancellor. This is why for Helmut Kohl the removal of Margaret Thatcher from power in 1990 was, despite their poor personal relations, so shocking and wrong (something he made publicly known at the time).

For the opposition, the selection of a chancellor candidate can often be a difficult decision. It is not, for example, axiomatic that the chairman of the party has an automatic right to the slot if he or she wants it. In 1998 Oskar Lafontaine was SPD party chairman and would dearly have liked to become chancellor, having failed to do so when he was the SPD's candidate in the election of 1990. But there was another big beast in his party in the shape of Gerhard Schröder, and

Schröder was, according to the opinion polls, much more popular in the country at large and had a better chance of beating Helmut Kohl.

Schröder himself had to face an election in Lower Saxony, of which he was minister president, in the spring of that year (the federal election was not due to take place until September), and he cleverly made use of it as a kind of primary. He declared that if he did not achieve a certain (in fact not very ambitious) result he would not consider himself to be a credible candidate for the chancellorship. In the event he comfortably exceeded the threshold he had set himself and was able therefore to present the result as in some way giving him wider legitimacy. His popularity ratings increased still further and Lafontaine decided not to stand against him at the party conference to pick the candidate.

Schröder's success led eventually to Lafontaine's defection from the party. In 2000, in an act of unexplained pique, Lafontaine resigned from his posts as party chairman and finance minister. After a long political sulk he joined Die Linke, the party associated with the former communist party of the GDR and was for a time their co-chairman. The SPD had less luck when it subsequently opted for a chancellor candidate who was not the party chairman. In 2009 the party opted for Frank-Walter Steinmeier rather than Kurt Beck and in 2013 Peer Steinbrück rather than Sigmar Gabriel. Both lost.

In the case of the CDU and CSU the selection of a chancellor candidate is complicated by the fact that the two parties are separate entities who have to agree on a common representative. This has twice resulted in the leader of the smaller party, the CSU, being nominated. In 1980 Franz Josef Strauss was chosen in preference to Helmut Kohl, in 2002 Edmund Stoiber in preference to Angela Merkel. Although both Kohl and Merkel were chairmen of the larger CDU, they were in each case fairly new in their jobs and had not achieved complete dominance of their party. So their internal party rivals were able to conspire to prevent them from getting the chance to become chancellor.

In neither case did the choice of a CSU, rather than a CDU, candidate result in electoral victory, and in both instances the

Bavarian identity of the nominee was held by many observers to have been a drawback. Perhaps so. But by historical standards they did not do badly. In 1980 the combined CDU/CSU share of the vote was their highest ever. In 2002 they came within a whisker of being the largest party in the Bundestag. And in both years they were facing popular and powerful SPD incumbents in the shapes of Helmut Schmidt and Gerhard Schröder.

* * *

The absence of a leader of the opposition is one reason why the Bundestag is not a confrontational body. Another is the character of the chamber itself.

It is arranged as a hemicycle and its members sit grouped together by party. Speakers address their colleagues from a lectern and are only rarely interrupted. Speaking slots and times are allocated in accordance with status and there is little spontaneity or passion. It is a parliament designed and programmed for rational debate among sensible people geared to finding consensus, rather than for the rough and tumble which characterises the House of Commons.

As a result, political rhetoric is not a skill which in Germany is highly prized. Reputations in the Bundestag are not made, or at any rate not principally made, by dexterity on the floor of the house or by the ability to pose, or respond effectively to, tough questions. Rather, they are made by expertise and hard work in committees, either committees of the Bundestag itself or in the *Fraktions* and their ancillary bodies.

Expertise is encouraged through a system which rewards specialisation. Each *Fraktion* has its chairman and vice chairmen and its own official spokesmen for the main policy areas (foreign affairs, defence, health, social policy, economics, taxation, etc.). In addition, individual *Fraktion* members are informally acknowledged as being responsible for particular topics or relationships.

Of course, in all parliaments individual members have personal interests or hobby horses. In the Bundestag this is more formalised. As a result, huge numbers of parliamentarians are bound into the system through a position of responsibility either in their own party group or in the Bundestag itself. This in turn means that there is a premium on acquiring expertise in something or other.

There is also less of a sense of frustration among backbenchers feeling they have no role to play and no prospect of promotion to ministerial rank. Indeed, such promotion is not necessarily the ambition of most Bundestag members. There are two reasons for this. First, there are far fewer ministers in Germany than in Britain, not all of them are elected and there is no tradition of the reshuffle (although ministers sometimes resign for personal reasons, the expectation is that once appointed they will serve for a full four-year parliamentary period). So the scope for moving onto or up the ministerial ladder is tiny. Second, the Bundestag itself is directly linked to the government in a way that the House of Commons, for example, is not. Legislation is discussed in advance with the *Fraktions* of the coalition parties, sometimes with those of the opposition as well, and the views of the *Fraktion* experts and office holders are taken very seriously. Their support is not automatic: it has to be earned.

A political career in Germany which is limited to the holding of parliamentary office is not a second-class one. The chairmanships and senior memberships of Bundestag committees are not allocated as consolation prizes to those who hoped for, or who have lost, ministerial posts. Prominence in the Bundestag is important in its own right. The post of chairman of a *Fraktion* is one of the most senior in German political life, second only to that of the chancellor in the case of a governing party and equal to that of party chairman in the case of a party in opposition. When it comes to media interviews and talk shows a Bundestag expert is as likely to be the focus of attention as a minister. The phenomenon of the disgruntled backbencher, thwarted by lack of ministerial promotion and fed up with being treated as lobby fodder by the whips, is not part of the German political scene.

* * *

If asked what was their primary purpose in the House of Commons, most British MPs would probably say (either because they believed it or because they thought it was the answer expected of them) that it was to represent their constituents. Their German counterparts would be more likely to say that it was to control the government. This is not because members of the Bundestag do not have constituencies but because their relationship with their personal electorate takes a different form.

The Bundestag has around 630 members. Half of them are directly elected by constituencies on a first-past-the-post basis. The other half are elected from regional (*Land*) party lists proportionately to the overall number of votes secured by their parties. The candidates who win constituency seats are elected irrespective of the performance of their party overall. But to be allocated seats from the list a party needs to achieve at least 5 per cent of the national vote.

There is no difference in status between a directly elected Bundestag member and one who is elected from a list. During his 16 years in the Bundestag as federal chancellor, Helmut Kohl was only once directly elected from his constituency. Gerhard Schröder never stood in a constituency at all.

The system has obvious attractions. It has the merits of proportional representation in ensuring that the composition of the national parliament broadly reflects the national party vote. It retains the link between parliamentarian and constituency. It makes it difficult for minority extremist parties to get elected. It has provided Germany since 1948 with remarkable political stability. Governments usually last their full four-year term. Coalitions are the norm, but they have only ever involved two parties; only once, in 1982, has the composition of a coalition changed in mid-term.

And German voters seem to understand what their Bundestag members can and cannot do. They do not expect them to sort out their housing problems or to involve themselves with local issues which fall within the competence of *Land* governments or local councils. Given that the Bundestag usually sits for only one week a month, German parliamentarians spend a lot of time in their local areas. Many of them hold the equivalent of constituency surgeries, where they listen to the views of their voters on a one-to-one basis. For the most part, though, they use their time back home to maintain their personal political popularity. It is the local party association which decides who will be the candidate in a particular constituency and the order in which candidates will appear on the regional list. A politician of real national prominence is unlikely to be deselected or relegated. For others, each election means a new challenge to ensure local party support.

As a result they are assiduous attenders at local party fora. When they refer to public opinion it is usually the views of the '*Basis*' (the party faithful) that they have in mind. Mavericks are not unknown but for the most part German parliamentarians see their prime loyalty to their party, rather than to their electorate.

* * *

The Federal Republic of Germany, which came into being in 1948, has always had a multiparty system. In the first Bundestag, elected in 1949, 12 parties were represented. In the Bundestag of 2013 there were five. During the intervening years eight parties disappeared from the national stage, one new party (the Greens) was born and one (Die Linke) reinvented itself.

For all this time the Bundestag was dominated by two blocs – the Christian Democrats and the Social Democrats – and one of these blocs, together with a minor party, normally formed the federal government. The exceptions were the periods from 1966 to 1969, from 2005 to 2009 and from 2013, when the two blocs combined to form a so-called Grand Coalition, in each case with a Christian Democrat chancellor.

Both the Christian Democrats and the Social Democrats have deep roots in German political history but they developed their present form and ideology in the first two decades of the Federal Republic. Both describe themselves as *Volksparteien* (people's parties), meaning that they aspire to represent a wide spectrum of popular opinion and to achieve a substantial percentage of any popular vote. They have generally succeeded in these aims. Neither of them has ever polled less than 20 per cent of the national vote (in the case of the Christian Democrats never less than 25 per cent); no other political party has ever polled more than 15 per cent.

The Christian Democrats are, as the name suggests, a conservative party whose original ethos was to support the moral values of the Catholic Church. The party's social outlook has been caricatured as reflecting the nineteenth-century concept of '*Kirche, Küche, Kinder*' (church, kitchen, children) and it has traditionally been strongest in those parts of Germany, notably the south, where the population is overwhelmingly Catholic. But it has been agile enough over the years to modernise itself and to continue to appeal to a wider spectrum of the electorate than simply churchgoers. It has, for all but ten years of the Federal Republic's history, always been the largest party in the Bundestag and it has provided Germany's chancellor for all but 20 years.

The CDU's sister party in Bavaria, the Christian Social Union, is traditionally more socially conservative and more protective of the rights of individual *Länder*, including the right to dish out subsidies. It dominates the politics of Bavaria. All Bavaria's minister presidents since 1957 have been from the CSU.

The Social Democrats are a single party. Its origins were Marxist but in 1959 at the party conference in Bad Godesberg it formally committed itself to the market economy by removing from its programme any references to nationalisation or to opposition to capitalism (the equivalent of the removal in 1995 of Clause 4 from the programme of the Labour Party in Britain). The party has traditionally had a large individual membership (usually larger than that of the CDU) and, though it has close links with the German trade union movement, it is not dependent on the unions for financing.

For much of the Federal Republic's history the only other party to form part of the German government was the Free Democrat Party. It was in office from 1949 to 1956, from 1961 to 1966, from 1969 to 1998 and again from 2009 to 2013, a longer period overall than either of the two main parties. From 1949 to 1956, from 1961 to 1966, from 1982 to 1998 and from 2009 to 2013 it was the junior partner in a CDU-led coalition and from 1969 to 1982 in an SPD-led one. For much of its time in government, under both types of coalition, it held the post of foreign minister.

The FDP represented classic liberalism: free market economics but socially tolerant. It generally polled between 5 and 10 per cent of the national vote, with its best performance in 2009, when it received 14.65 per cent and had 93 out of 622 seats in the Bundestag. Four years later, in the election of 2013, it failed to meet the 5 per cent threshold and disappeared from the national stage.

The FDP was seen as the most pro-European of all the German parties and this may have contributed to its defeat in 2013. That was not the only reason. The party chairman, Guido Westerwelle, found it hard to develop any profile as foreign minister under Angela Merkel and was forced to give up the leadership of the party. Neither of his two successors, Rainer Brüderle and Philip Rössler (unusual among German politicians in being of Vietnamese origin and adopted), made much of a mark as economic minister. By 2013 the party seemed to have lost its way and to have drifted into irrelevance.

It remains to be seen whether it can ever recover. So far the signs are mixed. In the European elections of 2014 it sank to 3 per cent and in the *Land* elections since then it has performed poorly. Without representation in the Bundestag or in many *Land* parliaments it has lost almost all of its state funding. In the national opinion polls it was by late 2016 hovering just above the 5 per cent threshold. It is hard to see what specific niche in the electoral market it can now hope to fill.

While some parties in Germany wither and fade, others spring into being. Mostly they achieve only local success and even that does not last long. Only one has established itself as a seemingly permanent feature of the national political landscape.

The Green Party was originally a protest movement. Its members are the linear descendants of the so-called Sixty-Eighters, the generation that became politically engaged through the student protests of that time, which left more of a mark on Germany than on any other European country. Whereas in Britain the 1960s are associated with music, fashion and sexual freedom, in Germany it was an era of political awareness and awakening: of anger, of radical revolt, of the alienation of a generation from their parents and from their parents' values. The protesters of 1968 in Germany were the first generation to have grown up with no personal experience of World War II, but with curiosity about what had happened to their country between 1933 and 1945, and why – and, above all, about what role their parents and grandparents had played.

There were protests and demonstrations elsewhere in Europe and America at that time. But in Germany it was more visceral and personal. Those who headed for the streets in 1968 and in the following years both displayed, and were confronted with, a level of violence which even nearly 50 years later still arouses strong passion and controversy among the German intelligentsia. They subsequently divided into three camps. Some, a tiny minority, chose the road of terrorism and morphed into the Baader-Meinhof gang or the Red Army Faction. Some just got on with life and joined the bourgeoisie. Others decided that the way to achieve political change was via what they called the long march through the institutions. So they formed a movement to provide the framework within which to do this.

It took a while for the Greens to decide whether they really wanted to be a political party and to exercise political power. Some of the individuals who were initially prominent in the movement resigned because of the compromises which this involved. But on the whole the party decided that power was indeed what it wanted to have. After successes in *Land* and European elections the first Green members were elected to the Bundestag in 1983 and the first Green *Land* minister, Joschka Fischer, was appointed in Hessen in 1985 (the training shoes which he wore when he took his oath of office are preserved in the Museum of German History in Bonn). Finally in 1998 the Greens entered the federal government as the junior partner in a coalition with the Social Democrats; the same Joschka Fischer became foreign minister and vice chancellor.

The Greens generally poll around 10 per cent of the popular vote. Like their counterparts elsewhere in Europe they focus particularly on environmental questions, and on social policy their perspective is a left/liberal one. They are more free market and less corporate in their approach to economic issues than the Social Democrats. They are fundamentally opposed to nuclear energy and to nuclear weapons.

In the past the Greens were a strongly pacifist party but their experience in national government changed that. The Green ministers in the government from 1998 to 2005 approved the participation of German armed forces in NATO operations in Kosovo and Afghanistan, and the party by and large supported them. They will never be enthusiastic about going to war but in some circumstances they will accept it.

The Greens are a normal party in the sense that other parties are ready to form coalitions with them. Their natural partners are the Social Democrats and their only experience so far of government at the national level was with the SPD. However, a coalition of the CDU and the Greens has held office in Hamburg (admittedly not a typical *Land*) and it is not inconceivable that one day such a coalition might emerge from the Bundestag. After the federal election of 2013 Angela Merkel, as chairman of the CDU, held talks with the Greens about the possibility of forming a government with them, for which there would have been a majority in the Bundestag. The talks came to nothing, as much from difficulties on the Green side as from the CDU, but the fact that they took place at all showed that from the CDU's point of view the Greens were in principle *koalitionsfähig* (suitable for forming a coalition with).

This is not true of the other party represented there, namely Die Linke (The Left). Its origins lie in the former Sozialistische Einheits Partei (SED) – the Socialist Unity Party – which was the name of the communist party in the GDR. After reunification the party changed its name to the Partei Demokratischer Sozialismus (PDS) and normally polled around 20 per cent of the vote in the eastern part of the country. In 2007 it merged with a breakaway group of left-wing Social Democrats to become Die Linke. At the 2013 Bundestag election it polled 8.6 per cent of the vote, down on its performance four years earlier, but still in third place.

Die Linke attracts votes from all over Germany and is represented in *Land* parliaments in several western *Länder*. Its real strength is in the eastern part of the country, though. It scores around 20 per cent or more of the vote in all the areas of the former GDR and has frequently been part of *Land* government coalitions there, including in Berlin. In 2014 a minister president from Die Linke was elected in Thüringen, the first time the party had ever held such a post.

The party is remarkably effective at the local level in looking after its supporters. I once spent a day with Uwe Klett, the *Burgermeister* (mayor) of Hellersdorf, a suburb of East Berlin. Klett came from a family of true socialist believers: his father had been an apparatchik in the GDR and Klett himself had joined the SED at the age of 22. He had, immediately after reunification, spent a couple of years at Glasgow University – an experience which did nothing to diminish his enthusiasm for radical socialism – and had on his return made a career in local politics with the PDS, the SED's successor. I had met him previously and mentioned that I had never been to Hellersdorf and he invited me to come and visit. We don't, he said, get many ambassadors in our part of Berlin.

His part of Berlin was indeed a different world. Hellersdorf is on the edge of Berlin on the border with Brandenburg and about 40 kilometres from the Polish border. Until the 1980s it was green fields and water meadows. Then, in the last decade of the German Democratic Republic, Hellersdorf was developed as a new housing project. The style was called Plattenbau – unit after unit of middle-to high-rise housing, uniform in style, devoid of any colour, charm or architectural merit. Functional and cheap (but not cheerful) accommodation for the citizens of a socialist republic.

West Berliners could never imagine living somewhere like Hellersdorf. But Klett was proud of it; so, more importantly, were the local residents. As he took me round people came up to him and chatted. He behaved like any engaged and experienced Western politician. He knew their names, asked after their families, discussed any local problems they had and promised to take up any issues they raised. If I had been a Hellersdorfer I would certainly have voted for him.

Despite its local successes at the national level no other party is willing to accept Die Linke as a coalition partner. This is partly because of its policies: it is opposed to Germany's membership of NATO and advocates the nationalisation of large swathes of the German economy. More broadly it is seen as too closely associated with the communist regime of the GDR and thus as not truly committed to the principles of German democracy.

The presence in the Bundestag of a party with which no one is willing to co-operate already makes government formation difficult. It meant that after the 2013 election only two options were available: either a coalition between the CDU/CSU and the Greens or a Grand Coalition between the CDU/CSU and the Social Democrats. Neither was a natural political fit.

The problems will be compounded if, as now looks likely, a new party is elected to the Bundestag in 2017. The party is called Alternative für Deutschland – Alternative for Germany (AfD). It was founded in 2013 by a group of middle-aged academics, most of whom were former members or supporters of the CDU. Its principal policy, and the reason for its establishment, was opposition to the euro. It was not, like the UK Independence Party (UKIP) in the United Kingdom, opposed to the EU as such. It argued that the creation of a single currency with such economically disparate members was a mistake and that the euro should either be abolished or replaced by a much smaller grouping limited to Germany, Benelux and Austria.

AfD was at first derided by the German political establishment. Commentators noted that all previous attempts to form a Eurosceptic party in Germany had come to nothing and that its leadership lacked any charismatic figure. But in the federal election in 2013 it gained 4.7 per cent of the vote and only narrowly failed to secure representation in the Bundestag. In the European election the following year it achieved 7 per cent of the vote and provided 7 of Germany's 96 successful candidates.

It was not an easy party to categorise in left/right terms. Its policies on European issues were reasonably clear. It opposed the euro but supported an EU which would do less and which would return certain competences to the member states. It was, therefore, against David Cameron's wishes and to the chagrin of Angela Merkel, accepted as a member of the European Conservatives and Reformists Group in the European Parliament, the group to which the British Conservatives also belonged. In other areas its positions were less clear. Many of its original leaders came across as economic and social liberals (one of them was Hans-Olaf Henkel, a former president of the Confederation of German Industry and a prominent supporter of Amnesty International), but others used a more populist rhetoric.

In the *Land* elections held later in 2014 AfD did even better, receiving around 10 per cent or more of the vote in Saxony, Thüringen and Brandenburg. Until the middle of 2015 it was polling 7–8 per cent nationally and looked set to be a durable feature of the German political landscape. But with its success came schism. Many of those who voted for it in the *Landtag* elections were nationalist in their outlook, and they gradually took over the party. In June 2015 it split in two. Its president and founder, Bernd Lucke, a mild-mannered economics professor who was a member of the European Parliament, was replaced by Frauke Petry, a more abrasive personality whose primary concern was immigration and who had been elected to the *Landtag* in Saxony. Lucke and several other prominent members resigned and founded a party of their own. Within months AfD's ratings were down to around 4 per cent; the other half of the party seemed to be going nowhere.

But the refugee crisis of the summer of 2015 gave AfD fresh wind. It was able to capitalise on public disenchantment with Angela Merkel's policy of offering asylum to any Syrian reaching Germany and it was the only party which identified immigration as the major threat to

Germany's way of life. By September 2015 it was back up to 7 per cent in the polls. Its popularity continued to rise in *Land* elections in 2016. In March in Sachsen Anhalt in the east it won 25 per cent of the vote and came second, behind the CDU. In Baden-Württemberg it won 15 per cent and in Rheinland Pfalz over 12 per cent. In September in Mecklenburg-Vorpommern (Angela Merkel's home province) it scored 20.8 per cent and pushed the CDU into third place and in Berlin in the same month it received 14.2 per cent of the vote. By the end of 2016 it was polling around 12 per cent nationally. No minor party has ever before achieved results on this scale. In all three elections immigration, and Chancellor Merkel's handling of it, was the principal pull factor in the AfD's favour.

The reaction of the other German political parties to the rise of AfD was first to ignore it and then to demonise it. Angela Merkel and others in the CDU ruled out any co-operation with it at either the *Land* or federal level. Within the European Parliament German members of all parties except Die Linke have conspired to prevent AfD representatives from securing the full share of committee posts to which they are entitled under the normal rules.

If AfD does enter the Bundestag in 2017, then treating it as a pariah will make coalition-forming even more difficult. If both a left-wing and a right-wing party are considered unsuitable partners, then the electoral arithmetic is likely to point to a permanent Grand Coalition. This will make many Germans uneasy. Unlike in Austria, where Grand Coalitions have been the norm for decades, in Germany they have traditionally been considered as something exceptional, to be entered into only as a last resort in exceptional circumstances. There would be fears that, if they occur regularly then, as in Austria, minor parties would prosper and that political extremism, on both left and right, would be strengthened.

Some in Germany worry that AfD could itself evolve in this direction. Since the ousting of its herbivore founders by the anti-immigrant carnivores it has certainly taken on a more nationalist tinge. At its party conference in April 2016 it adopted a programme which stated unequivocally that Islam did not belong in Germany and that minarets, the call to prayer and burkas should be banned. It also called for the removal of foreign troops and nuclear weapons from German territory.

AfD remains opposed to the euro. But immigration and Islam are now the main themes of its political campaigning. They undoubtedly resonate with sections of mainstream German public opinion, albeit not to the same extent as in Britain. But these are also the traditional concerns of Germany's far right. Inevitably therefore the success of AfD raises the question which has always hovered in the background of German politics: could a fascist party ever achieve power in the country again?

For Mrs Thatcher this was one reason for opposing German reunification. She did not fully trust the democratic instincts of the German people. She feared that they were imbued with some genetic psychological trait which made them susceptible both to sentimentality and to nationalism. She was mocked at the time for her beliefs but they were possibly shared by many people of her generation.

All the evidence, though, suggests that she was wrong.

* * *

The National Socialist Party was banned in Germany in 1945 and that ban remains in force. So too do strict laws outlawing the use of Nazi symbols or denial of the Holocaust. No political party which claimed to draw inspiration from Hitler or his ideology would be permitted to function in Germany today. However, that has not prevented the emergence over the years of a number of groups or movements of a – to put it mildly – pretty unappetising character; some of them have been associated with violence and criminality.

Far-right (to use a convenient shorthand term) political parties have existed in modern Germany since the late 1940s. They have usually had the words German, National or People somewhere in their names and have cultivated a populist image. Currently the

Nationaldemokratische Partei Deutschlands – the German National Democratic Party (NPD) is the best known and the most successful. It, or its predecessors, have from time to time won seats in *Land* parliaments – for example, in Sachsen Anhalt in 1998 with nearly 13 per cent of the vote – but they have never achieved the 5 per cent national threshold to secure representation in the Bundestag. (They did, in 2014, elect a single member to the European Parliament, but this was because the Constitutional Court had ruled that for European elections the threshold should be reduced to only 3 per cent.)

Attempts have often been made to have the NPD banned. On one occasion, in 2002, they failed because when the issue got to the Constitutional Court it transpired that most of the party's members were informants for, or indeed agents of, the Federal Security Service and it was therefore impossible to determine where responsibility for its activities really lay.

Right-wing extremism of the kind which the NPD represents has minimal public support or political impact in Germany, but its criminal element is alive and well. The Federal Security Service estimates that there are around 6,000 neo-Nazis in the country with a propensity towards violence, and that they have in recent years been responsible for some truly horrible attacks. In the 1990s there were a number of incidents of arson against hostels housing asylum seekers, one of which resulted in several deaths. More recently a cell calling itself the National Socialist Underground murdered ten immigrants or Germans of Turkish origin over a period of six years from 2004.

Such extremism is also publicly visible, particularly in the east of the country. Take a short drive outside Berlin and you find small run-down villages with groups of swastika-tattooed skinheads lounging around the local café. They have probably never seen a Jew or an immigrant but they mouth the same slogans of racial hatred as did their predecessors in the 1930s. Of course such gangs exist in most European countries but there is still something eerily sinister about seeing them on Hitler's own old territory.

None of the leaders of AfD has any extremist background. They reject any co-operation with nationalist or far-right parties. They do not support extra-parliamentary action and see themselves as a mainstream political party which has caught the zeitgeist in a way that the traditional ones have not.

Despite this, their focus on Islam brings them into contact with a popular movement whose activities are more dubious. PEGIDA is the acronym for Patriotische Europäer Gegen die Islamisierung des Abendlandes (Patriotic Europeans Against the Islamisation of the West). It was founded in 2014 by Lutz Bachmann, a public relations executive. It started off with a few small demonstrations which Bachmann characterised as evening strolls. Support grew and by January 2015 the gatherings were attracting crowds of 25,000. Its biggest rallies took place in Dresden and Leipzig, the cities in East Germany which had witnessed the demonstrations against communist party rule in 1989, a symbolism that was uncomfortable for liberal opinion.

PEGIDA attracted a hooligan element and provoked counter-demonstrations. But in 2015 it put up a candidate in the election for mayor of Dresden and got nearly 10 per cent of the vote. It never developed into a real political force and as the immigrant numbers declined, so too did PEGIDA's support. Its demonstrations in 2016 attracted hundreds rather than thousands of supporters. It survival seemed questionable.

What PEGIDA showed is that there is in Germany a latent hostility to Islam and to the presence of Muslims in German society which can be politically exploited. Many of those involved in PEGIDA were extremists, but that does not mean that hostility to Muslims is purely an extremist hobby horse. It touches a chord with some ordinary folk – conservatives, traditionalists, however one may choose to describe them – who do not want to see their country change in the way that, say, parts of Britain have changed.

An unspoken fear in German politics has been the emergence of a party on the right capable of attracting the support of these ordinary people. It is the nightmare in particular of the Christian Democrats. As the CSU exists as a separate party in Bavaria it is able as a result to advocate tougher social policies to its own electorate, which is on the conservative end of the spectrum, than would be acceptable in the more liberal northern parts of Germany.

Could AfD morph into, or pave the way for, a really popular nationalist party in Germany, similar to the Front National in France, the Freedom Party in Austria or Geert Wilders' party in the Netherlands? A few years ago most Germans would have dismissed the idea. Democracy and liberal values, they would have said, are simply too deeply entrenched in German society. And the experience of the Nazi era has made Germans viscerally antagonistic to any form of rabble-rousing populism.

Both of these points are still true. The sort of language used by Jörg Haider in Austria and by Jean-Marie Le Pen in France would simply not resonate beyond a minority audience in Germany. Germans are too suspicious of demagogy of this kind.

But a more thoughtful or middle-of-the-road approach might have a wider appeal. Opposition to spending German taxpayers' money on southern European wastrels, fears about excessive immigration and a concern to maintain Christian values in the face of an increasingly militant Islam are a powerful combination of political concerns. AfD has shown that it can translate its support into electoral success. It is not fanciful to imagine that, far from swiftly disappearing from the political stage like previous right-wing parties, AfD might become a permanent part of the political landscape.

The Greens have shown that it is possible in Germany to break the mould. Within two decades they developed from a fringe protest group to become part of a government coalition. Whether AfD manage to do the same will depend partly on events outside Germany – whether, for example, there is a new euro crisis or a new surge in immigration across the Mediterranean. Perhaps more crucially, it will depend on whether a charismatic figure emerges capable of catching the public mood. At the moment there is none. The new leadership of AfD is certainly more populist than its mild-mannered academic predecessors, but it does not contain any really strong personality.

Frauke Petry, its leader, is a sophisticated individual – she has a doctorate in chemistry and a successful career as an entrepreneur. She is virtually bilingual in English, having studied for her first degree at the University of Reading. However, she is not a natural media performer and she does not stir crowds. In addition, she is prone to gaffes. Once, in answer to a question about how Germany's borders should be protected, she offered the idea that police and border guards should be armed and should if necessary use their weapons. She tried subsequently to claim that she was merely quoting what the law prescribed and that using weapons did not mean killing people, but she was widely castigated for speaking in this way.

Even if she were to stand down, there is no one else in the leadership of AfD who looks to have a popular appeal beyond the party's current supporters. It is the party's programme, rather than its personalities, which currently attracts people to AfD.

This means that there is a potential in the future for a more powerful figure to give the party even more impetus. Not a demagogue like Le Pen, not a clown like Beppe Grillo of the Five Star Movement in Italy, not a loud-voiced man in a pub like UKIP's Nigel Farage, but someone with the ability to articulate the concerns of AfD voters in a way which makes them seem reasonable and natural. Someone from outside politics, perhaps, but with a reputation already made. A footballer? A CEO of one of the big corporations with the personality, if not the style, of Donald Trump? If, without such a figurehead, the party can reach 15 per cent in the polls, there is no reason why it could not reach 20 per cent or more under a more impressive leader. Were it to do so, German, and European, politics would be fundamentally changed.

It probably will not happen. This, at any rate, seems to be the calculation of the two main political parties in Germany, neither of which has so far shown much inclination to take AfD's agenda seriously. Questioning the euro is still a taboo for both of them.

Those few of their politicians who do speak out against Islamic values or who demand less tolerance of cultural diversity are treated as pariahs.

If AfD were to confound the commentators and increase still further its popularity, it would not mean that democracy in Germany was under threat – any more than the success of UKIP in Britain does. It is precisely because the party avoids – on the whole, at any rate – the language of nationalism or of contempt for others that it has prospered so far.

Extremism is definitely not alive and well and living in Germany. There's no revolution in the air. The country is not going to lurch to the right. The political landscape is serene, albeit more complicated than previously. The CDU seems set to remain the largest party on the national stage. What the rise of AfD has shown is that there is more discontent lurking beneath the surface than the pundits previously credited.

German politicians and commentators used to view with rather lofty disdain the travails of their colleagues in other European countries as they struggled with the likes of UKIP, the Front National, the Five Star Movement or Spain's Podemos. They were dismayed that the smooth course of European progress was perturbed by the recourse of some EU countries to referenda and the proclivity of electorates, not just in Britain, to deliver unanticipated referenda results.

Now they have to worry about their own country. Already there is talk that the CSU in Bavaria might turn itself into a national party and put up candidates elsewhere as well. Some in its leadership think that this would be the best way of harnessing the votes of those in their sister party, the CDU, who find Angela Merkel's policies on immigration too liberal and who might otherwise be tempted to shift to AfD.

It would be a huge gamble. The CDU would presumably put up its own candidates in Bavaria and the result would be unpredictable. But somehow or other the political system needs to accommodate the changing public mood. Both the Christian Democrats and the Social

Democrats in Germany pride themselves on being *Volksparteien*, meaning parties which have a broad appeal and which do not see themselves as representing any particular class or interest group. If they do not show more sensitivity to what many Germans feel about immigration and about Islam they may find that this status is called into question.

* * *

To anyone brought up in the German political tradition the world of Europe is, in terms of its governance, familiar. The role of the Commission is similar in function, though not in competence, to that of the federal government. The division of legislative responsibility between the Council and the European Parliament exactly mirrors that between Bundestag and Bundesrat. The appearance of the European Parliament's chamber in Strasbourg, and its procedures and operating methods, are those of the Bundestag in Berlin. The importance of committee work, the primacy of the political groups and the seemingly endless need for negotiation and compromise, all hallmarks of EU politics, are just what German politicians have been used to in their regional and national political life.

For many people in Britain, including many British Euro-parliamentarians, the workings of the EU seem alien and bizarre. For Germans they are a natural extension of domestic politics. No wonder that in recent years Germans have occupied so many senior positions in Strasbourg.

Equally familiar, from a German perspective, is the other major institution of the European Union, the European Court of Justice (ECJ). Its role, and the way it exercises that role, corresponds closely to that of Germany's own Constitutional Court. That court – the Bundesverfassungsgericht – enjoys enormous authority and respect. Its job is to interpret Germany's Basic Law and to ensure that all decisions of the country's government, legislature and judiciary are in accordance with it. Its role is that of judicial review. It is not an appellate court (of a kind like the Supreme Court in Britain) to which other courts routinely refer their cases. It acts on the basis of complaints, and these complaints can come from institutions such as the government, the political parties or individual *Länder* as well as from private citizens.

As a result, all manner of issues get referred to it and its rulings cover the whole spectrum, social, political and economic, of German life. Almost any piece of controversial legislation is likely to provoke a challenge to the court. Its judges are appointed by the Bundestag and the Bundesrat, and most of them have some sort of political coloration in that they have been nominated by one or other political party. But, unlike the Supreme Court in the United States, it does not routinely divide in its opinions according to the party political background of its members. Its reputation is that of a professional, almost pedantic, interpreter of a sacred text.

The court has no hesitation in striking down legislation, at either the national or provincial level, which it considers to be incompatible with the constitution or in ordering either the federal government or *Land* governments to revoke or amend decisions. It is not criticised for over-activism or for seeking to create, rather than interpret, the law. Germans seem to accept, for the most part, that the constitution has primacy and that it is up to the court to decide what the implications of this primacy are.

The court's rulings on issues relating to the European Union are followed with particular interest outside Germany. From time to time assertions are made, particularly from the anti-EU side of the argument, that the court has established, or re-established, the supremacy of national law over EU law or has set limits to the process of European integration. A close reading of the relevant texts, however, usually shows a more nuanced judgement.

The court has shown itself prepared, if necessary, to rule that EU legislation is incompatible with the German constitution. On issues where unanimity in EU decision making is required, the German government can prevent the adoption of any measure which would run the risk of provoking such a ruling. But in areas where decisions are taken by qualified majority vote and where there is thus a risk of Germany being outvoted, or pressurised by the possibility of being outvoted, into accepting an unsatisfactory compromise, the possibility of a successful challenge to the Constitutional Court cannot be excluded.

A recent example was over the Data Retention Directive of 2006. The court ruled in 2010 that the German legislation transposing the directive into national law breached the terms of the constitution and annulled it. As a result Germany was fined by the Commission for failing to fulfil its obligations. The reasons given by the court were effectively those of proportionality and detail, rather than of principle; the court did not challenge the right of the EU to enact legislation in this field or the broad purposes of the directive in question. It simply ruled that some aspects of its implementation were disproportionate in their impact on the individual freedoms to which German citizens are entitled.

The ruling thus does indeed show that in Germany the constitution, as interpreted by Germany's own Constitutional Court, takes precedence over anything enacted in Brussels. Some in Britain would argue that this is a good reason for having a written national constitution or at any rate a written Bill of Rights. But the practical impact so far of the Constitutional Court's rulings on EU issues has been limited. It has never challenged the right of the EU to legislate at all in any field in which legislation has been adopted.

It could in theory do so. The court is often concerned to protect the sovereignty of the Bundestag as set out in the constitution, but this tends to find expression in rulings which insist that the EU can only operate or legislate in accordance with the powers which the Bundestag has given it. The court does not challenge the right of the Bundestag to ascribe particular competences to the EU. Rather it seeks to maintain the doctrine that it is only by virtue of the Bundestag's decision that the EU has the power to act, and that EU actions are illegal if they depart from the terms under which the Bundestag has given it this power.

This is an important proviso. Taken with the court's rulings on issues like the Data Retention Directive it means that the court is the ultimate arbiter of whether EU legislation can be enacted in Germany. What it does not establish is the primacy of German parliamentary sovereignty. Nothing in any of the court's judgements so far could be interpreted as empowering the Bundestag to enact legislation incompatible with, or superseding, EU law.

The court's ruling on the legality of the European Stability Mechanism which it delivered in September 2012 is typical of this approach. It set out certain conditions which were necessary to ensure the compatibility of the mechanism with the German constitution. These were for the most part designed to protect the authority of the Bundestag; they did not call into question the right of the Bundestag itself to decide on the establishment of the mechanism or on its terms.

The Constitutional Court enjoys high respect in Germany. Its rulings are rarely criticised and there is no public mood of resentment that it is somehow usurping the function of parliament. Indeed, if anything there is a perception that the court sometimes serves as a bastion of individual rights against a state which is over fond of regulation.

Some of this respect seems to rub off onto German perceptions of the European Court of Justice. There are very occasional grumbles when an ECJ ruling strikes down some piece of German domestic tradition, as it did over the arcane beer production laws. But on the whole Germans seem to accept that the ECJ does a good job. Even in areas like Justice and Home Affairs, where the ECJ's involvement is relatively recent, there is no clamour in Germany for the Bundestag to retain the right to legislate or opposition to the idea that foreign prosecutors should be able to extradite German citizens.

* * *

The fact that the structures of power in the EU are so similar to those in Germany itself means that for most Germans Europe is familiar political territory. The doings of the EU may not be of burning daily interest, but they are easily intelligible and correspond in form and style to what Germans are used to at home.

The EU is also an institution of which Germany was a founding member and in which it has always been a major player. By contrast, Germany only joined NATO in 1955 and the United Nations in 1973. In both cases the rules and ethos of the organisations had been established without German participation and there was a sense in which Germany was initially under a kind of political probation – expected to demonstrate a period of good behaviour before it could aspire to assume a leading role. It took until 1988 for the first German politician (Manfred Wörner, the former defence minister) to become NATO's secretary general.

In the EU, on the other hand, Germany was involved in the original negotiations and was able itself to shape the organisation from the outset. The first president of the European Commission in 1957 was the former German foreign minister, Walter Hallstein (so far the only German to hold the post). Just as there is in Britain a historical pride in having been present at, and indeed actively responsible for, the creation of the institutions established in the 1940s which have helped shape the world ever since (the OECD and the Council of Europe as well as the UN and NATO), so too there is in Germany at having helped create the EU. And since in its early years the EU was an economic community, there were no restrictions on Germany exercising from the outset a strong influence on its policies, structures and procedures. Many of them are cast directly in a German image.

The statue above the Brandenburg Gate in Berlin is of a quadriga, a chariot pulled by four horses. It was erected to commemorate the Prussian victory over France in 1871. Today it could just as well depict the four key institutions of the modern Federal Republic – government, Bundestag, Bundesrat and Constitutional Court – all of which find a direct echo at the European level in the European Commission, the European Parliament, the European Council and the European Court of Justice.

The similarities go wider. Just as in Germany the Bundeskartellamt plays a central role in maintaining the rules of a market economy, so too one of the key elements of the original Treaty of Rome was competition policy. No separate institution comparable to the Bundeskartellamt was established at the European level, but within the European Commission the Directorate General for Competition (initially designated DGIV) has from the outset been the most powerful and autonomous department: the commissioner responsible for competition policy is able to take decisions on a quasi-judicial basis without the need for the collective support of his or her colleagues. For the first 20 or so years it was always headed, at official level, by a German (just as the Directorate General for Agriculture, DGIX, was for a similar period always in the hands of the French). The EU's approach to competition has consistently reflected German values.

So has the importance attached in the EU to the role of the so-called 'social partners', namely the employers and the trade unions.

Both employers and trade unions are organised at the European level, through Business Europe (formerly UNICE, the Union des Industries des Pays de la Communauté Européenne) and the European Trade Union Confederation. Their representatives sit on various EU consultative bodies and the Commission defers to their claimed expertise. They expect, as is the case with their German counterparts, to be informed about and to have the opportunity to influence any piece of draft legislation in the economic or social fields.

There is not, at the EU level, any equivalent of the German legal requirement for works councils and supervisory boards, but there is in EU employment law a presumption that it is the responsibility of employers' organisations and trade unions to negotiate together, and that governments and parliaments should accept whatever they collectively decide. This too reflects German practice more than that of any other member state.

* * *

It is often alleged by opponents of the EU that it is a French creation which is based on a French concept of the role of government. It is true that in the first 20 years or so of its existence French was the dominant language in the European institutions and the bureaucracy of the Commission worked in a French way. But when it comes to the structures of power, the nature of the bodies which exercise it, and the procedures through which they do so, the EU is not a French paradigm. It is Germany writ large.

⛩ FOUR ⛩

A Land Without a Past

In the 2002 film by the Finnish director Aki Kaurismäki, *Mies Vailla Menneisyyttä* (*A Man Without a Past*), the central figure is subjected to a violent attack which leaves him unconscious. When he wakes up he has lost his memory: he does not know his own name or anything about his previous life. He has to invent a new identity and to start all over again.

This is pretty much what happened to Germany after 1945. Neither the Federal Republic in the West nor the Democratic Republic in the East associated themselves with the Germanies which had gone before (although in terms of international law the Federal Republic accepted that it was a successor state), and neither sought to establish any continuity with the past. The emphasis was on reconstruction and renewal. Insofar as any looking back was allowed, it was to be done with shame and guilt.

In relation to the events of 1933 to 1945 this was understandable and indeed necessary. Acknowledging the truth about what happened during the Nazi years was vital in the development of democracy in the Federal Republic (it was not something to which much attention was paid in East Germany). What is surprising is that in the process of rejecting the inheritance of National Socialism, Germany has also, it seems, turned its back on the rest of its past as well.

* * *

Germany's only day of national celebration is 3 October, the date in 1990 on which the reunification of the country took legal effect. It is the occasion for *Festakts* throughout the country: solemn ceremonies

102

at which long speeches are delivered, interspersed by musical interludes of varying quality.

There is also, in terms of commemoration rather than celebration, 27 January, Holocaust Remembrance Day. Each year on this day the Bundestag is summoned to a special session at which all the leaders of the political parties make speeches in which they recall, and express their regret for, what happened to the Jews and others and their determination that Germany must never again allow the ideology which gave birth to the Holocaust to take root. The Bundestag is usually full for the occasion. No German parliamentarian would want to be accused of not acknowledging Germany's former sins. It is an occasion unique in the world. In no other country is there such a public recognition of past evil committed in the country's name. In no other country does the current generation of politicians accept the responsibility of public atonement of this kind.

The acceptance of this responsibility does not just apply to one day of the year or to the political class alone. It permeates all of modern German culture and discourse. German children, whose grandparents may have been born after the end of World War II, are taught in school about the Nazi period and the Holocaust and are, in many cases, taken on a visit to one of the many former concentration camps in Germany which have been preserved as monuments to terror. German historians and sociologists write prolifically about what happened and why.

Right in the centre of Berlin, between the Brandenburg Gate and the Potsdamer Platz, there is concrete reminder of it. The Holocaust Memorial is on a massive scale: a collection of sombre stone stelae which extends over four and a half acres. It was opened in 2005, 60 years after Hitler's death, and was visited by 3.5 million people in its first year. Berlin was not, as it happens, a city in which the Nazi Party enjoyed much support and Hitler did not like living there. But soon after the decision was taken in 1991 that Berlin should again become Germany's capital a competition was launched to decide how the memory of the Holocaust could best be publicly preserved there. Whatever the joy of reunification, it had to be accompanied by a visible reminder of Germany's past guilt.

It was not always so. In the two decades immediately after 1945 Germans paid little attention to their recent past. Many of the officials – judges, civil servants, teachers – who had served the Nazis, often enthusiastically, remained in office; although the most egregious war criminals were prosecuted there was little interest, either from the Allied occupiers or from the Germans themselves, in going after the smaller fry. Germany's second postwar chancellor, Kurt Georg Kiesinger, was a former member of the Nazi Party. Denazification certificates, cynically referred to as *Persilscheine* (Persil notes – after the detergent), were easily obtainable. People were more focused on survival and on the prospects for the future than on assigning guilt for former crimes or misdemeanours.

Things changed in the 1960s. The younger generation began asking questions, including questions about their own parents' involvement in the events of 1933 to 1945. One reason why the revolutionary atmosphere of 1968 and the following years was so intense in Germany was that it had a personal dimension to it. It was a revolt not just against the state or against the system but against the students' own families, and against the culture of silence which, as they saw it, had hidden the truth about the extent to which ordinary Germans had participated in, or at any rate turned a blind eye to, Hitler's excesses. The result was a catharsis of openness – in films, TV, books, press reporting and public discussion – about the Nazi years. It was uncomfortable at first for many of those who preferred to forget. But it allowed the country as a whole to feel more comfortable in its skin.

The way in which Germany has come to terms with its past is one of the many admirable features of modern German democracy. It stands in sharp contrast with the reluctance of other countries – Japan, Russia, China, Spain, for example – to examine their own history in the twentieth century.

Coming to terms with the past (for which the word *Vergangenheitsbewältigung* has entered the German language) has had wider implications for German public policy. It has led to a rejection not only of the Nazi period, but of the whole of previous German history. Nothing which happened before 1945 is accorded any public value or respect. No event – political, economic or social, let alone military – is commemorated, no achievement lauded, no individual lionised. The country has simply, like the character in Kaurismäki's film, moved on.

Of course there were many aspects of Germany before 1933 which were less than admirable. During the time of the Kaiserreich, the period from 1871 to 1918, anti-Semitism was rife – though probably no more so than in France – and the style of government was authoritarian, though less so than in Russia or Spain. But there was also a sophisticated legal system, the world's first social security network, the emergence of Europe's first social democratic party, the invention of the motor car and a host of other industrial and technical innovations. If one goes further back, why should the role of Blücher at Waterloo not be commemorated as much as that of Wellington? And why should Frederick the Great not be accorded the same respect as Napoleon?

But they are not. Of course history is taught in schools, and technological inventions are recorded in museums. Ordinary Germans, though, are not brought up to identify with any of this. In Germany the past is literally another country.

* * *

The way in which we recall history in Britain is rooted in our daily life. Our public events, our pageantry, our respect for our armed forces, the institution of the monarchy – all reflect our past and all contribute to our sense of Britishness. We celebrate enthusiastically the anniversaries which are involved. We like the fact that we can put on a good public show.

In Germany there is none of this. There are no national public events (even the reunification day celebrations are predominantly local in character), nothing remotely equivalent to the Trooping of the Colour or the State Opening of Parliament or the Remembrance

Day ceremony. The only parades which take place are local ones, such as the carnival processions in the Rhineland and in Bavaria, the Oktoberfest in Munich or the Love Parade which used to take place in Berlin but subsequently moved to the Ruhr area. They attract crowds but they are designed for fun, not for commemoration.

Perhaps because of the lack of any pageantry in their own society Germans are avid followers of such phenomena elsewhere. There is massive popular interest in the British royal family (and indeed, on a somewhat lesser scale, in the other European royal families) and Germans in their millions watch on their television screens whenever there is a British royal event.

I was once asked by one of the German news channels to provide a live commentary on one such event (the Queen Mother's funeral). The principal German expert on the British royal family was contracted to another channel and they were, they confessed, desperate to find someone who could describe what was going on. I did my best to explain in German the ceremonial arcana involved, though I am not sure that my translation of 'Silver Stick in Waiting' or my explanation of his functions left viewers much the wiser. But I could not help wondering whether it was a deliberate sense of irony which had prompted the Queen Mother, whom Hitler had once called 'the most dangerous woman in Europe', to choose Brahms's German Requiem to be played at her funeral.

Germans are also enthusiastic followers of the Last Night of the Proms – and no doubt slightly perplexed at the fact that these days it is not just the Union Jack which is waved there: many other flags, including German ones, are also on display. (And not just flags. The first non Anglo-Saxon to sing 'Rule Britannia' at the event, in 2015, was the German tenor Jonas Kaufmann. He was the recipient of various items of ladies' underwear thrown at him by appreciative female members of the audience, to which he responded by bringing on stage a pair of Union Jack underpants and delivering what is widely regarded as the most magnificent live performance of 'Nessun Dorma' in modern times).

Interest in events like these abroad does not translate into wanting to emulate them at home. It is almost as if Germans do not trust themselves to display en masse their own feelings, as if any big commemorative event might be construed as a kind of modern-day Nuremberg rally.

For those Germans who grew up in the East it is even worse. They have no history before 1989. Nothing from the German Democratic Republic has been retained in current German public life. No personality is revered, no sporting triumph celebrated, no social phenomenon admired. Only a few *Ampelmänner*, the little figures with hats which appear on pedestrian traffic signals in East Berlin, have been allowed to survive as physical reminders of the former regime.

The absence of public ceremony in Germany especially affects the German armed forces. No public pride is taken in Germany's past military achievements and no public respect is shown to those who died in the service of their country. There are here and there a few village war memorials, but nothing approaching the scale of those in Britain or in France, and there is no equivalent in Germany of the commemoration on 11 November of the end of World War I. There is a veterans' association, but it does not enjoy the public profile or esteem of the British Legion.

Germany, and in particular Prussia, was once the world's predominant military power. The most influential book on the art of war, *Vom Kriege*, was published in 1832 by the commandant of the Prussian Military Academy, Carl von Clausewitz. And the most successful military leader of the last several hundred years was, it could plausibly be argued, Field Marshal von Moltke the Elder, the man who achieved decisive military victories over, successively, Denmark, Austria-Hungary and France, who won, at Königgrätz, the biggest battle ever to take place on European soil and who, as he himself pointed out, in contrast to Napoleon or Frederick the Great, never had to undertake a retreat. He is sometimes described as the father of modern warfare.

The Wehrmacht, the German army in World War II, was instilled with the ethos of von Moltke. It was, many military historians would claim, the best fighting force the world has ever seen. The tactics of its key commanders – Manstein, Rommel, Guderian – are still studied in military academies today. But the awfulness of the regime they served has forever clouded their professional distinction. No one in Germany today would publicly call them heroes or express any feeling of pride in what they achieved.

In the early 1950s the question of German re-armament dominated the international political agenda. After World War I Germany had been disarmed under the terms of the Treaty of Versailles but was able to maintain a clandestine military programme (which depended to a large degree on the co-operation of the Soviet Union). In the immediate aftermath of 1945 there was a presumption that Germany must never again be allowed to pose a military threat to Europe's security, and the Wehrmacht was completely disbanded. But as the Cold War developed, the Americans realised that without a significant German contribution the burden of defending Western Europe would fall disproportionately on them. They therefore concluded that the German armed forces should be reconstituted, but with the sole purpose of playing a part in this common defence.

The British government of the time accepted the logic of this. The French were initially less enthusiastic, but eventually came round. The Bundeswehr, the name chosen to replace the old Wehrmacht, came into being in 1955, and Germany joined NATO the same year. The size of the Bundeswehr and the type of armaments which it and the German navy were allowed to procure were strictly limited (the limitations were relaxed over time), and its concept was that of '*Der Burger in Uniform*' (the citizen in uniform): it was to be staffed mainly by conscripts performing voluntarily a public service (other forms of public service were available), a far cry from the professional military ethos and sense of separateness of the officer caste of the past.

Germany's constitution was adjusted in order to ensure strict conditions, including crucially the requirement for Bundestag approval, under which the Bundeswehr could ever be deployed operationally. These too have evolved slightly over the years. The requirement for Bundestag approval remains, however, and the only circumstances in which the German government can seek it are the direct defence of Germany's own homeland, operations under the command of NATO or the EU, or UN-mandated peacekeeping missions.

For so long as the Cold War lasted, the issue of NATO operations was straightforward: they were only envisaged in the context of an attack on NATO territory in Europe. The Bundeswehr was equipped and trained to play a key role in NATO's defence strategy, its speciality being the conduct of armoured warfare. Although Germany spends less, in terms of GDP per head, on defence than Britain or France, its contribution to the NATO common defence has always been substantial. At the height of the Cold War Germany had over twice the number of tanks in its inventory than Britain; the tanks, designed and manufactured in Germany, the Leopard 1 and Leopard 2, were the best that NATO had.

German politicians and officials also played a crucial role in NATO's military planning. Four German generals, including two who served in World War II (one of them was sitting next to Hitler in his Wolf's Lair headquarters when the bomb meant to assassinate him went off), have been chairmen of NATO's Military Committee. Manfred Wörner, a former German defence minister, served as NATO secretary general from 1988 to 1994 and is generally regarded as one of the most distinguished holders of that office. Of all the heads of state or government in NATO countries during the Cold War, the one who made the most important personal contribution to the development of the Alliance's strategic doctrine, not least its doctrine on nuclear deterrence, was Helmut Schmidt, the German defence minister from 1969 to 1972 and chancellor from 1974 to 1982.

The fact that NATO never had to fire a shot in anger during the Cold War means that it is impossible to say how well the Bundeswehr would have performed in battle, but it was highly regarded by most British and American officers. On the one occasion when German

Special Forces had to undertake a hostage rescue mission – to free the captives taken by Palestinian terrorists on a Lufthansa flight in Mogadishu in 1977 – they were spectacularly successful.

German public opinion has always broadly supported NATO and Germany's role in it. German governments had their own perspectives on, and concerns about, certain aspects of NATO's strategy. They were always keen to emphasise the detente component of the Harmel doctrine of defence and detente. And though they endorsed the principle of the policy of flexible response, including the option of the first use of nuclear weapons, they were anxious to ensure that it did not translate into the acceptance of a protracted war involving tactical nuclear systems.

These were concerns rooted in clear German interests. Insofar as tensions between NATO and the Warsaw Pact could be eased, West Germans could enjoy more opportunities to visit their relatives and fellow citizens in the East; if tactical nuclear weapons ever came to be used they would be likely to be detonated in the first instance on German territory. Germany was thus directly affected by the realities of the Cold War in a way that no other NATO member state was.

In the early 1980s there were demonstrations, as there were in Britain, against the deployment of cruise and Pershing 2 missiles on German territory. But the German government, like the British one, held firm against them and the deployments took place. Even in the final stages of the Cold War, when negotiations were under way about the conditions for German reunification, the German government, and in particular Chancellor Kohl, resisted any suggestion that as a condition for reunification Germany should loosen its links to NATO or accept conditions which would damage NATO's ability to function as an effective alliance.

The end of the Cold War posed a greater challenge for the Bundeswehr and for German defence policy than for the armed forces of any other Western country. It took a long time for public opinion and the political class to accept that Germany might have security interests other than the direct defence of NATO territory. In the early

1990s a few German medical units took part in a UN peacekeeping operation in Cambodia and Somalia, but Germany took no part in either the Iraq War of 1990 or the UNPROFOR (United Nations Protection Force) operation in Bosnia from 1992 to 1996.

Things changed under the Red/Green government which took office in 1998. Contrary to the expectations of many outside observers, German forces participated in the NATO bombing campaign to force Serbian troops to leave Kosovo, in the subsequent NATO KFOR (Kosovo Force) operation to preserve peace there and in the NATO ISAF (International Security Assistance Force) deployment to Afghanistan. Taking part in these missions required great political courage on the part of both Chancellor Schröder and Foreign Minister Fischer. They had to overcome entrenched resistance within their own parties, a public opinion which was at best ambivalent and a CDU opposition which was concerned more with trying to secure political capital for itself than with a calculation of Germany's real strategic interests. In the case of the Afghanistan deployment, Schröder ran the risk of a vote of confidence in the Bundestag which his government only won by two votes.

The political courage shown by Schröder and Fischer in arguing for German participation in NATO operations in Kosovo and Afghanistan has not, however, been replicated by the governments of Angela Merkel which followed. The Bundeswehr remains in Afghanistan, but its activities are subjected to a range of caveats and exemptions. And Germany abstained in the UN Security Council, along with Russia and China, in the vote on the resolution authorising the use of force in Libya in 2011. Conscription has at last been abolished, but the nervousness about involving the Bundeswehr in anything which might be termed war still remains.

No attempt is made to give the Bundeswehr any public profile. Germany's armed forces are rarely seen outside their barracks. The air force has no display team, the army no ceremonial units. When, as occasionally happens in Afghanistan, German soldiers are killed on active service, their bodies are brought home inconspicuously. It would be unthinkable in Germany for any local community to do as the people of Wootton Bassett did and organise a spontaneous homage to the returning coffins.

When the Queen visited Germany in 2000 to open the new British Embassy we gave a dinner in her honour. One of the guests we invited was General Klaus Reinhardt. He had recently returned from service as commander of the NATO force in Kosovo, where he had succeeded the British general Mike Jackson. Reinhardt was the first German general to command British forces in war (Kosovo was an operational deployment) and this had been commented on, favourably, in the British press. The Queen and Prince Philip, as always well briefed, were aware of this, and of its historical significance, and spoke to him about his experiences. For Gerhard Schröder, the federal chancellor, and Joschka Fischer, the foreign minister, who were also present, it was all a bit puzzling. It was unclear whether either of them had actually met Reinhardt before and they could not understand why the Queen would be interested in talking to him.

* * *

The rejection of their past also affects the way Germans think about themselves. From time to time focus groups or the like are asked if they feel proud to be German. In Britain the answer would be a resounding yes. In Germany people are ambivalent. Politicians usually try to dodge the question. They reply that you cannot be proud of something over which you have no control. Or they say that they are proud of Germany's constitution or its political and economic achievements. They are reluctant to come out and say that they are proud of their country as such.

The one exception to the ethos of national diffidence is football. Virtually all Germans are passionate about it. The German team's victory against the favourites, Hungary, in the final of the 1954 World Cup in Switzerland is known as *Das Wunder von Bern* (the miracle of Bern). It was not only a remarkable sporting achievement (Hungary had beaten Germany 8–3 at an earlier stage of the tournament): it also was, for most Germans, the first time since 1945 that the country had something to celebrate and marked a turning point in the psychology of the nation. Since then Germany has won the World Cup two more times, most recently in 2014, and the European Cup three times and is consistently ranked as one of the leading football countries of the world, just as Bayern Munich is one of the leading clubs.

Football is something which unites the country. It also provides just about the only occasion on which Germans display any overt signs of national fervour. When the World Cup was held in Germany in 2006 the atmosphere was extraordinary. The German team was beaten in the semi-finals by Italy, but the play-off for third place against Portugal (which Germany in the event won) brought hundreds of thousands of young Germans onto the streets wearing t-shirts and with their faces painted in the red, yellow and black national colours. Many older Germans were clearly emotionally affected by it all. They had not expected in their lifetime to see their children's or grandchildren's generation able to show and share mass happiness in this way. Perhaps the reason why football is so important in Germany is that there is little else which brings Germans together and makes them ready to celebrate their nationality.

It is a nationality which is defined in a very particular way. The starting point of German nationality law is, to use the legal jargon, the concept of *jus sanguinis* rather than *jus soli*. In other words, it is your bloodline, not the place of your birth, which counts. The reasons for this lie in Germany's history. Britain, as an island, has always been a defined geographical entity. So, too, for over 500 years have France and Spain. But Germany only came into existence in 1871 and its borders have changed considerably since then. What gave Germans their sense of national identity was not the territory on which they lived, but a shared racial and cultural inheritance which they had developed over centuries and which complemented, and indeed sometimes subsumed, their local affiliations.

It was this inheritance which constituted the core feeling of belonging to a German nation. It persisted irrespective of the nature or name of the state in which the members of this nation resided and to which they were supposed to owe their allegiance. It united Prussians, Saxons and Bavarians, who lived under monarchies, the people of Hamburg and Bremen, which were self-governing city-states, and the citizens of all the other various principalities and dukedoms which existed for centuries on the territory of Central Europe.

Language plays an important part in this inheritance, but it is not the sole or defining feature. Those Swiss whose mother tongue is German do not think of themselves as part of the German nation: they are Swiss. The same is true of the majority of Austrians. But both Switzerland and Austria have existed for centuries as independent entities. Germany has not. The territories on which the members of the German nation historically lived were for a long time a patchwork of statelets and principalities. Even after the creation of the German Reich by Bismarck there were still millions of Germans living outside its borders.

The way in which Germans define their German-ness has had profound consequences both for their own country and for their neighbours. An identity which is dependent on bloodline can, by definition, not be acquired by those of a different descent. So it has never been easy for a non-German to obtain German nationality.

More ominously, in historical terms, such an identity cannot easily be renounced. The descendants of Germans remain German wherever they live, and they have tended to retain a loyalty to this German identity which transcends their allegiance to the state where they reside and of which they are, or were, supposed to be citizens. The wars which Bismarck instigated were not a response to a perceived threat to Prussia or even a desire to acquire material spoils in Schleswig-Holstein or Alsace-Lorraine. They were the product of a mindset which could not contemplate that the Germans who inhabited these territories could be natural or loyal citizens of Denmark or France.

Bismarck's empire was dismantled by the Treaty of Versailles, which again left millions of Germans living in countries to which they felt little allegiance. The sense of grievance at this was one of the many issues which Hitler exploited and which underpinned the doctrines of *Lebensraum* and racial purity. He undoubtedly invested them with remarkable ferocity and fanaticism but he was able to tap into a well of long-standing national feeling about German identity and German exclusiveness.

Of course there have been exceptions. The French Huguenots who were given sanctuary in various German states in the eighteenth century managed to assimilate into German society and became prominent in many areas of German life. The prime minister of East Germany immediately after the fall of communism, Lothar de Maizière, was a member of a former Huguenot family, as is his nephew Thomas, who became a cabinet minister in Angela Merkel's government. And the German-speakers of Alsace-Lorraine have been content, since the end of World War II, with their status as French citizens (unlike the Saarlanders who in a referendum in 1955 voted decisively not to belong to France but to return to Germany). By and large, though, members of the German nation have remained stubbornly attached to their German-ness and equally stubbornly reluctant to share it with others.

So long as Germany was a country without many immigrants this was not too much of a problem. As a result of Hitler's 'Final Solution' there were by 1945 only a handful of Jews and Gypsies left in the country, and reform of the nationality law, or political re-education on issues of national identity, were not seen as a priority by either the occupation powers or the new federal government. But Germany's economic success, and the constraints on its labour market caused in part by the losses of young men during the war, meant that the issue soon had to be addressed.

Immigration into Germany had already begun in the 1950s when numbers of Italians moved north to exploit the opportunities in the catering sector and elsewhere offered by Germany's booming economy. Greeks and Yugoslavs followed. They were called *Gastarbeiter* (guest workers). Some of them stayed and settled in Germany (Giovanni di Lorenzo, one of Germany's most distinguished journalists who became editor of *Die Zeit*, is the son of such an immigrant). Most left their families behind and returned home themselves in due course. They were not seen as any kind of social problem: those who did stay managed to integrate well. But the next stage of modern Germany's experience with immigration proved more complex.

The Turks began arriving in significant numbers in the middle to late 1960s. They were welcomed at first as cheap labour in those sectors of the German economy where there was at that time a shortage. The erection of the Berlin Wall in 1961 and the consequent isolation of the Western part of the city meant that many came to Berlin to perform jobs which the local population were unwilling to undertake. It was assumed, insofar as anybody thought about the consequences of their arrival, that – like the Italians (or indeed like the small *Auf Wiedersehen Pet* generation of British immigrants) – they would mostly leave their families behind, stay for a few years and then return home; or that those who did settle would quickly intermarry and assimilate.

Things turned out differently. Large numbers of Turkish immigrants decided to stay in Germany and sent for their families to join them. Their children also stayed, and when they reached marriageable age they, like many immigrants in other communities, tended to look for a bride or husband from their homeland, often from a rural or less-developed part of the country. Today there are over 4 million people of Turkish origin living in Germany and they constitute around 5 per cent of the population. They live for the most part in inner-city areas; in Berlin they dominate the area of Kreuzberg, parts of which have the look of a Turkish rather than a German city. The Turkish community are particularly visible in the Tiergarten park in the centre of the city on warm summer evenings.

The Tiergarten stretches from the Brandenburg Gate to the Sieger Säule, the Victory Column erected to celebrate the German conquest of Paris in 1871. Contrary to what one might expect in a country traditionally associated with good order and discipline there seem to be few rules about what activities may or may not take place there. People sunbathe, and even play games, naked; the Turks use it for barbecues. The spectacle of dozens of Turkish families, the women dressed traditionally in headscarves, grilling their sausages alongside a team of nude footballers in a public park only a few hundred metres from the Reichstag is one of Berlin's unexpected cultural peculiarities.

Some of these immigrants and their descendants integrated and thrived. There are successful Turkish/German businessmen, lawyers, politicians and footballers. The majority, however, have chosen to remain essentially Turkish. They live in their own areas and mix almost exclusively with their own kind. Fewer than half of them have taken German nationality. This is because to do so they would have to give up their Turkish nationality. There is a widely held view among Germans that a person can, or should, have only one nationality. German nationality law reflects this. Anyone taking German citizenship had, until recently, to give up his or her previous nationality, and any German who took up a new nationality had to renounce his or her German one.

The only circumstances in which it was possible in Germany to enjoy dual nationality was if someone had been born with it. Otherwise a choice had to be made. Thus the German politician David McAllister, the son of a Scottish father and a German mother, who was between 2008 and 2012 minister president of Lower Saxony and considered a possible successor to Angela Merkel, is entitled to a British passport as well as his German one. But Gisela Stuart, the German-born MP for Birmingham Edgbaston, had to give up her German nationality when she took British citizenship.

For many Turks living in Germany, having to renounce their Turkish nationality is too high a price to pay for acquiring a German one. The rules have been softened in recent years in the sense that for anyone born and living in Germany the choice does not have to be made until the age of 18. The underlying principle has been retained, though: if you want to become German you must be only German.

In early 1999, only four months or so after the Bundestag election which brought them into power, the Red/Green government of Chancellor Schröder introduced a draft bill which would have allowed dual citizenship. The introduction of the bill coincided with a *Land* election in Hessen. All the opinion polls suggested that the administration in power there, also a Red/Green one, would be re-elected. The minister president, Hans Eichel, was not Germany's most charismatic politician but he was well enough liked and was considered to have performed competently. At the national level the Red/Green government was still popular.

But Eichel's opponent, Roland Koch from the CDU, made opposition to the proposed nationality law the centrepiece of his campaign (despite the fact that citizenship in Germany is a federal, not a *Land*, issue). He organised a mass petition in which members of the public were invited to add their names to a list demanding that the bill be withdrawn. They did so in huge numbers. The television news showed pictures of skinheads arriving in droves in Wiesbaden, the capital of Hessen, demanding to know '*Wo können wir gegen die AusLänder unterschreiben?*' (Where can we sign against the foreigners?). It worked. The Social Democrats suffered big losses and a new CDU-led government was formed with Roland Koch as minister president.

I had lunch a few days after the election with a CDU politician who knew Koch well. He acknowledged that the petition ruse had been a bit '*unappetitlich*' (unappetising). But the issue was, he said, one which people really cared about and the federal government had only itself to blame.

Since then German governments have tiptoed around the issue. There has been some mild liberalisation of the rules for acquiring citizenship. Children born in Germany to a parent from another EU member state who has lived in Germany for over eight years now have the right, when they reach the age of 18, to apply for German nationality without having to renounce that of their mother or father, but this does not apply to the children of non-EU parents.

So the underlying principle of German nationality law remains: if you are a German, you should be only a German.

*   *   *

Not only does an applicant for German nationality have, in most cases, to renounce any previous one. He or she is also expected to assimilate completely into existing German society. There has never been in Germany any enthusiasm for the concept of multiculturalism. The term '*multi-kulti*', when used in German, has a derogatory sense. Most German intellectuals, even at the liberal end of the political spectrum, were aghast at the idea promulgated in some quarters in Britain in the early years of Tony Blair's government that different sets of cultural values could be considered equally British and that we should as a country celebrate our differences. They have watched with quintessential German *Schadenfreude* as the public mood in the United Kingdom has changed.

The expectation that immigrants should assimilate is of course not always easily compatible with other equally entrenched modern German values such as freedom of religion and freedom of expression. There is in Germany the same type of public debate as in Britain, or in most other European countries, about Muslim girls or women wearing distinctive clothing or being educated in a different way. Ninety per cent of the Muslims in Germany are of Turkish origin and the burka or even the niqab are not normally part of their traditions, but the hijab, the headscarf, is, and there are misgivings among many Turkish-German families about certain aspects of the German school system.

A number of cases end up in the courts and no comprehensive doctrine has yet been established. But the Constitutional Court has already ruled that individual *Länder* have the right, as several have decided to do, to ban headscarves in classrooms. A local court in Leipzig ruled in September 2013 that a Muslim girl could not be excused from mixed swimming lessons on the grounds that her parents objected to her exposure to the sight of bare-chested boys.

As the judge succinctly put it in his ruling, 'The social reality of life in Germany came above her religious beliefs.'

The belief that to be German means to be only German and that this German-ness is essentially a matter of genetic inheritance partly explains why there was so little questioning in Germany of Hitler's racial obsessions. It is also reflected in the attitudes of Germany's tiny, but spectacularly brutal, neo-Nazi community of today.

Demagoguery has not so far been a characteristic of modern German politicians. All three of the Social Democrat chancellors in the Federal Republic – Brandt, Schmidt and Schröder – were accomplished public speakers, and Brandt could sometimes bring great emotional force to bear, notably in his gesture of falling on his knees before the monument to the uprising in Warsaw. But none of their Christian Democrat counterparts – Adenauer, Kiesinger, Erhard, Kohl or Merkel – have had particularly impressive oratorical skills. Their personae have reflected more homely virtues. They have sought to reassure, not to inspire.

Germany is a country which, despite its historical experiences, still feels deep down that the bloodline matters. But the bloodline is getting thinner. Germany's biggest challenge in the coming years is demographic. The birth rate has plunged and the population is shrinking. Currently there are around 82 million Germans. In 50 years' time there will on current projections be only 70 million. Germany will then be only the third biggest country in Europe after Britain (80 million) and France (72 million). And within Germany those of pensionable age will outnumber those who work. The consequences for the affordability of Germany's generous social security system and for the availability of a skilled workforce will be profound.

Unless, of course, there is more immigration. Until recently, German politicians tended to argue that '*Deutschland ist kein Einwanderungsland*' (Germany is not an immigration country). By this they meant that Germany was not a country with a tradition of immigrants from former colonies in the way that Britain and France were, nor was it a country, like the United States or Australia, which depended on settlers for its growth. They did not as a result oppose all immigration but they assumed that immigration would be only on a limited scale and that immigrants would be few enough to assimilate easily into the existing national culture. To have to accept that Germany needs immigration on a large scale in order to sustain its current levels of prosperity would be a huge psychological shock.

It may happen. Already in the last 10 or 20 years the appearance of many of Germany's big cities has changed. None of them is like London in the extent of their multinationality, but in Berlin now different skin colours are commonplace on the buses and the metro, and employers argue that they need to be able to recruit globally in the way that their American and British counterparts do. The underlying dilemma remains, though. In Britain and America it is commitment to a way of life that most people regard as the fundamental requirement of citizenship. In Germany it is descent.

Some commentators claimed that one reason why Germany was willing in 2015 to throw open its doors to Syrian refugees and accept another 1 million immigrants in a single year was that it was an opportunity to add a large number of active, and mostly well-educated, young men to its workforce. This may turn out to be the effect, but it was certainly not the intention. No German politician has ever advocated large-scale immigration as a way of dealing with Germany's demographic problem. Immigrants have been tolerated, and even welcomed. But they have not been seen as a solution.

Accepting 1 million immigrants, mostly Muslims, in a year, as Germany did in 2015, is a challenge which no other European country has so far had to face. In defending the decision to open Germany's borders to Syrian refugees, Chancellor Merkel confidently predicted, '*Wir schaffen das*' (We can do it).

In material and organisational terms she was right. Germany has been able to mobilise the resources needed for housing and educating the newcomers and providing them with health care. Despite some local grumbles there is not, on the whole, resentment in the country about the cost involved.

What is less clear is how they will be treated in the longer term. It takes four years before an asylum seeker in Germany has the right to work; even then, few jobs are available without a good knowledge of German. Dependents of refugees are not guaranteed entry. The system was originally designed to provide temporary shelter to people who would ultimately return to their country of origin, not for the sudden arrival of a million new permanent residents.

For those refugees who consciously try to integrate – learn the language, get a qualification, work hard and dress like Germans – there will be few problems. They will be welcomed into society and their neighbours will probably be proud to have them. But those who cluster in their ghettos, insist that their wives and daughters wear the headscarf and do not mix outside their own community will not find things easy. If you want to be German you are expected to buy in to existing German social culture, not to maintain an identity of your own which is different.

* * *

For a country which has renounced its past, a new political entity like the EU offers a particular opportunity. The more that it becomes the vehicle through which identity is expressed, aims pursued and influence exercised, the less important is the historical baggage of its individual members.

This is, for many Germans, the underlying attraction of the EU. As EU citizens they feel on a par with their fellow Europeans. They are comfortable discussing Europe's role in the world, Europe's interests and how Europe should pursue them. They would feel much less comfortable discussing such things on a purely national basis. As Germans they are constantly reminded of their past. As Europeans they can escape from it. Europe can be admired, extolled and celebrated in a way that Germany itself cannot.

In the EU's early days Germans politicians and officials would defend the European project (the term that was commonly used in order to connote a process rather than an end-state) on the grounds that it was the only way to accommodate the reality of German power. By the 1950s it was clear that Germany was going to become Europe's leading economy and was expected to play a leading part in Europe's defence. For the Germans themselves, as well as for their neighbours, this was a daunting prospect. Would it mean a rerun of what happened after World War I? Or was there a way in which German power could be taken out of German hands and shared with others?

It was of course not only the Germans for whom history called into question reliance on the traditional structure of the nation state. All the original six signatories to the Treaty of Rome had suffered occupation and destruction during the period from 1939 to 1945. In all of them there was the feeling that their governments had failed and that some new system of political order was required. There had been wars and defeats before, but the cataclysmic character of World War II meant that for those who were affected by it there could be no going back to the simple interplay of national interests.

Fortunately, a generation of political leaders emerged who were able to, in the fashionable phrase, ride the zeitgeist. Adenauer, Monnet, Schumann, Spaak and Di Gasperi were responsible for giving form to the new Europe. They tapped into a widespread popular appetite for change.

Neither the political class in Britain nor British public opinion shared this mood. Understandably so. Our democratic institutions had not failed, our political leadership had not let us down, our self-belief had not been shattered. On the contrary, we were proud of how we had endured and we felt that we had deserved our victory. It was indeed our finest hour. We did not emerge in 1945 convinced that the European nation state had had its day. Or certainly not as far as Britain was concerned.

In the EU's early days the notion of an ever-closer union, a journey which, long though it might be, was destined to involve increasing transfers of power to the European level was unchallenged. In Germany it was an act of faith that integration at the European level was desirable in its own right and that the direction of travel was one way and irreversible. Few Germans asked whether their own country was really ready for such a journey.

Yet, of all the member states of the EU, Germany is the least suited to the sort of integrationist future which its founding fathers and its early visionaries had in mind. Not just because of the financial burdens which might fall on German taxpayers, but because of how Germans view themselves. A nation which defines itself through the bloodline, and which is reluctant to accept dual citizenship, cannot easily submerge itself into something else. Co-operation, even the sharing of sovereignty, with other nation states is perfectly compatible with German identity. But expecting Germans to give up their inherent sense of German-ness and to regard themselves as Europeans with an allegiance to a wider European *Volk* is counter-intuitive. Of all the nations of Europe, Germany is the one which is most attached to genetic exclusivity.

This is not to impute any stigma of racism or Aryan superiority to modern Germany. It is one of the most tolerant civic societies in the world. Equality before the law and a high regard for human rights are now deeply embedded in the German psyche. So is openness to the wider world and respect for other cultures. It is simply that they define themselves by their ancestry not by where they live.

There is thus an in-built conflict in Germany's approach to Europe. On the one hand there is a wish to escape from the past and forge a new identity. On the other hand there is an inherited identity which cannot be renounced.

Of course many Germans would deny that there is such a dilemma. It is perfectly possible, they would say, to be both a German and a European. This is not the same as having two nationalities because one is a subset of, indeed a condition for, the other. There is no incompatibility involved, just as there is no incompatibility with being both Bavarian and German. This is true, provided that one of the nationalities is accepted as decisive. Despite its federal character, Germany is a state in which all citizens would describe themselves as German and would accept a first loyalty to the German state. As long as the European Union does not seek to replace this primacy, Germans can enthusiastically support it. So far they have been willing to do so.

At some point this enthusiasm may come under strain. Germans accept, even advocate, many things in the EU which people in Britain find profoundly unwelcome and which contributed to the vote to leave. British concerns reflected a concept of the irreducible sovereignty of the nation state. Germans have fewer hang-ups of this kind: they are, for example, quite prepared to see Europe operate as an actor on the world stage in its own right. But Germans will not be prepared to stop thinking of themselves as German. This will inevitably set limits on how far they will be prepared to be governed as Europeans. When exactly these limits will be reached, and whether German politicians will be capable of discerning them in advance, is unclear.

It is a pity, in retrospect, that the experience of the appointment of the Commission president in 2014 did not cause any deeper reflection in Germany about the nature of popular allegiance in Europe. In Germany the procedure whereby the candidate nominated by the biggest party grouping in the European Parliament got the job was hailed as a triumph of democracy.

Few Germans asked themselves how they would have felt if they had been British. Someone was appointed for whom no one in Britain had voted, who was opposed by all the main British political parties and who did not receive the support of a single British member of the European Parliament. This is democratic on the assumption that there is a single European demos whose citizens consider themselves essentially European and who therefore accept that majority decisions can be taken to which they may be personally opposed. But when, as with the British electorate, this was not the case, it is hard to argue that democracy has prevailed.

It was curious that in all the discussion in Germany about the election of Jean-Claude Juncker, no one raised this issue of democratic legitimacy. There was plenty of comment, mostly critical, about David Cameron's failure to vote for him. But not one journalist or commentator pointed out that Cameron's position reflected the expressed will of the British people.

For Germans, of course, things look very different. It is, in current circumstances at any rate, inconceivable that Germany could be outvoted in this way. Germans are dominant in the European Parliament and it is hard to imagine circumstances in which a candidate for the Commission presidency could be selected who did not enjoy a high level of German support.

The failure to address the issue of compatibility between different identities, national and European, has been a feature of the way in which all German politicians discuss Europe. Because their own country takes no pride in its past, they assume that an EU can be developed which equally has no collective past to be proud of. They even make a virtue of it. The EU is characterised in Germany as the guarantor of Europe's stability. Franco-German reconciliation is seen as the precursor to this. The underlying assumption is that the nation states of Europe failed in the past to prevent wars and that therefore the nation state is itself inadequate as an instrument of governance.

What they fail to understand is that Germany is unique. No other country in Europe has turned its back on its past in the way that Germany has. For most of Germany's EU partners, history still plays a significant role in their national consciousness and in their sense of national identity. Britain may be an extreme example of this but it applies to many others as well, including, for example, Italy – which came into being as a nation state at about the same time as Germany itself.

The two attempts in Europe to construct a new political entity without any common historical heritage, the Soviet Union and Yugoslavia, both ended in tears and in a return to nation statehood, in the latter case after a terrible war. Many Germans would argue that in both cases the countries were dictatorships, that it was the end of dictatorship which prompted their demise and that no valid comparison with the EU can be drawn. They would point to the

United States as showing that a democracy can develop a new national identity without reliance on the past.

But America was a country of individual immigrants who had deliberately chosen to make a new life. The EU consists of existing member states most of whose citizens are comfortable with their existing nationalities. These citizens, or at any rate many of them, can be persuaded of the need for a new form of supranational co-operation in Europe involving voluntary sharing of sovereignty. What they are reluctant to accept is that they should be expected to renounce or downgrade the identity to which they are attached.

Hitherto when German politicians talked about the EU they tended to say that of course they had no wish to abolish its member states and that they accepted that the French would always feel French and the British would always feel British. But they did so in a way that suggested that this was an idiosyncrasy which needed to be appeased, rather than a fundamental limiting factor in the process of the EU's political development. They were also reluctant to acknowledge that the Germans would also always feel German. Germany's leadership of Europe reflects a mindset in which the past has no relevance and in which the construction of Europe can proceed from *Stunde Null* in the way that the reconstruction of Germany did after 1945. Their admirable rejection of their own historical baggage has made them insensitive to the attachment which many of their partners have to national pasts which evoke pride not shame.

They may also have underestimated the extent to which the inherited notion of German-ness still holds sway in the minds of their own public. The fact that Germans do not glory in their past does not mean that they feel any less German.

It remains to be seen whether the impact of British withdrawal from the EU will cause Germany's political class to think again. So far there is no sign of it. There has been much talk of the need for the EU to change, but no indication of how, and certainly no recognition that the issue of national identity is central to the challenges which the EU faces.

For the last 60 years Germans have been brought up to see the EU as an essential part of the political framework in which they are governed. But if it develops in a way which requires Germans to subordinate their national identity to a European one, then popular discontent may grow. And if the issue of identity is linked to that of money – that is, if Germans are expected to pay more into an enlarged EU budgetary kitty – then discontent may develop into more outright hostility.

This should worry the German government. At the moment they are shutting their eyes to it.

✿ FIVE ✿

Looking After the Relations

German dominance of economic policy making in Europe is now a fact of life and is likely to continue for the foreseeable future. There are four reasons for this. First, the relevant treaty provisions were drafted, and agreed unanimously by all member states, in such a way as to reflect German practice and values. The Commission has become over the years thoroughly imbued with German economic thinking. Second, the model which Germany represents is a successful one. Germany itself has shown enough resilience to cope effectively with a range of passing shocks while still maintaining a high rate of economic growth and a high level of social provision for its citizens. Third, Germany is the EU's most populous member state and the largest contributor to the EU's budget. Piper-payers generally call tunes. And, fourth, there is no rival model available which commands credibility. Whatever the intellectual merits of economic policies based on demand stimulus or deficit financing, there is no example, at any rate in Europe, of a state which has successfully implemented them.

So, enthusiastically or reluctantly, Germany's EU partners go along with the discipline which the EU, at German behest, requires.

This does not mean that Germany has no need to pay attention to the other states' concerns, but German readiness to do so has in recent years become more circumscribed.

* * *

It was not always so. Germans like to be liked; for many decades a key feature of Germany's EU policy, in addition to the relationship with France, was a determination to position itself as the friend of the smaller member states. Helmut Kohl as chancellor personally articulated this approach, arguing that it was precisely because of Germany's power (and its history) that Germany should be especially sensitive to their interests.

As a result, Germany was on several occasions reluctant to use its weight in the EU in support of decisions which, though sensible and in Germany's own interests, would have been unpopular with others. It would, for example, have been open to Germany to insist in 1981 that Greece was not ready for full membership of the EEC (as it then was). Following the restoration of democracy in Greece in 1975, the Commission had analysed the state of the Greek economy and, more importantly, its public administration and had concluded that they did not justify early accession. Rather, the Commission submitted a so-called 'reasoned opinion' proposing a form of special partnership which would allow time for the membership conditions to be properly fulfilled.

However, the Council – i.e. the member states – took a different view and judged that Greece was fit to join. It was the first time in the EEC's history that a reasoned opinion of the Commission on an important issue had been rejected. The reason was purely political. As President Giscard d'Estaing of France put it to François Ortoli, his fellow Frenchman, who was president of the Commission at the time, '*On ne dit pas non a Platon*' (You don't say no to Plato).

There was widespread sympathy with this view, but if the German government had insisted that the Commission's judgement was right and should be respected, it could probably have ensured a delay. With the wisdom of hindsight it would indeed have been in the wider European interest to ensure that before a new member state joined it should have a functioning system of tax collection and a public service not based on cronyism and corruption.

Similarly with the accession of Cyprus in 2004. It was foreseeable that accepting into the EU a divided island would create huge political complications with Turkey – a country with which Germany had particular interests and connections. German officials warned at the time that taking in Cyprus would bring trouble. One of them even tried at the last minute to persuade Germany's foreign minister, Klaus Kinkel, who was on a skiing holiday at the time, to look at the issue again. To no avail. The German government decided not to cause a fuss. (Of course, the British government should have known better as well. But at least Britain had a concrete interest at stake in the form of two military bases in the Greek part of the island.)

When it came to the euro Germany again decided to go with the flow. It voted in 1998 in favour of an initial euro membership which was far too wide. It voted in favour of accepting Greece in 2002 and Cyprus in 2008. In all three cases economists in Germany warned of the risks. In all three cases the government decided to ignore them.

In dealing with the current euro crisis the German government has been much more hard-nosed. Wanting to be liked is hardly the leitmotif of current German policy. The caricature pictures of Angela Merkel with a Hitler moustache which proliferated in 2012 on street hoardings in Athens would in the past have caused consternation and self-questioning in Germany. Instead they seem merely to have served to reinforce the German government's determination to ensure that Greece complied with the terms of its EU bail-out

This new toughness on Germany's part may reflect a determination to learn from the mistakes of the past. But it is also because what is at stake now is fundamental to the way Europe is economically governed; this touches directly on Germany's own national interest.

It is not only the small countries like Greece who are affected by the change. France too is feeling it. France has always been Germany's most important EU partner. The Elysée Treaty signed in 1963 by President de Gaulle and Chancellor Adenauer came after the 1957 Treaty of Rome and was about the two countries' bilateral relationship, but it committed them to co-operate within the framework of the common market as well. Ever since, at least until recently, they have done so.

This co-operation has traditionally taken two forms. At the senior political level successive French presidents and German chancellors have developed joint positions and launched joint initiatives on all aspects of EU business. They have described their relationship as constituting the motor of Europe and have regularly presented joint papers or proposals in the immediate run-up to European Council meetings. This has been the case irrespective of the political affiliation of the personalities concerned. Adenauer and de Gaulle both came from a conservative tradition. But their relationship was continued by Helmut Schmidt and Valéry Giscard d'Estaing, by Helmut Kohl and François Mitterrand and, after a certain hesitation, by Gerhard Schröder and Jacques Chirac, whose party backgrounds were different from each other.

This relationship at head of government level has been underpinned by a network of contacts among other ministers and civil servants. Indeed, it is the civil servants' working habits which have made the Franco-German relationship so unique and so effective.

For decades, virtually every French and German civil servant was expected to know his or her opposite number. They telephoned and emailed each other regularly. They knew that whenever they offered a piece of advice to their own government they would be asked what the French or Germans thought about the issue in question. So they made sure that they found out early on and, to the maximum extent possible, they devised policies which were compatible with the interests of their partners.

In Britain, civil servants, when confronted with an EU issue, tended to seek ministerial guidance as early as possible. Once they knew what their ministers wanted, or thought they wanted, they tried to find allies in achieving it. But of course once the policy has been set, any departure or deviation from it represented a defeat – all the more so if by then the original policy had become public.

By contrast, French and German officials have traditionally spoken to each other before seeking any ministerial decision. If at all possible they would, when they made a recommendation to ministers, offer one which they knew would not cause friction with their partners. By operating in this way they ensured that their ministers could take a view from the outset on what a common position acceptable to the two governments would look like. If they found it acceptable, they could endorse it without having to go through the hoops of subsequent compromise or climb-down.

Of course this is only possible against a political background supportive of Franco-German co-operation. It would be impossible for officials to proceed in this way if the likely reaction of their ministers would be to ask why the views of another government were being given such deference and why they were not identifying the country's national interests and pursuing them vigorously. But in the past officials knew that in practice the reverse was the case. Their ministers would much prefer not to have to deal with a dossier which offered the prospect of a Franco-German row.

* * *

The Franco-German relationship undoubtedly served the interests of both countries and facilitated EU decision making more widely. If the two biggest economic powers in Europe (which were France and Germany for most of the last 50 years) already agreed, then getting others to fall in line was not usually too difficult, not least because any Franco-German deal was likely to represent not just a compromise between those two countries but the balance of opinion within the EU as a whole.

But the relationship became an exclusive one. Joint papers would appear just before European Council meetings not because the two governments had anything very novel to propose, but in order to show that they controlled the agenda. The Franco-German motor became an end in itself: a sign of who was at the wheel, rather than a means of getting anywhere.

This was made apparent during the time of Margaret Thatcher's premiership. When she took office in 1979 European decision making was dominated by Helmut Schmidt and Valéry Giscard d'Estaing. Both had been in power for five years and had developed a close personal rapport. They expected that the new British prime minister, whom neither of them knew, would show them appropriate deference. They tried indeed to patronise her, particularly when she insisted that something needed to be done about Britain's excessive net contribution to the EU's budget.

It was the worst possible approach and it did not work. Mrs Thatcher arrived at European Council meetings better briefed than either of them and was not afraid to contradict them when they got their facts wrong. She treated them as if they were no different from the other heads of government in the room. This was not something that they were used to. As Hans-Dietrich Genscher, the veteran German foreign minister, put it in a wry private remark to his British colleague Lord Carrington: 'Your Prime Minister has hurt my Chancellor's masculine pride.'

In the end Mrs Thatcher got her way on the British budget problem and secured in 1982 a rebate which remains in force on pretty much the same basis today. Schmidt and Giscard's successors, Helmut Kohl and François Mitterrand, always treated her with respect, but they remained determined to ensure that the Franco-German relationship was what drove Europe.

The big EU issue of the later 1980s was the completion of the single market. Within the Commission the prime movers were Jacques Delors, its French president, and Lord Cockfield, the responsible British commissioner. Among the member states Britain, and Mrs Thatcher personally, was particularly supportive.

In the run-up to the European Council in Milan in 1985 the United Kingdom circulated a paper setting out some proposals for pushing ahead with the single market initiative. The Germans were supportive and it looked initially as though the British paper would be the main item on the agenda for this part of the European Council meeting. But at the last minute the Germans withdrew their support and presented together with France a rival paper which they suggested should be the basis of discussion.

It was not that the Franco-German paper proposed a different approach. Much of its content was along the lines of what the United

Kingdom had already suggested. Rather, it was put forward to establish a principle: only a Franco-German initiative should serve as the basis of the discussion at a European Council meeting.

This notion of exclusivity for the Franco-German relationship continued for as long as Helmut Kohl was chancellor. When he left office there was a brief period during which it looked as though it might be challenged.

Gerhard Schröder, when he became chancellor, knew little about France. He had visited it, he told me when I first called on him, only once when on holiday. Within the Social Democratic Party relations with the French were the responsibility of the chairman, Oskar Lafontaine, who as a French-speaker and minister president of Saarland, a province on France's border, knew France well. Schröder's natural political counterparts were President Clinton in the United States and Prime Minister Tony Blair in Britain.

Schröder and Blair even developed something of a political philosophy together. Known as the Third Way in Britain and Die Neue Mitte (the New Centre) in Germany, it was a form of social democracy which emphasised the role of the state as an active facilitator of training and participation rather than a passive provider of benefits.

The ideological and personal relationship between Schröder and Blair was also reflected in a closeness of approach on EU issues. Some of the traditional working habits of French and German officials began to be adopted by German and British ones. For a time it seemed that a shift in power within the EU was underway.

It all came to grief over Iraq. Blair was careful not to criticise Schröder for his government's position on the war. But for Schröder, Blair's – as he saw it – unthinking subservience to George W. Bush was a big disappointment. More significantly it meant that Germany was lined up with France in the UN Security Council (of which Germany was a member in 2003) when it came to the vote on the second UN resolution. The big fear of the German government was that France would at the last minute change its position and decide to participate in the military operation as it had done in the Gulf War of 1990, leaving Germany isolated in its opposition.

As a result Schröder aligned himself with French positions in the EU as well. He went along with a decision to maintain funding for an unreformed Common Agricultural Policy, and he made clear that he saw his political relationship with Blair as effectively over. He resumed the habit of frequent meetings with the French President which had somewhat fallen by the wayside; by the time Angela Merkel came into office in 2005 the Franco-German motor was back on full throttle.

* * *

Like Schröder, Angela Merkel is not someone who carries any historical or emotional baggage about France. Before 1990 she had no opportunity to visit the West or to learn much about other Western European countries. She speaks, in addition to German, decent English and Russian, but no French. When she goes on holiday it is usually to Italy or Austria. She did not find Jacques Chirac, who was the French president in 2005, and who saw himself as Europe's senior statesman, particularly sympathetic.

Still, she followed the practice of Helmut Kohl, in whose government she had served as environment minister, in making ritual references to the importance of the Franco-German motor. When Nicolas Sarkozy succeeded Chirac in 2007 she had a French interlocutor with whom she was better able to do business, not least because Sarkozy in his early days seemed committed to a more market-oriented economy in both France and in the EU as a whole. So they resumed the habit of joint papers and joint positions for EU meetings. The term 'Merkozy' was coined to describe their approach.

As the banking crisis and the subsequent euro crisis developed, it became clear that the positions which 'Merkozy' advocated were German ones. This emerged during the course of 2011 when decisions needed to be taken about how to deal with those members of the eurozone whose public finances were out of control, and how to ensure that such situations never recurred in the future. The policy of Angela Merkel was straightforward. The countries which needed financial support – initially Greece, Ireland and Portugal – should be given it, but with strict conditions involving massive reductions in their public expenditure, increases in taxation and a timetable for a return to balanced budgets. In addition, all eurozone countries should sign a legally binding agreement, the Fiscal Treaty, obliging them for ever to respect the original Maastricht criteria on deficits and borrowing.

Whether Sarkozy was intellectually convinced that this was a sensible approach is unclear. Previous French presidents would probably have favoured less austerity and more measures to encourage growth. But he went along with it. Quite possibly he recognised that the German government was not going to be swayed from its path; it was better for France to be seen as jointly controlling the agenda. What was certainly in Sarkozy's mind was a determination that it should not be left to the Commission to set the terms of the debate. He had for some time become convinced that the EU should be led by its member states rather than by its institutions.

Having to play second fiddle to Germany over the euro may have been unwelcome, but in foreign policy France under Sarkozy was able to play a substantial leadership role. In the negotiations at the UN over Libya it was France, Britain and the United States that set the agenda. Russia and China were ambivalent, but abstained on the crucial resolution authorising the use of force for humanitarian purposes. Germany kept the lowest of low profiles and in the end abstained as well.

The fact that France and Germany voted differently on such a crucial issue showed the limitations of the Franco-German relationship. It also meant that as the Libya crisis unfolded the EU played no role at all. Military action was undertaken in a NATO framework, but with France and Britain, rather than the United States, in the lead. Germany might dominate the EU's economic policy making, but when it came to hard power it was France and Britain who, literally, called the shots.

Whether the Franco-German relationship would have survived if Sarkozy had remained in office after the presidential election of 2012 can of course never be known. By then it was already beginning to look a bit frayed. France's own economic performance compared to Germany's was poor – to the point where there were suggestions that France might itself one day need some form of bail-out – and there was no evidence of any particular French imprint on EU decisions. Angela Merkel herself seemed to find her French counterpart's capricious nature somewhat trying.

In François Hollande, Sarkozy's successor, however, she found an even less kindred spirit. Before the election Hollande had criticised the Fiscal Treaty, the show-piece of Angela Merkel's EU policy, and Mrs Merkel had declined to meet him (as had David Cameron). He had undertaken at least to seek changes to it if he was elected.

On the day of Hollande's inauguration Angela Merkel issued a statement in which she said bluntly that the treaty had been signed and that no changes to it were possible. In response to calls for measures to promote growth, her spokesman made clear that in Germany's view these should be measures of labour market reform, not deficit spending.

Hollande quickly accepted that the Fiscal Treaty was sacrosanct. But at the first European Council following his election he tried to organise a majority in favour of measures to promote growth. He ostentatiously aligned himself with the prime ministers of Italy and Spain and a so-called Compact for Growth and Jobs was eventually endorsed by the Council as a whole. For a French president to manoeuvre in this way against Germany on a euro-related issue was unprecedented. There were articles in the German press speculating that some new constellation of power in Europe might be emerging and that Germany's influence might thereby be reduced.

It did not happen. The underlying realities of the EU's economy soon reasserted themselves. If Germany is disinclined to introduce eurobonds or other measures of debt communitisation, then they will not be introduced. And if Germany chooses not to stimulate imports or consumer expenditure, no one can force it to do so. President Hollande, like others before him, had no choice but to adjust to Germany's priorities.

* * *

Relations between France and Germany will remain crucial to the EU's development. Angela Merkel may be unsentimental about France and not much personally taken with François Hollande, but she will maintain at least the appearance of continuing the policies of her predecessors.

The special importance of France is embedded in the psyche and the working practices of German officials but it has become a relationship of unequals, of two countries with different interests and different political agendas. This will condition the way in which the EU as a whole will develop. Both countries favour more integration, but they want it in different fields. Germany wants more pooling of sovereignty in areas like taxation and banking and stricter rules on fiscal discipline. Beyond that, Germany is not looking to expand the EU's own budget or to pool its member states' debts. It is in foreign policy and defence that Germany would like to see more EU common action and would be willing to give up its own sovereignty to achieve it.

France's aim, by contrast, has always been to exploit German's economic strength to the benefit of the EU as a whole. A French-inspired EU would involve eurobonds, commonly funded infrastructure projects, a bigger role for state aid and the acceptance of a higher risk of inflation. France in principle favours more EU foreign policy as well, but not if it means a reduction in France's own ability to play an international role. No French government has so far shown any willingness to give up France's permanent seat on the UN Security Council in favour of an EU one.

One underlying, even if not explicitly acknowledged, bargain in the relationship is likely to endure: the acceptance by France of an EU external trade policy which is essentially liberal, and the acceptance by

Germany of an agricultural policy with high levels of subsidy for the EU's own farmers. It is sometimes asserted that this bargain represents a sacrifice on both sides: that France is inherently protectionist and only signs up to a free trade agenda because of Germany's insistence, and that Germany only endorses the need for extensive payments to farmers under French pressure.

The truth is more subtle. Many French politicians and officials are indeed suspicious of what they sometimes describe as an Anglo-Saxon international economic agenda and use liberalism as a term of reprobation rather than approval. But as France has developed its own export-oriented industries in fields like aerospace and automobiles, the attitudes of the French business community have evolved. The French *patronat* (the employers' organisation which is the equivalent of the Confederation of British Industry in Britain) believes (rightly) that in most industrial sectors French firms can compete internationally. It therefore tends to argue in favour of reducing tariffs rather than erecting them.

There are, of course, areas where, when it comes to international trade negotiations, France is hyper-sensitive. Agriculture and culture are the two most prominent examples. The French defend their interests in these areas vigorously and are sometimes almost paranoid in their determination to ensure that the Commission sticks to agreed negotiating positions and does not seek to develop compromises behind the Council's back. In the end though they usually tend to look for a solution and not just hold out in isolation. Their protectionist bark is more impressive than the actual bite.

Similarly with Germany and agriculture. The reason why reform of the EU's Common Agricultural Policy has been, and still is, so tortuous and slow is that Germany has never made it a priority. This is partly because of the relationship with France, but it is also because Germany is less hostile to spending money on farmers than it likes to pretend.

In the EU's early days the Common Agricultural Policy served the convenient political purpose of camouflaging resource transfers between Germany's north and south. German agriculture in Bavaria was concentrated mainly in small units, often run on a part-time basis, and was uncompetitive internationally. Bavaria at that time was one of Germany's poorer *Länder*, and small-time farming played a big part in its economy. The Common Agricultural Policy meant that the money needed to support Bavarian farmers could come through the EU. Otherwise it would have had to form part of the national *Finanzausgleich* (the general budgetary equalisation mechanism) and would have been politically controversial.

Since reunification the structure of German agriculture has changed. The small Bavarian farmers are still an important lobby group, although they no longer dominate German agricultural policy making. Instead Germany's main concern is for the interests of farmers in the eastern part of the country.

During the days of the GDR, agriculture was collectivised. Farms were large, but inefficient. Their machinery was old-fashioned and their productivity low. The upside to this is that the East German countryside is relatively unspoiled. DDT and other pesticides were not widely available or used and as a result the local flora and fauna have flourished. Wildflowers abound in the fields and the range of birds and animals is remarkable. Boar are to be found in the parks of Berlin and ospreys breed on, and sea eagles regularly visit, one of the city's main lakes. In Brandenburg wolves and great bustards, creatures normally associated with the remote regions of Russia, have survived. One of the many delights of Germany's capital is the ease with which one can escape to open countryside: the fact that the western part of the city was hemmed in for so long meant that the type of ribbon development which blighted so many of Europe's cities did not occur.

With the demise of the GDR the collective farms were returned to private ownership. Many of them remained large in size and this altered the German government's perspective on agricultural subsidies. Whereas previously its main concern had been to protect the interests of small farmers in Bavaria, it was now to ensure that the owners of large estates in the east were not disadvantaged. In the years since reunification Germany has therefore consistently opposed any suggestion that the EU's Common Agricultural Policy should be focused primarily on small producers, something for which there is a cogent social case. Instead it insists that the size of the holding is irrelevant and that whatever subsidy is granted should be available to all.

In this respect Germany's position was similar to that of the United Kingdom. One of the hypocrisies of successive British governments was to pretend that they were in favour of reducing spending on agriculture within the EU. This was the case in relation to products like olive oil, wine or tobacco, which are not grown in Britain, but when it came to the really big-ticket items like cereals and milk the zeal for reform vanished. It was the interests of the big barley barons of East Anglia which prevailed.

It is France which usually gets the blame for the iniquities of the Common Agricultural Policy. But just as France is less protectionist on international trade than is sometimes portrayed, so too is Germany less committed to agricultural reform than it likes to pretend.

* * *

Next to France, the country to whose EU interests Germany has in recent times paid most attention is Poland. The German–Polish relationship is not one of equals; it is not underpinned by any legal base comparable to the Elysée Treaty and does not involve the same close working links between officials. Yet German ministers still try wherever possible to keep their Polish counterparts onside.

The reasons are both geographical and historical. For Germany the defining effect of the end of the Cold War, apart from its own reunification, was the fact that the country was now surrounded by friends and allies. Germany has common borders with nine other countries (Denmark, the Netherlands, Belgium, France, Luxembourg, Switzerland, Austria, the Czech Republic and Poland). The border with Poland is the longest.

It is also the most fought over and the most politically fraught. Large chunks of what is now Poland were once part of Prussia or Saxony, the forerunners of the German Reich, and many of the people who lived in these territories were Germans. The sensitivities of their loss were far more pronounced in Germany than that of Alsace-Lorraine.

Of all the atrocities committed by the German army in World War II, those which took place in Poland were the worst. According to the doctrines of National Socialist ideology Poles, like Russians, were '*untermenschen*' (sub-human) and were treated as such. Around 6 million Poles, half of them Jews, died at German hands between 1939 and 1945. Nearly all of them were civilians who were murdered in cold blood.

Unsurprisingly therefore Germans feel a particular sense of guilt towards their eastern neighbour. One of the most arresting visual images of the Cold War is that of Willy Brandt, the chancellor of West Germany, on his knees before the monument to the Warsaw Ghetto uprising. Brandt was on a visit to Poland the principal purpose of which was to sign the treaty which finally recognised the frontiers of Poland as they had emerged in 1945, the crowning moment of his policy of Ostpolitik. His decision to kneel was apparently taken quite spontaneously and came as a surprise to all those present. He said afterwards that it was all he could do when words failed him.

Brandt's gesture, known in German as '*Der Kniefall von Warschau*' was controversial at the time. According to an opinion poll published in the magazine *Der Spiegel*, 48 per cent of West Germans thought it was excessive, 41 per cent thought it appropriate and 11 per cent had no opinion. Today, though, it is regarded as an act of real statesmanship which had a lasting impact both in Brandt's own country and more widely in Eastern Europe. It must have been in the minds of the committee which awarded him the Nobel Peace Prize the following year.

Even after Brandt's visit and the ratification of the treaty on Poland's frontiers, relations between the two countries were, for the remaining 20 years of the Cold War, difficult. Acceptance of Poland's borders, particularly the Oder–Neisse line between Poland and the GDR, meant the definitive renunciation of German claims to the territories of East Prussia and Silesia which had been home to Germans for centuries. Cities like Breslau (Wrocław) or Stettin (Szczecin), both only a couple of hours by train from Berlin, were for many Germans part of their families' history. Accepting their loss in practice was one thing. Signing a treaty recognising this loss as legal was, in the view of some, a step too far.

Opposition to the Warsaw Treaty was strongest on the right wing of German politics. It was encouraged by an organisation called the Bund der Vertriebenen (Association of Expellees), formed in 1957 to protect the interests of those Germans and their descendants who had been expelled from countries in Central and Eastern Europe in the years immediately after the war. Many of the early leaders of the Bund had a Nazi past. Its founding charter makes no reference to the historical background to the expulsions.

So, although the treaty was eventually ratified by the Bundestag in 1972, Polish concerns about the risk of some form of German revanchism were never completely assuaged. The treaty contained a clause which made clear that it did not prejudice an eventual treaty constituting a final settlement to World War II. Hence the possibility that Poland's borders might one day be changed was still theoretically open.

It was only after 1990 and the conclusion of the so-called '2 plus 4' agreement establishing the principles of German reunification that the issue of Germany's eastern frontier was definitively settled. For a time there were worries in Poland that some Germans might try to recover or buy back property which their families had possessed in East Prussia or Silesia before 1945. Once it became clear that this was not going to happen, relations improved dramatically.

This did not mean that the Poles never tried to exploit the past. On a notorious occasion in 2007, when the issue of voting rights in the EU was under discussion, the Polish prime minister, Jarosław Kaczyński, suggested that Poland's entitlement should be based not on its actual population, but on what its population would have been had so many Poles not been killed in World War II. Angela Merkel, the German chancellor, was reportedly not amused, but left it to others to remind the Poles that the underlying purpose of the EU was to escape from the past, not to perpetuate it.

Occasional hiccups of this kind aside, German governments now see Poland as a country for which they have a natural affinity and whose views and concerns they take seriously. In Poland, too, sensitivities over the past are declining – to the point where in 2013 the former president, Lech Wałęsa – admittedly no longer an accurate barometer of his country's public opinion – suggested that Poland and Germany should join together in a federal union.

One reason why Germany's relations with Poland have prospered is that when Poland joined the EU the German government insisted on a seven-year transition period for the full application of the EU's rules on the free movement of labour. As a result when, in 2011, the restrictions were lifted, Poland's own economy was stronger and the propensity of young Poles to leave the country was somewhat less.

This does not mean that Polish immigration is not a political issue in Germany. It is. But the concerns are not, as in Britain, with the overall numbers but rather with questions such as entitlements to social security benefits, particularly for children in Poland, and the circumvention of Germany's strict rules on professional qualifications. There are in fact far more Poles resident in Germany than there are in the United Kingdom (1.5 million as opposed to 850,000), but fewer of them are recent arrivals and they are more spread out across the country. German agriculture, particularly in the eastern part of the country, has long been dependent on Polish seasonal workers.

An attempt to stem the flow was made in Brandenburg in the early 2000s when employers were told that before they could employ any Poles on the asparagus harvest they had first to take on Germans from the unemployed register, who in turn were told that they would lose their benefits if they refused to take the work. The result was a disaster. Most of the Germans lasted only one or two days in the fields. They complained that the work was too hard and they preferred to live without benefits.

Polish agricultural workers in Germany have tended, unlike their counterparts in Lincolnshire and East Anglia, not to settle permanently. Their presence has not therefore become a sensitive issue with the local indigenous population. Nor are there in Germany the ubiquitous examples of the '*Polski Sklep*' found in parts of England. Maybe Poles in Germany are happy to consume German gherkins and ham rather than import their own.

The fact that Germany, like Poland, has a head of government with personal experience of life under a communist dictatorship undoubtedly helps relations at a personal level. The departure from the scene of the Kaczyński twins was followed by the arrival of a new generation of political leaders in Poland who were seen in Germany as ideologically sympathetic. They shared the German belief in open markets, free competition and Atlanticism while remaining strong supporters of the European Union and the euro.

When in 2015 the Law and Justice Party returned to power in Poland, relations became more strained. The new Polish leadership was not afraid to criticise German policies, particularly in relation to immigration, and was more sceptical about joining the euro any time soon – not least when it became clear that Germany's vision of the EU does not involve resource transfers or loan guarantees. Nonetheless, many in Germany still see Poland as, after France, the country to whom particular attention should be paid.

Indeed, since 1991 the three countries, Germany, France and Poland, have been linked together through a form of trilateral co-operation known as the Weimar Triangle. It is only a loose type of relationship, based initially on occasional meetings of heads of state/ government and foreign ministers. Its importance was for 20 years largely symbolic, but more recently the frequency of its meetings has increased; they now include gatherings of environment, economics and defence ministers. There is even a small Weimar Triangle combat group (though it does not seem to have any clear military mission).

The grouping also played a more practical role during the early phase of the Ukraine crisis in 2014. The foreign ministers of

Germany, France and Poland, accompanied by the EU's so-called high representative for foreign affairs, attempted to broker a deal between President Yanukovych and the leaders of the opposition. Had it been implemented, the deal might have allowed for a change of regime to come about more slowly and in a calmer atmosphere, and thus without provoking the scale of unrest in the eastern part of the country and the Russian annexation of Crimea.

Instead, the opposition rejected it, President Yanukovych fled the country and events took their course. What was interesting about the episode was that for the first time the three countries acted together in seeking to bring their collective influence, coupled to that of the EU, to bear. The fact that they were unsuccessful on this occasion does not mean that they will not try again.

Surprisingly, this operational manifestation of the Weimar Triangle received little attention in Britain. The idea of a small group of EU countries acting together with the EU's high representative was not of itself a novelty. It is the model which has applied for several years in relation to Iran. What was novel on this occasion was that Britain was not involved. Although a member of the UN Security Council and a signatory of the 1994 Budapest Agreement guaranteeing Ukraine's territorial integrity in return for its renunciation of nuclear weapons, the United Kingdom was in effect sidelined.

Whether this form of trilateral co-operation will ever amount to anything more substantial is unclear. There are a number of other informal groupings within the EU – Benelux, Nordic and Visegrad (Poland, Hungary, Czech Republic and Slovakia), for example. But, even before the United Kingdom's decision to leave, Germany, France and Poland had shown in relation to Ukraine that it had no acknowledged right of foreign policy pre-eminence which made it an indispensable actor in projecting the EU's influence abroad.

* * *

There is no other EU country apart from France and Poland whose concerns Germany feels it has any automatic obligation to accommodate. This does not mean that Germany is indifferent to those of its other partners: merely that in considering how to address them Germany's starting point is their effect on its own interests. In other words, Germany behaves in this respect just like any other member state.

This is the way in which Germany traditionally dealt with the United Kingdom on EU matters. And this is how Germany is likely to do so in the future now that Britain has voted to leave. With the exception of the brief flirtation (as it turned out to be) between Gerhard Schröder and Tony Blair, no German chancellor has felt particularly warmly towards his or her British counterpart. This lack of personal empathy did not prevent the two countries from co-operating well together on many issues, particularly in the defence and security fields, but it was always a co-operation based on mutual interest, not on sentiment: one of the head rather than the heart.

West Germany's first postwar chancellor, Konrad Adenauer, disliked the British intensely. He had good reason to do so. In May 1945 he had been installed as mayor of Cologne, a position he had previously held from 1917 to 1933, by the Americans, who were at that time the occupiers of the city. Under the agreements reached later that summer, however, Cologne was transferred to the British zone of occupation, and in October 1945 the British Military Government dismissed him for incompetence.

The dismissal probably helped Adenauer's political career since it characterised him as someone who could stand up to the occupying powers. But it hardly fostered any fondness he might have had for the United Kingdom. He records in his memoirs the low opinion he had of the abilities of the British military officers with whom he had to deal – by contrast he was complimentary about the American ones – and his conviction that for Germany to re-establish itself as a respectable, and respected, sovereign state the relationship with France was crucial.

It did not prevent Adenauer from supporting British membership of the European Iron and Steel Community and later of the EEC itself. Even when the British government of the day decided against membership of these organisations Adenauer ensured that the ratification of the 1957 Rome Treaty by the Bundestag contained a reference to the possibility that Britain might eventually join.

When, a few years later, under Harold Macmillan's prime minister-ship, Britain changed its mind and tried after all to join, Adenauer made clear that it was France who needed to be convinced. Germany supported the British application but it was not prepared to have a row with France to bring it about. It was similar in 1970 when negotiations for British entry resumed. Willy Brandt was by then the German chancellor and he had none of Adenauer's historical baggage of anti-British feeling. But he too made clear that, though he and his government were fully in favour of British membership, it was President Georges Pompidou with whom the key conversations needed to take place. Germany was not prepared to undertake any heavy lifting on Britain's behalf.

The most egregious example of Germany protecting its own inter-ests and declining to help the United Kingdom was on the occasion of Britain's exit from the Exchange Rate Mechanism (ERM) of the European Monetary System in September 1992. It can of course be argued that Britain should never have entered the mechanism in the first place, certainly not at a rate of 2.95 Deutschmarks to the pound; or that the real cause of Britain's exit was its failure to control inflation and to improve its productivity. It is also true that Germany had no legal obligation to help out a fellow member of the ERM which was finding it difficult to live with the discipline which the system involved.

However, the brutality with which the German government, and the Bundesbank, responded to appeals from the British prime minister, John Major, was striking. Chancellor Kohl declined to intervene; the president of the Bundesbank, Helmut Schlesinger, refused point-blank either to buy sterling or to lower German interest rates by more than a quarter of 1 per cent.

Whether, as has been alleged, Schlesinger actually encouraged George Soros, the principal speculator involved, to move against the pound will probably never be known. But he not only refused any practical support; he was not even prepared to say anything publicly to give comfort to the British government. He even at one stage made himself unavailable on the telephone to the British Prime Minister.

Schlesinger's behaviour was perfectly in accordance with the Bundesbank's mandate, which was to control inflation, not to act as some kind of pan-European lender of last resort. The Bundesbank had operational independence and was not subject to instruction from the federal government. But it is hard to believe that if it had been France which had asked for help the response would have been so dismissive.

A more trivial example of German reluctance to offer special help to Britain came during the period when Gerhard Schröder and Tony Blair were in power. The Commission had presented a proposal for the imposition throughout the EU of a system of artists' resale rights. All living artists, and the descendants of those who had died within the last 70 years, would be entitled to a percentage of any subsequent sales of their works.

The justification for the proposal was that it would harmonise practice within the whole of the EU and thus contribute to the achievement of the single market. But the new rule would affect most substantially the art market in Britain. Some 70 per cent of art sales in the EU took place in London, where the world's two biggest auction houses had their headquarters, and the British art industry was bitterly opposed to the scheme. They argued that its only result would be to drive sales out of London to places like New York or Geneva, where the tax would not apply.

It was a typical example of a Commission proposal which focused on achieving conformity within the EU itself rather than improving the competitiveness of EU enterprises in the wider world. And it was introduced against the wishes of the one member state which would be affected by it more than any other. So the British government launched a vigorous campaign of opposition to the proposal. Tony Blair lobbied Gerhard Schröder personally about it.

To no avail. The Germans were willing to support the idea of a somewhat longer transition period than the Commission were initially proposing, but they were not prepared to oppose it in principle. Such a tax already existed in Germany and the German government had no interest in preventing its introduction elsewhere.

In its way the issue of artists' resale rights was a microcosmic forerunner of the arguments ten years later over the regulation of financial services. Which is more important – harmonisation within the EU or the ability of EU enterprises to compete with their American or Swiss counterparts? And should the interests of a member state upon whose territory the vast bulk of the economic activity in question takes place be given any special consideration?

In both cases there was no specific German interest at stake. And in both cases the German government saw no reason to be particularly accommodating to the country, the United Kingdom, which was principally affected.

This does not mean that Germany was indifferent to the concerns of the United Kingdom about the EU. Germans in all political parties valued British membership and would have emphatically preferred Britain to stay engaged. They recognised that Britain is Europe's second or third largest economy (the statistics of British and French economic performance vary from year to year), that it contains Europe's largest and most prosperous city, and that it is the EU's oldest democracy.

In addition, the UK's economic values are in many respects close to those of Germany itself. Britain does not follow the German model of industrial relations and its market in services is more open than Germany's but it has traditionally stood for free trade, for robust rules on competition and for the effective use of taxpayers' money.

There are also wider reasons which make many ordinary Germans feel well-disposed towards Britain. Britain played a role as an occupying, later a protecting, power in Germany which earned a great deal of respect. In the immediate aftermath of 1945 the British government made a conscious decision to devote resources to the political re-education and civic infrastructure of the zone for which it was responsible. Newspapers like *Die Welt* and magazines like *Der Spiegel* were founded and were given real editorial independence. Young politicians and journalists were encouraged to learn the practices and values of liberal democracy – a conference centre called Wilton Park was established in Sussex for the purpose – and trade unions were supported. Whereas the Americans toyed for a while with the Morgenthau Plan (according to which Germany would have been reduced to the status of a non-industrial peasant society), the British government set out from the beginning to restore German industry and to reintegrate Germany into mainstream European life.

Some of the judgements made by the British military authorities in the 1940s were quixotic. A British major, Ivan Hirst, was responsible for converting the Volkswagen factory in Wolfsburg to the produc-tion of civilian cars and for ordering the first 20,000 of them. His superiors, however, having failed to offload the plant onto the Ford Corporation, gave it away for free to its German managers on the ground that the model it was building had no commercial future and the company therefore had no value. In the end over 5 million Beetles were produced and Volkswagen became the biggest and most profitable car manufacturer in the world.

The enlightened approach of the British occupation regime was mirrored by the subsequent behaviour of the British military units which remained stationed in Germany for the following six decades. Whereas their American counterparts stayed for the most part on their bases, socialised with each other and led lives centred on the PX and the base cinema, the British military integrated far more with the local community. They gave local Germans access to their sports facilities, invited them to their events and developed close relations with local civic leaders.

German mayors in towns where a British unit was stationed were particularly cultivated. Not only would they on occasion attend mess dinners, they were also sometimes invited to visit their local unit when it was on operational deployment in Bosnia or Kosovo. I was once taken on a tour of the big British military training area at Sennelager near Paderborn. Two local councillors from the Green Party, not traditional friends of the military, were also on the trip. As we drove around we were shown not only the rusty tanks used for target practice, but also some of the local wildlife – goshawks, black storks, woodlarks – which bred happily among the firing ranges. As our guide pointed them out, and noted that if public access were not restricted they would probably soon disappear, I could sense my Green companions becoming more and more uncomfortable.

Many British soldiers, of all ranks, married German spouses. Some of them stayed on in Germany after the completion of their military service to work either as civilians on British bases or in the wider German economy. David McAllister, the former minister president of Lower Saxony, is the child of one such marriage.

The British military presence was of great benefit to the local German economy. Many of the goods and services which the British army in Germany needed were procured locally. When the last British units leave Germany in 2019 after a presence there of 74 years there will be genuine regret in many towns in North Rhine Westphalia and Lower Saxony. Unlike their Russian counterparts in the East, the British soldiers were seen as protectors and friends.

Defence was indeed the area in which British and German links were traditionally the closest. In the 1980s the term *Die Stille Allianz* (the quiet alliance) was used in academic foreign policy circles to describe a relationship which was much less publicly visible than the Franco-German one, but which nonetheless played an important part on guiding NATO policy.

Of course the United States was, and still is, the dominant military power in the North Atlantic Alliance, and nothing can be achieved in NATO against American wishes. But the strong British–German security relationship during the latter days of the Cold War meant that there was always something of a counterweight to total American hegemony.

Mrs Thatcher's forlorn and quixotic attempt to block German reuni-fication meant that in the post-Cold War era British–German relations got off to a poor start. But there remains among the German public a surprisingly high level of respect for the political culture, the institutions and the achievements of the United Kingdom.

Even if most German politicians do not share the underlying reservations about the democratic legitimacy of the EU which prompted British withdrawal, there was some sympathy for British concerns at the extent of EU legislative activity. David Cameron's remark after the 2014 European elections that the EU had become 'too big, too bossy and too interfering' would find an echo with many German voters.

Indeed, in a guest article for *Die Welt* on 30 May 2014, the German finance minister, Wolfgang Schäuble, suggested that what was needed was not more Europe, but a more 'intelligent' Europe, an EU which concentrated on a limited number of core functions and discarded some of its previous responsibilities. The list of core functions which he advocated pointedly did not include social or judicial policy.

Those in the Conservative Party in Britain who advocated the reform of the EU rather than withdrawal from it took encouragement from voices such as Schäuble's. They saw Germany as the key ally in an attempt to refashion the EU into something more like the original European Economic Community. They did not seek to prevent the countries of the eurozone from integrating further in the fiscal and budgetary field but they hoped that Germany in turn would be willing to support the establishment of a clear differentiation between the core obligations of EU membership and the much wider ones of the single currency.

They were disappointed.

*   *   *

When David Cameron became prime minister he hoped that Britain's relationship with the EU could be subsumed into such a reshaping of the whole organisation. He assumed that before too long the members of the eurozone would need to negotiate new treaty provisions applicable to themselves and that this would provide an opportunity for Britain to press for a loosening of the commitments which applied to non-eurozone members.

It did not turn out that way. Once the Fiscal Treaty had entered into force, enthusiasm within the eurozone for going further, at any rate in legal terms, evaporated. Governments recognised that the popular mood had changed. It was not going to be possible to secure support for new provisions imposing more budgetary discipline or surveillance from Brussels. No one wanted to lose another referendum. The eurozone would just have to soldier on with the powers which already existed. So, if new arrangements were required for the United Kingdom, they would have to be negotiated separately. This in turn meant that the position of Germany and of the German Chancellor would be the critical factor.

Thus in the run-up to the British general election of 2015 a curious shadow dance took place. The British Prime Minister had already committed himself and his party to the principle that if they were in government after the election they would seek to renegotiate the terms of Britain's membership of the EU and ask the British people to endorse the result in a so-called in/out referendum to be held by 2017.

The Conservative leadership hoped in this way to lay the issue of Europe, which had proved so toxic for the party in the past, to rest until after the election. It was not to be. The success of UKIP in the 2014 European elections, in which it secured the highest share of the vote, and then in two by-elections, brought the issue back into the foreground of political debate. So David Cameron felt obliged to be more specific about what changes he would seek and tried to stake out a clear position on the question of EU immigration.

He needed a position which would stand a chance of being negotiable with the other member states, and this meant securing the agreement, or at any rate avoiding the opposition, of the German Chancellor to what he had in mind. So before he made any firm commitment on the subject he had to be confident in advance of

Angela Merkel's reaction. For several months ideas were ventilated, options evoked and trial balloons flown. Might there be a correlation between the right to free movement in the EU and the convergence of member states' economies? Could there be an emergency brake mechanism if migration to a particular destination exceeded a certain amount? Was there scope for differentiating between different types of prospective EU immigrants?

But as soon as any new idea was raised, the German reaction was the same. Mrs Merkel's spokesman, and sometimes Mrs Merkel herself, would reiterate the fundamental importance of the principle of free movement and Germany's opposition to anything which called this principle into question. In the end, therefore, the British Prime Minister was forced to fall back on measures which restricted the rights of EU immigrants to benefits as his preferred way of dealing with the problem. He abandoned any attempt to set binding numerical limits. UKIP, and many Conservative backbenchers, were predictably withering in their response.

So too later was Iain Duncan Smith, who until his resignation in March 2016 was the secretary of state for work and pensions. In the course of the EU referendum campaign he complained, in an article for the *Sun* newspaper, that Angela Merkel had sabotaged Britain's attempt to renegotiate its membership of the EU by rejecting any serious measures to control immigration. It was, he said, as if they were 'sitting in a room even though they weren't there. There was a chair for them, a German chair. They had a veto over everything.'

His language may have been somewhat colourful, but in essence he was right. So great was the British Prime Minister's concern to have the Germans on side that they were able to set the terms of Britain's renegotiation of its EU membership even before that renegotiation had started. Nothing could be more illustrative of the dominance which Germany now exercises over the EU's internal affairs.

David Cameron's so-called renegotiation of the terms of Britain's membership of the EU was inept. So too was the way he conducted the referendum campaign. No one can know whether the British people could ever have been persuaded to vote to remain in the EU but David Cameron bears a heavy responsibility for the wholly negative way he made the case. Project Fear failed.

However, Angela Merkel and the German government did nothing to help him. It was clear all along that the issue of immigration was going to be a key issue in the British debate about the EU. A British government which was unable to offer any mechanism to limit it would be seen to have failed to respond to its voters' concerns.

It would have been possible for the German government to insist that something needed to be done, that there was an issue which needed to be addressed seriously. Of course the Central and Eastern European countries would have been suspicious and there would have been legal complications. There is, though, a long history in the EU of finding solutions to political problems through special or transitional arrangements and the like. The German government could at least have suggested that an attempt should be made.

They did not. Neither Chancellor Merkel nor any other German minister put any pressure on the Commission or on the Poles and others to be more accommodating to British concerns. All that they were willing to offer was some marginal change to the social security entitlements – a change which in the course of the referendum campaign was derided and shown to be of no real significance in terms of the numbers.

This is perhaps surprising. Immigration is, after all, an issue on which German public opinion is also quite sensitive. There are more EU immigrants in Germany than in Britain and there have for a long time been concerns about their impact on the labour market and on social services. During the negotiations for the entry into the EU of Poland, the Czech Republic and others, the Germans insisted on a long transition period before the provisions on free movement came into force and applied the period in full in Germany itself. (By contrast, the British government chose not to apply the transitional regime in the UK, with the result that the first wave of EU immigrants from the new member states came predominantly to Britain.)

This was therefore an issue on which the German government might have been expected to show some sympathy for British demands. But sensitivity to immigration does not, in Germany, mean calling into question the right to free movement. Ensuring that immigrants do not abuse the social security system is, in German eyes, one thing. Preventing them from coming at all is something else. The firmness of Germany's position was due partly to a genuine belief in the sanctity of free movement as one of the fundamental principles of the EU. It also reflected Germany's own self-interest. If the free movement of people were called into question by the imposition of limits, however temporary or circumscribed, on immigration, then there might at some stage be calls for similar limits to be applied to the free movement of goods – through import surcharges or the like. This for Germany would be hugely damaging.

Germany of course had a national interest in retaining the United Kingdom as a member of the EU. Without Britain's involvement in shaping its policies the EU is likely to be somewhat more protectionist in its foreign trade agenda, somewhat more profligate in its budgetary choices and less influential as a foreign policy actor. Germany will lose a natural ally in many areas of EU decision making.

But in the one field which matters most to Germany, the future of the euro, Britain was not a player. As the German Chancellor and other German ministers spent more and more of their time on euro-related business, the absence of Britain from the table meant the absence of Britain from their thoughts. Keeping Britain in the EU was an aim of the German government, but it was not an overriding priority.

Nor was it an issue on which personal relationships were decisive. Angela Merkel does not reveal her private views about her foreign colleagues (or indeed about much else), but as far as is known she found David Cameron easy to deal with. She was annoyed by his decision in 2009 as party leader to remove the Conservative Party from the CDU-dominated European People's Party group in the European Parliament, but once he became prime minister she treated him with courtesy and respect.

In the end, however, her willingness to help him, as would have been the case with any other British prime minister, depended on two things: her assessment of Germany's national interest and the domestic political context in Germany. In her volte-face over the appointment of Jean-Claude Juncker as president of the European Commission she showed that she was prepared if necessary to let a British prime minister be humiliated.

Britain was, by the time of its EU referendum, already a semi-detached member of the EU; there was little to suggest that this would change even if the British people voted to stay in. We were not going to join the euro or the Schengen Agreement on borders. We would retain our opt-outs from many of the EU's policies on justice and home affairs. We would not take part in EU schemes to distribute refugees. We were sceptical about improving the EU's role in foreign policy and opposed to giving it any more responsibilities in defence.

The prize of retaining Britain as an EU member was thus not exactly glittering. In weighing up how big a price to pay for it, the German government no doubt considered how Britain could help secure the sort of EU which Germany would like. They would have calculated that when it came to the internal market and international trade policy Britain would indeed be a valuable ally. But on the two issues which currently dominate the EU agenda, the euro and immigration, Britain was, from a German perspective, irrelevant.

The Germans are of course disappointed that in the end the UK has decided to leave. It is a blow to the prestige and authority of the EU which they lead and thus, indirectly, to that of Germany itself. They worry that there may be some ripple effect on the commitment of others to the EU itself or to the euro. But they are not agonising about whether they should have offered Britain better terms on the issue of free movement of EU workers, for example. Their judgement of the price the EU should pay reflected their assessment of the value of continued British membership.

When asked in a British television interview in March 2016 how Germany would react if Britain left, Wolfgang Schäuble replied, 'We will cry.' Having metaphorically cried, the German government is getting on with life. This includes a willingness to negotiate some kind of trade agreement between the EU and Britain, but the rapid conclusion of such an agreement will not, compared to managing the euro and dealing with the immigration crisis, be at the top of their list of priorities.

Nor will they feel any need to be overly generous about its content. They were not willing to pay more than a modest price to keep the UK in. They will certainly not be willing to pay any more to make things comfortable for the UK now it has voted to leave.

* * *

The EU, and the issues which directly affect it, now dominate the attention of the German political class. They spend much less time worrying about what used to be the central concern of their foreign policy, namely their relationship with the United States. During the Cold War the United States was the guarantor of Germany's security. Substantial numbers of US servicemen, and US nuclear weapons, were stationed on German territory. NATO planning for the defence of Western Europe against aggression by the Warsaw Pact focused on the central front area of Germany, particularly the Fulda Gap salient, which was considered to be the likely *Schwerpunkt* (focal point) of any attack.

Hence German politicians paid close attention to anything which happened in America, particularly if there was any evidence of a slackening of the US commitment to the defence of Western Europe or of a wish to bring American forces home. German officials and the leading lights of German think-tanks cultivated contacts with their American counterparts. Each year a big security conference took place in Munich (it still does), for which a dozen or so senators and congressmen would be flown over. A post was created of special co-ordinator for German–American relations, usually held by a leading politician, with a remit to ensure that the relationship was kept in good repair.

It was a relationship based on genuine popular support. Affection and respect for America was widespread across the country. It received a boost in 1989–90 when George Bush as president showed an understanding of the German people's wish for reunification. His public support for it and his determination to help bring it about was in stark contrast to François Mitterrand's suspicion and Margaret Thatcher's downright hostility.

American popularity remained high in Germany throughout the 1990s. It culminated in 2001 in the aftermath of the attack on the Twin Towers on 11 September. There were demonstrations of support all over the world but the one in Berlin was the biggest. Half a million people gathered spontaneously at the Brandenburg Gate waving American flags and placards with statements of solidarity. It was the biggest demonstration to have taken place in Germany since World War II. I remember standing in the crowd, listening to the speeches and watching the mood. You could feel the goodwill, the sympathy and the shared grief. It was real, raw emotion.

The Iraq War drained away some of this support. George W. Bush never replicated in Germany the respect felt for his father. But with the election of Barack Obama the pendulum swung back again. In a poll taken in 2010, 88 per cent of Germans expressed support for his policies. Things changed dramatically, however, in the years that followed. By 2013 Germany's national broadcaster, ARD, reported that support for Obama had dropped by half, to 43 per cent; 61 per cent of Germans saw the United States as untrustworthy and only 35 per cent viewed America as a good partner, a figure only marginally higher than that of Russia.

The main reasons for the collapse in support for the United States were the reports of American espionage in Germany and of American surveillance activities in the wider world. The revelation by Edward Snowden that the US National Security Agency had been listening to Angela Merkel's telephone provoked outrage. So too did the subsequent revelation that the CIA had recruited a member of Germany's own external intelligence agency, the Bundesnachrichtendienst (BND).

The German government reacted with uncharacteristic firmness. In the past, behaviour of this kind would have resulted in a private complaint. This time the head of the CIA station in Berlin was publicly named and expelled and the BND employee was prosecuted. Intelligence co-operation was suspended.

The damage to the intelligence relationship can no doubt be repaired in time, but the effect on German public opinion will be more lasting. Sixty per cent of Germans regard Edward Snowden as a hero. There is no longer the instinctive sense of common security and common interests.

This does not mean that Germany is moving away from its traditional Atlanticism or that support for NATO is on the wane. Among the political class there is a healthy awareness of the security realities in Europe and in the wider world. They know that without NATO, and the American commitment to European defence which it embodies, Europe would be a precarious place vulnerable to blackmail, if not direct aggression, from a resurgent Russia.

So they will take care to keep the relationship with the United States in good order. The business community too is anxious not to provoke any trend in Washington towards protectionism. No one in Germany argues that America no longer matters or that its concerns and views should not be heeded, but they do not show up on the radar as brightly as they used to. Germany today is focused on the problems of the euro and immigration. These are not areas where America is involved. Inevitably therefore the old familiarity with American politicians and officials is not what it used to be. There is simply less to talk about.

The approach of the Obama administration did not help. The much-vaunted pivot to Asia carried with it the message that Europe did not loom so large any more in the United States' perception of its strategic interests. Shortly before he left office, President Obama described Angela Merkel as his closest international partner during the past eight years. This may be so, but there were few visible signs at the time of the closeness of the relationship.

If Hillary Clinton had succeeded Barack Obama as president of the United States the relationship with Germany would probably have become somewhat warmer. She was a well-known figure who, from a German perspective, had performed well as secretary of state and who would have represented continuity with the traditional ethos of Atlanticism and commitment to Europe in American foreign policy.

Donald Trump, by contrast, is an unknown quantity. Most Germans were horrified by some of the things which he said on the campaign trail: there is no tradition in Germany of the kind of abuse which he engaged in and neither racism nor misogyny feature in German political debate. Angela Merkel's message of congratulations to him was probably the coolest he received from any NATO ally, emphasising as it did the values which linked the two countries rather than any personal regard. His lack of enthusiasm for free trade and his transactional concept of NATO seemed to set him apart from all his predecessors. The fact that he is the first American president of German heritage since Eisenhower has not made either his personality or his policies any more endearing in German eyes.

American presidents have on many occasions earned the respect and gratitude of the German public. President Truman did so by initiating the Berlin airlift in 1948, President Kennedy with his '*Ich bin ein Berliner*' speech in 1963, President Reagan by publicly calling on President Gorbachev to tear down the Berlin Wall in 1987 and President Bush by his support for German reunification in 1990. It seems unlikely that President Trump will join their number or that he will find Angela Merkel a soulmate.

This does not mean that there will be any crisis in German–US relations. Both countries have objective interests, in the fields both of trade and security, which bind them together. Presidents and chancellors come and go but these interests remain. The trend over the last decade or so, though, has been for German politicians to focus more on their European concerns. The old familiarity with the Washington establishment is vanishing.

Things would be different if there was a direct attack by Russia on a NATO member. In this case NATO would be the focus of consultation and action, and the United States would be expected to exercise the leadership role which it has traditionally played. There would be no suggestion from the German government that somehow the EU should seek to cope with the crisis on its own.

In the meantime, relations between Germany and the United States remain, at the governmental level, correct rather than cordial. They are like a long-married couple who have found that in retirement they have less in common with one another than they previously thought. There is no question of separation and there are ties that still bind. But overall they have tacitly agreed to pursue parallel lives.

₥ SIX ₥

The Ever-Closer Union

The EU, and the euro, have brought Germany huge economic advantages. The political structures and priorities of the EU reflect those of Germany itself. The EU enables Germany to escape from its own past and offers it a framework for influencing the world without appearing nationalist in doing so. No wonder, therefore, the political class in Germany is whole-heartedly in favour of it. Being in favour of something translates easily into wanting more of it. So no wonder too that, when confronted with a new political or economic challenge, German politicians instinctively look to the EU as a potential vehicle for finding a solution.

What is strange, however, is the uncritical nature of their professed commitment to more European integration, their reluctance to spell out what such integration might eventually mean and the huge gulf between what they say about Europe and how they behave within it.

* * *

Officially, Germany favours what it calls a political union. This has been the position of successive German governments for decades. The term has, in Germany at any rate, a nice sound to it – sufficiently vague not to worry those in other member states who might have reacted badly to more precise concepts such as federation or confederation. In the past (though less so nowadays), German politicians often used to add the caveat that in speaking of a political union they did not of course mean a United States of Europe, still less to call into question the existence of Europe's nation states.

Efforts by outsiders to tease out the nature of such a political union have always failed. In 1997, the last year of John Major's government in

Britain, the then foreign secretary, Malcolm Rifkind, tried specifically to get a German answer to the question of what was the destination of, to use the jargon, the European project. He embarked on a short mini-tour of Germany in which he gave several speeches, mainly to student audiences, in which he argued for greater clarity about the aim of further European integration and greater honesty on the part of governments about its limitations as well as its opportunities. He received no answers. The audiences themselves seemed puzzled as to why it was necessary to know where Europe was going: they seemed content just to be on a journey. The German government thought it wrong to raise the issue at all.

Chancellor Kohl was particularly incensed. When I paid my introductory call on him as ambassador the following year it was the first subject he raised. He made clear that he considered it discourteous and unacceptable for a British minister to come to Germany and ask questions of this kind. He jabbed his stubby fingers on the table to emphasise the point and his German, never the most limpid at the best of times, became almost incoherent. It was almost as if a blasphemy had been committed in a place of worship.

The analogy is an apt one. The European Union is to some degree Germany's state religion. Yes, there is freedom to criticise it. But to do so is frowned on in polite society. It is as if the sensitivities of those who owe allegiance to it take precedence over the normal habits of public discussion.

A visiting minster trying the same thing today would fare no better than Malcolm Rifkind. There is no official text or keynote speech in which the German government has spelled out the nature of a political union or has explained which powers should eventually be exercised at the European level and which should be left in the hands of the individual member states.

Naturally, there are innumerable articles in the German press and speeches by German politicians about Europe, and all the country's many foundations and think-tanks pontificate regularly on the subject. There are lively debates about the policies of the European

Central Bank, about the nature of an eventual banking union, about the conditions for the European Stability Mechanism, about the terms under which Greece or Spain should be bailed out, about trade policy or regional policy, and so on. In all these areas there are well-thought-out and well-argued views, and there are differences of opinion both between and within the political parties.

When it comes to the fundamental question of what sort of institution the EU should be in the future, though, the German political and intellectual class seems collectively to have adopted the approach of Ludwig Wittgenstein – '*Worüber wir nicht reden können, darüber müssen wir schweigen*' (Whereof we cannot speak, thereof we are obliged to remain silent).

Such reticence would be understandable if Germany had a vision of the EU's future which was too ambitious for most of its partners; it would be understandable also if it were too restrictive. But the truth is that there is no vision at all. There are vague indications of some new powers which Germany would like the EU to acquire, but they are mostly fairly technical in character and designed clearly to satisfy Germany's own interests: more centralised control of national budgets and more tax harmonisation. There is no suggestion of any fundamental shift in what the EU does.

There is of course nothing wrong with favouring the status quo and being averse to change, but it is bizarre that the most powerful country in Europe feels it necessary to profess attachment to a process of further political integration, while being unable to indicate even in outline where such integration might lead. Even the shock of Britain's departure has brought no clarity. There has been plenty of talk of the need for a fundamental reflection about the EU, but no proposals so far for what the outcome of that reflection might be.

*   *   *

It is possible, for illustrative purposes, to extrapolate from the German constitution the possible outlines of an EU organised on a German model. Its basic principles would be that those policies which directly affect the individual are the responsibility of the member states, that all citizens must be treated equally and that policies which benefit from collective action are the responsibility of the EU centrally.

Specifically this would mean:

- Foreign and defence policy would be conducted by the European Commission, responsible to the European Parliament. The member states would have no role to play, just as the *Länder* have no role to play in Germany's foreign and defence policies.
- Immigration and citizenship rules would be set collectively through co-decision, under majority voting, by the member states and the European Parliament.
- There would be a single currency throughout the EU and only the central government of the EU would have the right to borrow.
- Most taxes (income tax, VAT, excise duty, corporation tax) would also be levied on the basis of common rules established by co-decision. They would be administered by the member states, but the revenues would accrue to the central budget. The member states would be free to raise additional taxes to finance their own expenditure.
- Social security (unemployment, housing, pensions, health care, disability benefits, etc.) policy would also be set centrally by co-decision. It would be administered by the member states on the basis of common rules and entitlements and funded through resource transfers via the central budget.
- Major infrastructure projects would be funded centrally, though the member states would have to give their approval to them.
- The only significant policy areas which would be the exclusive prerogative of member states, and for which they would have to find the financing themselves, would be education, policing, local infrastructure and culture.

This is the sort of vision of Europe which prompted Mrs Thatcher's 'No, no, no' in 1990. It is a Europe in which nation states of the traditional kind no longer exist. They would be reduced to subordinate entities of a federal superstructure.

Is this what the German government means by a political union? It would never admit to it. No German politician, not even the most ardent Europhile, has ever advocated the complete replication of Germany at the European level. To do so would, in domestic terms, be political suicide. The federal budget of such an EU would be huge in comparison to the budgets of its member states – just as Germany's federal budget is vastly bigger than the budgets of its individual *Länder* – and taxpayers in Germany would pay the brunt of it. There is no popular enthusiasm whatever in Germany for resource transfers on this scale.

As a result there is no discussion among the German political class about federal options of this kind for the EU. Whatever form a 'political union' might take, it does not mean, for Germans, raising money in Germany for the benefit of others.

Equally, there is no discussion of the other implication of a federal Europe, namely the consequences for the future of Germany as a nation state.

In Britain the ability to conduct a national foreign policy, and above all the ability to take the decision to commit armed forces to a military operation, are seen as an irreducible characteristic of sovereignty. That is why under successive British governments the condition for co-operation with European partners in the defence and security fields was that it should be voluntary and intergovernmental and that it should not call into question the right of the United Kingdom to act nationally if it so chooses.

But that is not how many German politicians talk about it. Their starting point is the logic of the federal principle: that tasks should be undertaken at the level where value can best be added. It seems to them self-evident that Europe acting together in the defence and security fields would be able to achieve more than its individual member states acting separately. To them, foreign policy, far from being the most sensitive area where progress should only be made cautiously and incrementally, is portrayed as the quintessential candidate for the pooling of sovereignty at the European level.

The implications of this are rarely analysed. It is unusual for a German politician to be pressed on what such pooling of sovereignty would in practice mean and they can normally get away with a fudged answer. Only once has a senior German politician acknowledged the truth. During the federal election campaign of 2002 Edmund Stoiber, the minister president of Bavaria, was challenging Gerhard Schröder for the chancellorship. Stoiber had the reputation of being, in German terms, something of a Eurosceptic. He had from time to time spoken out against interference by the EU in matters which, he claimed, were not its business, and he criticised the Brussels mentality of wanting to do more at the European level irrespective of whether there was any practical advantage in doing so.

His remarks echoed an earlier comment made by Douglas Hurd when he was UK foreign secretary that the European Commission seemed to want to penetrate into too many nooks and crannies of British life. Some British Conservatives thought that in Stoiber they had found a kindred spirit. They were probably unaware that the aspects of EU interference to which Stoiber took exception were in many cases issues of competition policy: how public contracts in Bavaria were put out to tender, how subsidies were used to attract inward investment and whether the Bavarian Land Bank was in compliance with the EU's state aid rules – not exactly the concerns of a free marketeer.

They would have been even more disappointed if they had heard Stoiber's answer to a question at a press conference about a position paper which he had published during the campaign, setting out his vision for the future of the EU. The paper was pretty much in line with the traditional thinking of the German political establishment. It contained inter alia the perspective of a fully integrated European foreign policy, with a single European seat on the United Nations

Security Council and the development of a common European defence policy.

Where Stoiber was different was in his willingness to endorse the logical corollary of such an approach. He was asked by one of the journalists present whether what he was advocating did not mean the dismantling of the Auswärtiges Amt (the German Foreign Ministry) and the incorporation of the Bundeswehr into a European army. Most German politicians would have somehow brushed the question aside. But Stoiber, whose political qualities included candour, did not. Yes, he said, that was indeed what it would mean. It was not something which was going to happen in the near future. Rather, it was what he saw as the long-term logical outcome of a political union in Europe.

* * *

So is this what the Germans themselves really want? Do they want their country to disappear from the international stage altogether? Are they prepared to have German soldiers sent to war as a result of a decision-making process which excludes the Bundestag and against which all German members of the European Parliament might have voted?

Almost certainly not, but they have never been asked. No hard questions have up till now been discussed in Germany about the eventual destination of European integration. Politicians have therefore been able to advocate a direction of travel and focus on the next steps on the way without having to explain what might lie at the end of the journey.

For many German commentators, this reticence is a virtue. The European Union, they would argue, has always proceeded by concentrating on the immediate challenge and finding an answer to it, rather than by worrying about what might come afterwards. The single market, the abolition of frontier controls, the single currency, and now the banking union, all came about because governments could see, or at any rate thought they could see, an obvious current need for them, not because they were part of some detailed long-term plan. Public opinion accepts, or can be brought to accept, individual steps of this kind, whereas it would react negatively to a full prospectus.

This is not a disreputable thesis. The EU has indeed developed gradually over the last five decades. Flexibility has been shown in the form of opt-outs, exemptions, special arrangements and the so-called enhanced co-operation procedure in order to take account of the special concerns of particular member states (often, but not exclusively, the United Kingdom). But until the United Kingdom decided to leave, the show was somehow kept on the road. The founding fathers of the EU may have been visionaries, but their successors have been pragmatists. One step at a time has worked in the past. Why, with the British gone, should it not in the future?

Perhaps it will. Perhaps after the banking union there will be a fiscal union in the eurozone involving the full harmonisation of taxation. This would suit Germany well. But the scope to go much beyond this in pursuing integration is limited, unless decision makers in Germany are prepared to address two key issues: how much more would Germany have to pay into the EU's budget? and would Germany still remain a sovereign state?

So far no one has been prepared to do so.

When Angela Merkel calls for a political union and predicts, as she did in an address to the European Parliament in November 2012, that the European Commission is bound to become the government of the EU, the European Parliament its source of democratic accountability and the Council of Member States its upper chamber, most observers would assume that she envisages an EU which will take on not just new policies but also substantial new financial responsibilities. So far, however, neither she, nor any other senior German politician, has given any hint of what these responsibilities might be.

Quite the reverse. In all the negotiations about the future of the eurozone and the conditions under which the Stability Mechanism might be applied, the principal concern of the German government has been to avoid, or at any rate to limit to the minimum the scope for, any pooling of EU member states' debts. Germany has been prepared, reluctantly, to accept that in the cases of Greece, Ireland, Portugal, Spain and Cyprus bail-out packages were necessary, and, even more reluctantly, that the European Central Bank should play a limited role in bond purchases. But these decisions have been discussed and agreed in Germany on the basis that they were necessary for the survival of the euro, not because they were intrinsically desirable. There has been no suggestion from any German representative that developments of this kind are welcome as natural precursors of a big-budget EU or of more collective European policy responsibility.

When Finance Minister Wolfgang Schaüble suggested, as he did in a newspaper article on 12 January 2013, that a European commissioner should be given a personal veto power over the national budgets of member states, in the way that the competition commissioner has powers over mergers, subsidies and cartels, it was not because he wanted to encourage common European decision making on, or common European responsibility for, their content. He just wanted to ensure that individual member states cannot escape the disciplines of the fiscal pact.

So is the use by German politicians of the term 'political union' just a slogan?

Yes and no. Yes, in the sense that it is a concept which is not fleshed out, not specific and not therefore susceptible to critical examination. Without knowing what the powers of a political union might be or how individuals would be affected by it, it is difficult for electorates to make rational choices about whether they support such a union or not. Many voters who might be in favour of, for example, more pooling of sovereignty in the field of foreign policy would be fundamentally opposed to the idea that the amount of income tax they pay should be decided by a majority vote in the European Parliament. Unless they are given some clear picture of what a political union would in practice mean, they cannot logically be asked to express a view on whether they want it.

On the other hand, even a direction of travel has a certain resonance, a certain notion of what the future might hold. In expressing support for a political union Angela Merkel and her colleagues are conveying at least a subliminal message: that they are not afraid of more decision making at the European level and that they have confidence in the fairness and the efficiency of the European institutions. Brussels is not portrayed as an alien bureaucracy, but as a natural, and benevolent, extension of the German state itself.

What they never allude to is the possibility that, given that the EU institutions operate in large measure through majority voting, laws could be made or decisions taken to which the German government was opposed. This may be because they are so confident of Germany's power in Europe that they assume that none of their partners would really dare to overrule them on an important issue. It may also be because, never having had to explain how a more integrated political union might work, they have simply never thought it through.

German politicians have been able to get away with this vagueness about the EU's future because until recently the German electorate has allowed them to do so. German public opinion, measured by opinion polls, has for decades been consistently in favour of German membership of both the EU and the euro. Europe never featured as a key issue in internal German politics. Yes, there were grumbles and complaints from time to time, and all German governments have had to take account of a lack of enthusiasm on the part of its taxpayers for spending money on foreigners, including European ones. But until the emergence in 2013 of the AfD party German governments did not have to worry about whether the fundamental nature of their European policies risked falling foul of the instincts of the German electorate.

In part, of course, this is because the electorate is not directly consulted. The German constitution is a careful construct of checks and balances, but it is institutions which constitute these checks and balances. True, Article 20 of the constitution states that 'All state authority is derived from the people. It shall be exercised by the people through elections and other votes and through specific legislative, executive and judicial bodies.' However, the only 'other votes' for which the constitution makes specific allowance are referenda on a single issue, namely the new delimitation of federal territory.

Two such referenda have been held. In 1951 the electorates in the states of Württemberg-Hohenzollern, Baden and Württemberg-Baden endorsed a proposal that their *Länder* should merge into the new *Land* of Baden-Württemberg. In 1996 the electorates of Berlin and Brandenburg rejected a proposal that their two *Länder* should merge (Berlin voted in favour, but Brandenburg against). Curiously, there was no referendum on the biggest change to the delimitation of the national territory, namely the reunification of the country in 1990.

From time to time local politicians organise petitions on specific issues. Roland Koch, when campaigning to become minister president of Hessen in 1999 did so on the question of immigration and citizenship and was helped thereby to win the vote, against expectations. And in 2011 the city of Stuttgart organised a consultative vote on whether to build a new railway station. But to conduct a legally binding, or even legally authoritative, referendum at the national level would, most expert jurists agree, mean an amendment to the constitution.

* * *

Even though German public opinion has been broadly positive about the EU, it has never been wildly enthusiastic. The EU is tolerated, rather than loved. It is a fact of life, not something of which the average German is proud in the way that he or she genuinely is about the country's own constitution and system of governance. And some of those German politicians who advocate more European integration are conscious of this.

Indeed, schemes for filling the so-called democratic deficit of the EU abound in the German political debate. Two German politicians in particular have thought hard about it and have set out in public their ideas on how to strengthen the link between the EU and its citizens.

They are Joschka Fischer and Wolfgang Schäuble. Though they come from different ends of the political spectrum their conclusions are remarkable similar.

Fischer is one of the most interesting politicians of modern Germany. His background was the revolutionary student movement of 1968 (though he was never himself a university student – after graduating from high school he worked on and off as a taxi driver) and in the street politics and demonstrations of the 1970s. Some of his associates from that time found their way into the Rote Armee Fraktion (Red Army Faction), the terrorist organisation which succeeded the Baader-Meinhof gang. Fischer himself opted for traditional politics.

He was one of the founder members of the Green Party in 1980, was elected to the Bundestag in 1983 and became a minister in the Hessen government in 1985. He was co-chairman of the Bundestag parliamentary group of the Greens from 1994 to 1998 and in 1998 became foreign minister and vice chancellor. When the Red/ Green coalition of Gerhard Schröder came to an end following the federal election of 2005, Fischer, like Schröder, resigned his seat in the Bundestag and retired from politics. He is now a pundit and occasional university teacher.

Both during and after his service as foreign minister, Fischer took a particular interest in European politics. He was the representative of the German government at the convention which prepared the first draft of the ill-fated Constitutional Treaty. A speech he made at the Humboldt University in 2000 is still one of the reference points for German thinking on the future of the EU.

Wolfgang Schäuble is a more conventional politician. A lawyer from Baden-Württemberg born in 1942, he became a member of the Bundestag in 1972 and a cabinet minister in 1984. He served as minister for inner German affairs and later as interior minister under Helmut Kohl and was the key interlocutor on the West German side in the negotiations for German unity. During the federal election campaign of 1990 he was shot in an assassination attempt by a mentally disturbed man and as a result has spent the rest of his life in a wheelchair. He resumed his political career and was chairman of the CDU parliamentary group from 1991 to 2000 and chairman of the party from 1998 to 2000.

His speech in the Bundestag debate in 1991 about whether to move the capital to Berlin or stay in Bonn is reckoned to have been decisive. Most of his CDU parliamentary colleagues from southern Germany had spoken in favour of Bonn. Schäuble argued passionately that this would be wrong and that only by opting for Berlin could the country really be reunified. As the man who had carried out the detailed negotiating work on reunification, and as a southern German himself, he was listened to with respect.

I asked Schäuble years later whether he had realised that his speech would be so influential. He said no. He had spoken off the cuff without any notes as he had not planned to intervene in the debate at all. It was almost his first time back in the Bundestag after the assassination attempt and he was still taking things easy. But when he heard so many of his colleagues arguing the case for staying in Bonn he felt he had to remind them of what was at stake.

He was of course right. By the time the move to Berlin actually happened, in the summer of 1999, no one, not even those who had argued in favour of Bonn eight years earlier, denied that it was the correct decision.

It was assumed that if and when the CDU came back to power Schäuble would become chancellor, a job which he would undoubtedly have performed well. Instead he was obliged to resign his party positions as a result of a scandal over party financing which erupted in 1999. Schäuble's role in it had been minor by comparison with that of Helmut Kohl, but he admitted receiving party donations which had not been properly declared (there was no suggestion that he had himself in any way profited from them) and the mood of the party was for a fresh start.

His relations with Angela Merkel, who succeeded him as party chairman, were at first cool. But, somewhat to the surprise of most observers, she appointed him interior minister in the Grand Coalition which she formed after the 2005 election and finance minister after 2009 and again after 2013.

For Schäuble, politics has been his life; his disability seems only to have strengthened his political appetite and energy. In his younger years he had a reputation as something of a political attack dog: he could certainly be coruscating in his put-downs of his opponents in Bundestag debates or in other public fora. But he is also one of the most thoughtful and intelligent of German politicians, and one of the issues on which he has reflected the most is the question of the EU's democratic governance. When Larry Siedentop's book *Democracy in Europe* was published in Germany Schäuble presided over the book launch and was clearly fascinated by Siedentop's views.

Fischer and Schäuble were both early advocates of the need for the EU to introduce some formalised system of variable geometry, the doctrine of what came to be called enhanced co-operation, whereby a group of countries within the EU can pursue in the EU's name and with the EU's resources a policy in which not all member states participate.

Indeed, Schäuble can with some justice claim to be the intellectual father of the idea. In a 1994 article which he wrote together with Karl Lamers, the then foreign policy spokesman of the CDU, entitled 'Reflections on European Policy', he called for the establishment within the European Union of a new entity based on the model of a federal state. This core Europe would be centred around France and Germany. It was unclear whether its membership would be self-selecting or whether it would be identical to the membership of the eurozone when the euro was introduced (the timing of which in 1994 looked pretty uncertain). But it was taken for granted that the United Kingdom would not wish, or would not be considered qualified, initially to take part.

The theme of a core Europe was also taken up by Joschka Fischer in his Humboldt University speech. He too advocated the formation of a federation within the EU for those countries which were willing to integrate further or faster. But he speculated that the government of this federation might not necessarily have to be the European Commission. Rather he implied that the Council – i.e. the member states acting collectively – might somehow be able to take on this role.

Both Fischer and Schäuble recognised that if the EU were to develop in the way they proposed, its citizens would need to be more committed to it and more involved in its governance. They have both therefore in recent times advocated the idea of direct popular elections to the post of either president of the Commission or president of the European Council. Neither of them seems to find anything odd in the adoption at the European level of a political mechanism, direct election, for which there is no provision in Germany's own constitution.

The idea of such a direct election sounds superficially attractive. If there is a democratic deficit or a legitimacy problem in Europe, what better way to deal with it than to give people the right to vote for Europe's chief political figure?

If the proposal were that individual national electorates in the EU should each vote for their own commissioner, the idea might have some merit. It would of course be hated by the European Parliament, since with their own direct electoral mandate commissioners would not be dependent on the Parliament's support. But it would certainly be a way of involving citizens directly in the EU's governance in a way they could comprehend.

The idea is not, however, feasible for Europe as a whole. The problem, of course, is that Europe is not a single electorate. For democracy to work there needs to be a body of people, a demos, who feel sufficiently connected to each other to allow decisions about how they are governed to be taken collectively by majority voting – and to accept the validity of those decisions even when they personally disagree with them. There also needs to be a sufficient degree of common awareness among the electorate to enable them to make informed judgements about the people or parties who present themselves for election.

At the European level this is not the case, or at least not to the extent that permits the operation of the democratic rules which apply in the EU's individual member states. Hence the reluctance of many EU governments to allow the further extension of qualified majority voting beyond the areas in which it currently applies. If the population of the EU saw their primary identity as European, then there would be no difficulty with the decision-making structure which already exists: it provides a perfectly effective vehicle for the transmission of popular will into political governance.

But they do not, and no amount of tinkering with the procedures can change this reality. If people do not feel an instinctive solidarity, or sense of common belonging, to one another, they will not accept the legitimacy of decisions which are collectively taken. Within the United Kingdom the normal rules of democracy – majority voting – do not apply in Northern Ireland for precisely this reason.

Germany's own sense of national identity, with its distinctive emphasis on descent, is particularly inimical to the emergence of a European demos. No German politician has so far been willing to acknowledge this.

When it comes to direct elections there is a further problem: the absence of widespread name recognition beyond a limited number of categories of potential candidates. Footballers and rock musicians are well known across national borders, but few other professions can boast this. A direct popular election for the post of president of the European Commission or European Council could only work if the candidates were reasonably well known to all the voters. A contest between, say, Cristiano Ronaldo and Mick Jagger would be an interesting event. It is probably not the sort of election which the enthusiasts for the idea would have in mind.

In the past Wolfgang Schäuble at least seemed to accept that the absence of a European demos set limits to the extent that democratic politics could operate at the European level. More recently both he and Joschka Fischer have resurrected the idea that Europe's governance problem can be overcome by involving its citizens more directly in the process of selecting its leaders. They do not, however, offer any examples of the sort of people who might be expected to stand in such an election. Nor do they explain how voters in, say, Estonia could be motivated to choose between a German and an Italian candidate.

Of course the problem of how to cope with recalcitrant electorates is not new in German political thinking. In his poem 'Die Lösung' ('The Solution'), published in 1953 after the bloody suppression of the workers' uprising in East Berlin, Berthold Brecht ironically suggested that rather than accuse the people of having forfeited the confidence of the government (as the secretary general of the communist Writers' Union had done):

> *Wäre es da*
> *Nicht doch einfacher, die Regierung*
> *Löste das Volk auf und*
> *Wählte ein anderes?*

(Wouldn't it be simpler for the government to dissolve the people and elect another one?)

* * *

How robust is the German consensus on Europe? Will Germany's politicians continue indefinitely to argue for more integration without having to spell out what exactly this would mean? Will its electorate always be willing, even if unenthusiastic, to go along with whatever next step is proposed along the road of ever-closer union?

For decades there were no signs of doubt. Of the five parties represented in the Bundestag before 2013 (Christian Democrats, Social Democrats, Greens, Free Democrats and Die Linke), only the latter, Die Linke, had any qualms about the EU, and even they did not advocate Germany's withdrawal, merely that the EU should be more socialist. All the others endorsed the idea that more should be done at the European level, that the EU should be given more power and that its decision-making arrangements should be adjusted in order to facilitate this.

Nor were there within these parties any mavericks or lone voices who suggested a different approach. No one of any prominence in the traditional German political parties has so far described himself or herself as a Eurosceptic. Even at the level of regional politics there has been little or no dissent from the traditional wisdom.

Occasionally in the recent past one of Germany's nationalist groupings, whose policy platforms – insofar as they are discernible – imply a more Germanocentric view of the world, has achieved representation in a *Land* parliament. But they have never achieved any real political momentum and have usually disappeared from view after a single term. Even the Freie Wähler (Free Voter) movement, a loose organisation akin to British Ratepayers' Associations, which sometimes do well in German communal elections and which grumble about the burden of legislation and regulation, do not advocate any fundamental change in Germany's relationship with the EU.

It is curious, though, that despite their professed devotion to the cause of Europe, few ambitious German politicians have so far actually chosen to go and work there. The first president of the European Commission, Walter Hallstein, was a former German foreign minister but since then the only German commissioner to have held cabinet rank was Martin Bangemann, a Free Democrat who was economics minister from 1984 to 1988. The two main German parties, the CDU and the SPD, have never sent to Brussels a real political heavyweight. Their commissioners have been *Land* politicians, trade unionists or party functionaries. Many of them have been perfectly competent and have held important portfolios in the Commission, but none has gone on to achieve further prominence in German political life.

Nor have many German members of the European Parliament. One or two former MEPs have made the transition to the national stage. Bangemann was leader of the Liberal group in the European Parliament before becoming economic minister and Peter Altmaier began his political career in Strasbourg before being elected to the

Bundestag and becoming minister for the environment in 2012. Martin Schulz, the former president of the European Parliament and SPD candidate for the chancellorship in 2017, is the first German politician with a European background to aspire to a truly senior role in German national politics. On the whole, though, German MEPs see European politics as an end in itself.

It remains to be seen whether David McAllister, the former minister president of Lower Saxony and a real heavyweight in the CDU, can also achieve prominence in both fora. Following his loss of office after the *Land* elections of 2013, McAllister chose not to remain as leader of the opposition in his *Land* nor to stand for election to the Bundestag. Instead he was chosen to head the CDU list of candidates for the European Parliament. Whether he still has ambitions to return to national politics in Germany is unclear; he is certainly young enough to do so. Within the European Parliament itself he has so far only been elected to one middle-ranking position.

Many of his compatriots have. Within European parliamentary politics Germans play a highly influential if not dominant role. The two main political groupings in the European Parliament, the Socialists and the European People's Party, correspond to the two big parties in Germany, and Germany usually provides the biggest national contingent in both.

As a result, Germans occupy more senior positions in the European Parliament than any other nationality. Of the presidents of the Parliament in the last 20 years, five have been German. Germans have frequently been the chairs of one of the two main political groups. In the Parliament elected in 2014 there has been a German president and a German chairman of the European People's Party, the biggest parliamentary grouping. Germans hold more committee chairs than any other nationality. Germans are also disproportionately represented in the key roles of committee rapporteur.

Few, if any, of the individuals concerned have been household names in Germany itself; awareness in Germany of what goes on in Strasbourg and Brussels is probably no higher than it is in Britain. The two worlds of national and European politics exist within their own highly encapsulated bubbles. German MEPs, as many of their British counterparts used to do, vote cheerfully for increases in expenditure through the European budget to which their colleagues at home are fundamentally opposed.

Such a divergence between the ways in which the same electorate is represented is not, in the long run, healthy. Either German voters want more EU expenditure or they do not. It is bizarre that in Berlin their views should be portrayed in one way, but in Brussels and Strasbourg in quite another.

The year 2013 saw the first signs that things might one day change. The success of AfD and the decline of the Free Democrats in both the federal election of 2013 and the European election of 2014 undoubtedly reflects a change in the German public's mood on Europe. There is virtually no hostility to the EU as such: not even AfD advocates German withdrawal. But there is a certain scepticism about the euro which AfD has successfully exploited; there is also a greater inclination to question the mantra of more Europe as the answer to every problem.

Whether this mood will persist, grow or disappear is hard to predict. The initial response of the traditional parties to AfD was to characterise it as extremist and to rule out any form of co-operation with it. The hope was that it would soon fade away. The immigration crisis quickly dashed that hope. It also raised further questions in Germany about the EU's policies. On the one hand there was a demand, from all sides of the political spectrum, for the EU to find a solution to the problem. On the other hand there were calls for Germany to suspend the Schengen Agreement and close its borders.

As a result, both the Christian Democrats and the Social Democrats have become more circumspect in the language which they use about the EU's future. When they argue for action at the European level, it is in more precise and measured terms than in the past. They even on occasions acknowledge the possibility that some powers could be returned to member states.

Wolfgang Schäuble's admission that it might have been better for Greece to leave the euro rather than to have to negotiate terms for a further bail-out was an illustration of this. For the first time a senior German minister acknowledged that membership of the euro might not be irreversible.

But so far no one in the German government has addressed the underlying question: is more European integration compatible with sound money?

*   *   *

It is this dilemma which in the long run will determine the course of Germany's EU policy. For most Germans it is axiomatic that the euro must be like the former Deutschmark. Their reluctance to contemplate pooling of the eurozone's debts or other schemes such as eurobonds is not just a sign of lack of generosity. It reflects a fear that to go down this path would be to acknowledge that the euro is not a naturally sound currency. If some governments in the eurozone are not capable of financing their debts without relying on the creditworthiness of others, then in the eyes of most Germans it is not the kind of currency which the Deutschmark was. And if the European Central Bank is obliged to take measures, such as bond purchases, which have nothing to do with the maintenance of low inflation, then it is a different sort of institution to the Bundesbank.

Commentators may claim – indeed, many do – that it was obvious all along that the euro could only prosper if Germany was willing to lend it credibility, and that this is a price which Germans ought to be prepared to pay to enjoy the advantages which it brings them. After all, the French made no secret of the fact that the ability to benefit from the strength of the Deutschmark was one of the reasons why they pursued the goal of a single currency in the first place. It was never just about minimising transaction costs.

This is not how Germans see it. In order for other countries to benefit from a German-financed solidarity mechanism, they need, in the view of most Germans, to conduct fiscal policies similar to those of Germany itself. Solidarity, they argue, must be earned and this means low debt, low borrowing and low deficits.

The paradox is of course that if every member of the eurozone maintained a high level of discipline over its public finances, there would be no need for bail-outs or eurobonds or stability mechanisms. It is perfectly possible for small or even poor countries to have low borrowing costs. What the markets are interested in is their ability to repay, not the size or nature of their economy. The whole ethos of the Fiscal Treaty agreed in 2012 is that in order to be able to benefit from European instruments of financial solidarity, member states must show that they are on track to meet certain specified criteria for debt, borrowing and deficits. Assuming, hypothetically, that in some years' time all these criteria have been satisfactorily met, then the requirement for the solidarity instruments will fall away.

At that point discussions about more integration in Europe should in logic be focused on the intrinsic desirability of the Europeanisation of particular policies, rather than on the need to save or sustain the euro. Fiscal discipline and better banking regulation are obviously directly linked to the euro's future. Some of the other issues which are sometimes raised in this context are not.

One obvious example is tax harmonisation. German governments have long argued for it as if it is a necessary concomitant of a single currency. They have made clear that a proper fiscal union should involve at least the establishment of common rates of corporation tax and of VAT.

Their motives, however, have nothing to do with safeguarding the health of the euro. Rather, it is all about enhancing Germany's own economic competitiveness. German governments do not want their consumers to be able to shop in other EU countries where prices are cheaper, and they do not want their companies to be able to move their headquarters to countries where corporation tax is lower.

It is perfectly rational, and perfectly legitimate, for a member state to seek to promote EU policies which are to its own advantage. France has done so for years over agriculture; Britain used to do so over free trade. There is nothing wrong in arguing that there is a wider common European good behind what is in fact a national interest. What is different about Germany's use of the EU agenda in this way is that so much of its effort is aimed at reducing the competitiveness of firms in other countries, rather than enhancing the competitiveness of firms in Germany itself.

This is particularly true of the EU's social and environmental agenda. In both these fields German representatives in the Council and in the European Parliament consistently argue for the introduction throughout the EU of regulations which mirror those of Germany. On issues like workers' rights, working time, the role of trade unions or pollution standards Germany is instrumental in generating European legislation which imposes costs on companies which cannot afford them in the way that German companies can.

James Dyson, the inventor, vacuum-cleaner manufacturer and a prominent campaigner for Britain to leave the EU, has complained bitterly about how, in his view, German companies are able to dominate the way in which the EU sets standards in this field. They do so partly through their own lobbying, but partly also because they can call on a network of German officials in the Commission and German members of the European Parliament to show sympathy for their case.

When defending proposals for EU legislation in the social or environmental fields German politicians use lofty European rhetoric about social progress and responsible environmental stewardship. In reality they want to ensure that Germany's competitors are not able to benefit from laxer rules than apply in Germany itself. They recognise that harmonising pay rates across the EU up to German levels would be a step too far, but they want at least to try to ensure that when it comes to non-wage costs the gap is kept as small as possible.

Self-interest thus plays the dominant role in Germany's EU agenda. This was particularly apparent in the behaviour of the German government in 2012 in relation to an issue – a planned merger between the aeronautical company EADS and the defence manufacturer BAE Systems – which, though not strictly speaking one of EU policy, nonetheless was directly relevant to the future of a key European industry.

EADS had come into being in 2000 in the aftermath of the breakdown of merger talks between BAE and DASA, the German aerospace company. At the time BAE and DASA both had shares of 25 per cent in Airbus, one of the world's two (along with Boeing) major manufacturers of civil aircraft. A merger of the two would have significantly altered the balance of power within the Airbus consortium, giving the new entity half the shares.

The main reason for the breakdown was that at the last minute Dick Evans, the CEO of BAE, decided to make a bid for Marconi, a British defence company. His motive seems to have been anticompetitive – to prevent Marconi falling into the hands of one of BAE's rivals – rather than the intrinsic attraction of Marconi itself (indeed Marconi subsequently proved something of a burden for BAE as many of its programmes ran into major technological or financial difficulties). Digesting Marconi while at the same time merging with DASA would have been difficult, and the addition of Marconi would have significantly increased BAE's size and thus the balance of shareholding in the new company between an enlarged BAE and DASA. So the prospective merger collapsed.

BAE's senior management claimed at the time that after a few years DASA would return to the BAE negotiating table. We in the embassy warned that this was a mistaken assumption, that DASA would be more likely to do a deal with the French and that this would have far-reaching consequences for the European aerospace sector. We also suggested that there was a British national interest in this and that the government should not just leave the decision to BAE's management.

As a result I was summoned to a bizarre meeting in Downing Street chaired by Tony Blair. It was bizarre in that no papers for the meeting had been prepared and the department supposedly responsible for aerospace, the Department of Trade and Industry, was not represented. Nor was the Ministry of Defence.

Instead there was a bevy of political advisers from No 10 and a couple of outsiders. The issue was discussed in a roundabout way and there was a certain sense of unease about what BAE was doing. But the suggestion that it should be explicitly warned off acquiring Marconi was not pursued and no subsequent action was taken. Nor was any record of the meeting issued. It was just the sort of sofa government which Lord Butler and Sir John Chilcot criticised in their reports on the Iraq War.

Thereafter things developed exactly as we had predicted. DASA merged with the French company Aerospatiale and EADS was born. In the years that followed, BAE divested its Airbus holding and its other civil aircraft manufacturing capabilities and sought to become a transatlantic defence contractor. But by 2012 the contraction of defence budgets in both Britain and the United States, and the difficulties which any non-American company faces in penetrating the American defence market, meant that BAE was looking to diversify back into the civil sector. A merger with EADS seemed to its board to make commercial sense.

The management of EADS was also enthusiastic, particularly Tom Enders, its German chairman, who as it happened had been DASA's main negotiator during the abortive merger attempt with BAE ten years earlier. He and his colleagues also saw such a deal as a way of diluting further the French and German governments' shareholdings in EADS.

It was assumed that the most likely opposition to a BAE/EADS merger would come from the British and/or French governments – the former out of a concern over the implications for the UK's access to American defence technology, the latter over a possible loss of French influence within the new group. The German government, by contrast, was thought by most commentators to be disposed to favour the deal. It symbolised, after all, two key German policies: the need to create a European defence and aerospace industry capable of competing with the United States, and the right of the managements of private sector companies to decide what is in their own commercial interests.

The opposite occurred. The British and French governments were prepared ultimately to accept the merger but the German chancellor, Angela Merkel, vetoed it. She never clearly explained her reasons for doing so. It seems, though, that she feared that in a group with more of a defence profile French and British views would be likely to be more influential than those of Germany and that German national interests would therefore suffer.

Whether a BAE/EADS merger would have prospered without Mrs Merkel's veto is open to question. The key lesson of the episode was that in a choice between European vision and German national interest it is not the European vision to which the German government gives priority.

*   *   *

So perhaps, in thinking about how a German-led Europe may develop, it is better to ignore what German politicians say and focus instead on what they do. It is not German rhetoric about political union which matters. It is German national interests and the way in which German governments are likely to interpret them.

In the economic field the track record is clear. Germany's national economic interests, as perceived by German politicians, have hitherto consisted essentially of the following:

- the survival of the eurozone with most, even if not necessarily all, of its current members;
- the further development and enforcement of mechanisms for maintaining fiscal discipline in all eurozone states;
- the completion of a eurozone banking union;
- a euro based on sound money and low inflation;
- measures of tax harmonisation to limit the ability of other eurozone states to attract business away from Germany;
- the avoidance of any mutualisation of eurozone countries' debts or borrowing abilities;

- resistance to any moves to turn the EU or the eurozone into a 'transfer union';
- an EU external trade policy which aims at further international liberalisation;
- some limited opening up of the EU's internal market in services, designed to ensure that big German companies can exploit opportunities in other member states, while protecting small enterprises in Germany's domestic market from competition;
- the limitation of any further EU legislation in the environmental and social fields to measures which do not require changes to Germany's own practice.

Both CDU- and SPD-led governments have over the years pursued these aims and have sought to promote, or avoid, EU policies accordingly. In so doing they have used language which appears to imply more action at the European level. They have called for more EU economic governance and for more powers for the EU institutions in ensuring the effectiveness of this governance. They have argued that this is necessary for the euro to prosper.

But not all the things they have argued for have anything to do with the credibility of the euro. Fiscal discipline on the part of its member states and the creation of a banking union certainly do; other elements of Germany's EU economic agenda are designed to promote Germany's own national economic interests. Often this means the advocacy of measures which prevent other member states from competing with Germany.

This is particularly true in the case of tax harmonisation, where Germany has already tried, so far unsuccessfully, to force Ireland to change its corporate tax regime as the price for access to EU bail-out funds. It applies also to social and environmental policy and to the extension of the single market into the area of services.

In the social field Germany's aim has always been to try to ensure that enterprises in other member states have to bear non-wage costs as near as possible to those in Germany. However, Germany has never supported any EU initiative which would involve any change to practices in Germany itself.

Similarly with environmental policy. Germany is at the forefront of those calling for EU action in setting high standards. But the German government is also resistant to anything which might impact negatively on Germany's own industrial interests. This was evidenced in the quiet lobbying which the German Chancellor undertook in the summer of 2013 to mitigate the impact of new emission rules for automobiles. When the German manufacturers complained that the rules would disproportionately disadvantage Germany because of the way they penalised diesel cars, Angela Merkel went to great lengths to ensure that changes were made to the Commission's proposal.

It subsequently became clear that German manufacturers had reason to be worried. In September 2015 Volkswagen admitted that it had programmed the software in millions of its cars to ensure that under test conditions they performed better than on the road. There was an outcry in the German press and the firm's chief executive had to resign. But in all the analysis of what had happened there was curiously little disposition to ask searching questions about the EU's testing regime and why it was that Volkswagen, and perhaps others, had been able to get away with it for so long.

Likewise when there are proposals for freeing up the market in services. In the sectors dominated by large companies Germany has traditionally been on the side of liberalisation. The two big German utilities, E.ON and RWE, have been major beneficiaries from the opening up of national energy markets, and the big international firms in advertising and accountancy are well entrenched in Germany itself.

When it comes to small entrepreneurs and artisans the picture is different. Traders such as plumbers, electricians, hairdressers and the like are highly regulated in Germany and the market is tightly protected. Everything has to be licensed and it is virtually impossible for a non-German resident to obtain the qualifications required. The

German professional bodies defend their monopolies on the grounds that the regime ensures quality and protects consumers. In reality it is a means of preventing access by outsiders to the German market. The German government has never itself shown any disposition to take on the lobby groups concerned. It has resisted attempts at the European level to do so.

The German economic blueprint for Europe is simple. The EU should be as similar to Germany as possible. Those member states who might be tempted to stray outside the constraints of a German model of fiscal discipline should be forced to stay in line. Those who might seek to compete through lower taxes or standards of regulation should be forced to comply with German norms.

*   *   *

In the fields for which the EU has always had responsibility – economic, social and environmental policy – Germany's priorities are easy to identify. There is a long history of discussion and negotiation, and the positions taken by successive German governments, of whatever political persuasion, have been remarkably consistent. There is therefore every reason to suppose that German governments in the future will continue to interpret Germany's national interests in the same way.

But in those areas where EU responsibility is more recent Germany's performance has been less predictable.

In the field of internal security – Justice and Home Affairs, as it is termed in the EU treaties – Germany has hitherto been a contented follower rather than a leader. Germany has land boundaries with nine other states, eight of which are members of the EU. Cross-border crime is therefore a daily reality and Germany benefits directly from measures which help to deal with it. So Germany has been supportive of initiatives to enhance police co-operation, facilitate the exchange of data and so on.

Germany has also signed up to the European Arrest Warrant. This was not straightforward because in the past Germany's constitution had been interpreted as precluding the extradition of a German citizen from German territory. But by appending to the European Arrest Warrant a requirement for proportionality – i.e. a condition that German citizens would only be extradited for crimes of a certain level of seriousness – the problem was overcome.

Nor does Germany have difficulties with limited encroachments on its sovereignty whereby police forces of neighbouring countries would have rights of hot pursuit across its borders or whereby some form of pan-European police entity would be able to conduct investigations in cases involving either the activities of EU institutions or instances of transnational crime. In these areas pragmatic self-interest overcomes any reservations about the idea of German citizens being arrested or investigated by foreigners.

But there has not been, in this field, any of the proclaimed ideological commitment which has characterised Germany's approach to the EU generally. No German politician has argued that a European police force is a good thing in its own right because it embodies a nobler ideal than national (or in the case of Germany provincial) forces or that responsibility for all civil or criminal justice issues should be transferred to Brussels because the EU is intrinsically better placed to legislate in these fields. This is not, as in relation to social security, because of cost. Rather it reflects an awareness by the political class that there are limits to the extent to which German voters are prepared to accept the imposition of 'Europe' on their daily lives. These limits may be more flexible than they turned out to be in Britain, but they exist nonetheless.

On immigration and asylum issues Germany was, until the summer of 2015, also more of a contented follower. This changed when tens of thousands of refugees began turning up in Germany and German policy making became uncharacteristically chaotic. The EU's policies on immigration and asylum are a function of the Schengen Agreement on the abolition of internal border controls. This agreement was originally an arrangement outside the EU Treaty framework involving only five countries (Belgium, Luxembourg, the Netherlands, France and Germany) but it has subsequently been incorporated into the EU and applies to 24 countries, including two, Norway and Iceland, which are outside the EU. The United Kingdom was not a participant, nor is Ireland.

The agreement has brought enormous practical advantages to the citizens of the countries involved. Individuals and businesses were able to exploit the new freedom to cross borders unhindered and rapidly did so. When the common currency came into force the opportunities of Schengen increased even more. It became commonplace in border areas to go shopping or to a restaurant in the country next door.

Borderless travel within the EU does not just benefit EU citizens, however. It also enables foreigners to travel unhindered, and this in turn leads logically to the establishment of common rules for who is entitled to enter the EU from the outside. As a result, the Schengen countries introduced their own visa system and their own procedures for dealing with immigrants. For legitimate business travellers and tourists this was a big attraction. With a single visa it was now possible to obtain access to all the countries of the Schengen area. For illegal immigrants, whether asylum seekers or those just seeking economic opportunity, it also added to the EU's appeal. Once across its external frontier they could disperse to anywhere within the Schengen area.

So common rules were also introduced for dealing with them. A key element of the rules, the so-called Dublin Regulation, is the provision that asylum seekers can claim asylum in only one member state, normally the first EU country they reach, and that once their claim has been registered and their fingerprints taken they can be returned to that member state if they leave it while their asylum claim is being processed.

The system never functioned perfectly. Countries like Greece, Italy and Spain with thousands of kilometres of coastline could not prevent migrants from Africa and Asia from slipping in unnoticed, and many of those who did made their way north. Germany was the biggest single destination. In 2014 around 200,000 people applied for asylum in Germany, more than in the rest of the EU combined. Most of them entered Germany overland and should, in theory at any rate, have made their applications elsewhere before they arrived on German territory.

This led to grumbles in Germany about the numbers of migrants who turned up in the country without having claimed asylum on the way, and to complaints that the Italian authorities were sometimes encouraging them to move on rather than process them themselves. But although the EU's asylum policy was creaking at the seams there was no widespread feeling, in Germany or elsewhere, that it was fundamentally unfit for purpose.

In the summer of 2015 all this changed. The floodgates opened, the rules were ignored and the system collapsed. It began with immigrants crossing from Libya to Sicily and to other Italian islands. Their numbers were soon exceeded by those crossing from Turkey to Greece. Some of them were escaping from the war in Syria. Others came from elsewhere in the Middle East, from Afghanistan and Pakistan and even from further afield in Africa. The distinction between asylum seekers and economic migrants became rapidly eroded.

So too did the ability of the Italian and Greek authorities to cope with the influx. As thousands of people poured onto their coasts every day the officials were unable to register and process them in an orderly fashion. The focus was on saving lives and on providing food and shelter. Taking fingerprints and checking identity cards were, understandably, lesser priorities.

It would in any case have been impossible for all the immigrants to have waited in their first country of arrival in the EU until their individual asylum claims could be assessed. There were simply too many of them. So they were shipped to the Italian and Greek mainlands and from there they headed north by bus, by train or even on foot. Television screens all over Europe were filled with images of them snaking their way along hot dusty roads. There were many families with children, but the majority of them were fit young men.

Most of them wanted to get to Germany or Sweden, which meant crossing several other frontiers on the way, some EU, some non-EU. The governments of the non-EU countries concerned, Serbia and Macedonia for example, were under no legal obligation to let them in and only did so if they could be sure that they would be able to pass them on rapidly to the next country up the line. For the EU countries the legal situation was different. They should, under the terms of the Dublin Regulation, have registered them and provided them with accommodation while their status was reviewed. But with one exception they did not; they simply moved them on.

The one exception was Hungary. The Hungarian government did exactly what it was supposed to do and started registering the immigrants as soon as they arrived on its territory. The result was a series of mini riots. The immigrants refused to submit to registration in Hungary for fear that it would prevent them from claiming asylum elsewhere. The Hungarian government responded by rounding them up and confining them on the premises of the central railway station in Budapest. For this the Hungarian prime minister, Viktor Orbán, a man of robust and nationalistic views, was vilified in much of the German and other European media. His response was to start building fences along his country's borders, first with Croatia then with Serbia, to keep the unwanted hordes out.

It might have been expected, on the analogy of its behaviour in the euro crisis, that the German government would have urged its partners in Schengen to respect the agreed rules and procedures for handling the influx of immigrants. Quite the reverse. To the surprise of everyone, including her own cabinet colleagues, and without any consultation with other governments, Angela Merkel announced that what was happening was a humanitarian tragedy of such proportions that exceptional measures were needed. Germany, for its part, would offer asylum to all immigrants from Syria.

The result was more chaos. Every Syrian refugee headed for Germany, and many who were not Syrians tore up any documents they had and claimed Syrian nationality. The people-smugglers in

Turkey who organised the perilous voyages across the Aegean Sea saw their trade increase further. The countries along the route to Turkey became even more concerned about the numbers who turned up on their frontiers and even more determined to hustle them through as fast as possible.

Quite why the German Chancellor announced such a generous policy towards Syrian refugees is unclear. In one sense she was merely recognising the inevitable. Most of them were heading for Germany anyway and they would all be likely to qualify for asylum. But to accentuate the pull factor in such a dramatic way was uncharacteristically bold.

None of the psychological speculation about her motives – folk memories of the Germans expelled from Central and Eastern Europe in 1945, her Christian upbringing, guilt about Germany's hard line on Greece, a wish to become the next secretary general of the United Nations – seems particularly convincing. Maybe the answer is more straightforward: having thought about it for some time, she simply concluded that it was the best thing to do.

It made many Germans feel good about themselves and their country. But, as the numbers increased, so too did the domestic backlash. Once it became clear that Germany would in the course of 2015 receive around 1 million immigrants, with the prospect of even more in 2016 unless the situation in the Middle East improved, public opinion started to shift. Villages who had never seen a foreigner before now found a thousand of them settled in their local community. Fears about Islamic extremism grew. It was not long before the political mood turned sour.

Most of the refugees arriving in Germany came through Bavaria. The minister president there, Horst Seehofer, took the lead in demanding limits on the numbers of refugees. He argued that Germany should accept no more than 200,000 asylum seekers in any one year, and he overtly criticised the policy of the federal government.

Angela Merkel's response was to demand that Germany's EU partners should shoulder more of the burden. The Commission duly came up with a proposal for a mandatory distribution of 120,000 refugees among the members of the Schengen zone. Under the decision-making procedures which apply to that part of the EU Treaty the proposal could be adopted by a qualified majority vote.

Most of the EU's Central and Eastern European members were adamantly opposed to the idea of being forced to accept a specified number of asylum seekers on their territory. The Hungarian Prime Minister forcefully pointed out that Hungary was a Christian country with no experience of Muslim immigrants and no wish to receive any. His Slovak counterpart was equally vociferous and threatened to ignore the decision if it was taken against Slovakia's wishes.

To no avail. The Commission, under German pressure, maintained its proposal and it was brought to a vote. The Polish government caved in and voted for it – with the lame explanation that it was going to happen anyway. But Hungary, the Czech Republic, Slovakia and Romania voted against. The German interior minister, Thomas de Maizière, expressed his satisfaction at the outcome. He went on to suggest that countries which failed to take their quotas of refugees should be denied access to EU structural funding on the grounds that the obligations of solidarity cut both ways. Neither he nor Chancellor Merkel showed any disposition to question the wisdom of forcing through a decision of this kind by majority vote. This was an issue where Germany had a direct national interest and was determined to impose its will.

It is still unclear whether the compulsory redistribution scheme will actually happen. Even if it does, its impact on the overall numbers involved will be marginal. In Germany public discontent continues, given even more impetus by the events at the end of 2015. In Cologne and in several other big cities, New Year's Eve was marked by a large number of sexual assaults, including one alleged rape, on women revellers in the street, carried out by what seemed to be organised gangs of North African- or Arab-looking young men. The police were accused of looking the other way.

Whether any of them were actually recent arrivals who had benefited from the open-door policy on Syrian refugees is still unclear, but it was grist to the mill of those demanding a tougher line – either by limiting the numbers allowed to come in or expelling those who were convicted of criminal offences. Angela Merkel's immediate reaction was to suggest the need for tougher action or tougher laws enabling criminals of this kind to be deported.

Meanwhile the Schengen Agreement continued to erode. In December Sweden imposed border controls on people crossing the Øresund bridge from Denmark. The Danish government responded by imposing similar controls on the Danish border with Germany. In both cases the motive was to stop refugees who had reached Germany from making their way further north. Even Germany itself introduced controls, supposedly temporary, on some of its borders, including the border with Austria.

The attempt was also made to persuade Turkey to cut off the flow to Greece. In March 2016 an agreement was provisionally reached that Turkey would take back any illegal immigrant from Greece who did not claim asylum or whose asylum claim was rejected. In return the EU would accept a number of Syrian refugees equivalent to the number returned from Greece to Turkey; Turkey would be granted visa-free travel to the Schengen area and a speeding up of its accession negotiations, as well as a 6 billion euro grant to help with the accommodation of refugees in Turkey.

The agreement was negotiated directly between Angela Merkel and the Turkish president, Recep Tayyip Erdoğan – much to the chagrin of Donald Tusk, the president of the EU Council, who thought that he was responsible for dealing with the Turks on the subject, but whose efforts Chancellor Merkel found inadequate. It did indeed slow down the flow, at least initially. But it soon ran into difficulties. Public opinion in Europe was clearly against visa liberalisation for Turks, let alone any prospect of early EU membership. There were legal challenges, too, on human rights grounds, to the forcible repatriation of refugees to Turkey. It seems unlikely that it will ever be implemented. President Erdoğan's increasing authoritarianism following the failed coup of 2016 has soured the atmosphere even further.

*   *   *

The issue of immigration will remain a live one in German politics. Germany has two main interests: to somehow stem the flow of migrants reaching Germany; and to preserve, or restore, the functioning of the Schengen Agreement, from which Germany, with land borders to nine countries, is a major beneficiary. The two aims are not easy to reconcile. Short of abandoning Schengen and erecting permanent fences and border controls around Germany itself, there is little Germany can do to stop refugees from arriving on its territory once they have entered the EU. Even further measures of compulsory redistribution would not solve the problem. Once granted asylum or residence status in, say, Slovakia or Poland, refugees could simply cross the border into Germany anyway.

So Germany is likely to look for measures to contain the flow at the source. In the long run this means finding solutions to the push factors involved – the wars and instability in Syria and elsewhere, the prevalence of poverty and poor governance. The resolution of these issues does not lie within Germany's, or the EU's, power, so Germany will seek to make the EU's external frontier less porous.

Under EU law, responsibility for the surveillance and control of external borders lies with the member states. But in 2004 an EU agency, FRONTEX, was established to facilitate co-operation and provide support. Initially it focused on risk analysis and training but it later expanded its activities to include the provision of border guard teams who could be deployed to particular pressure points. In 2015 it provided help to Greece and Italy in coping with migrants in the Mediterranean.

In the event the help mostly took the form of humanitarian rescue. If immigration into the EU is to be effectively controlled there needs to be a willingness to take more coercive measures such as preventing boats from landing on EU territory. This in turn would probably mean the establishment of processing centres outside the EU – for example in Turkey or Tunisia – where applications for asylum could be processed.

In December 2015 the European Commission proposed the establishment of an EU coastguard to replace FRONTEX. It would have an enforcement rather than a support role and would even have the right to intervene without the agreement of a member state. Germany welcomed the proposal. So indeed at the time did the United Kingdom. It is the sort of collective action which makes practical sense. If individual EU countries are overwhelmed by the numbers of migrants fetching up on their shores, why not let the EU take on the job and give it the financial and material resources to do so?

Whether the EU coastguard force will ever come into being is still unclear. So too is its exact size and role and the rules of engagement under which it would operate. But the impact on Germany of having to accommodate over a million refugees in one year with the prospect of similar influxes to come has been traumatic. The Germans will be looking for EU action to stem the flow.

They will be prepared to pay for it, provided that others do so as well. They will also be willing to use their political and economic muscle to get their way. The suggestion that those member states who did not fulfil their obligations on refugee quotas should lose their access to the EU's structural funds was not followed up, but it was an indication of how Germany might in future seek to impose its will.

What is less clear is whether Germans would have the stomach for a really hard-nosed EU policy on immigration. Deporting asylum seekers from Germany when they have committed serious crimes is one thing and would certainly be welcomed by the mainstream of German public opinion. But the sight on television of an EU ship with a German crew towing boats full of distressed women and children back from the promised land of EU territory and forcibly depositing them back on the Turkish or Libyan mainland would conjure up uncomfortable memories.

Facing up to a need to apply coercive military force is not something for which the German body politic is well prepared. This would be true for any policy of forcible return of, or denial of entry to, illegal immigrants. But it applies even more directly to any attempt to construct an EU foreign and security policy. This is the other big area where German rhetoric about the EU has been out of kilter with its actual performance. It is also the key factor in determining the nature of the political union which Germany professes to want.

🏛 SEVEN 🏛

Will the EU Army Ever March?

Foreign policy was not mentioned in the Treaty of Rome in 1957. But in 1970 the member states of the EEC instituted the practice of what was then called European Political Co-operation.

Such co-operation was conducted on an intergovernmental and voluntary basis outside the structures of the EEC Treaty itself. The Commission was present at meetings, but only as an observer. The European Parliament and the European Court of Justice played no role at all. The member states were under no formal obligation to act together. However, they chose to consult and to try to reach agreement on issues where all of them had common interests.

It is sometimes claimed that the EU which Britain joined was a purely economic institution and that only later did it move into the political field. This is true as far as the treaty itself is concerned, but foreign policy co-operation was already part of the EU's activities in 1973 when the United Kingdom's accession took effect.

In fact, Britain's involvement with the political side of the EU predated its formal membership. The United Kingdom, along with Ireland, Denmark and, until its referendum, Norway, began participating in European Political Co-operation immediately after signing the treaties of accession in January 1972 but before their accessions had been ratified. (The first EU meeting which Britain attended took place later that month. It was of a low-level sub-committee dealing with the Conference on Security and Co-operation in Europe, a project which at that time the Soviet Union and its Warsaw Pact allies were pursuing. The Belgian chairman began the proceedings by noting that hitherto discussions in Political

Co-operation had taken place in French without interpretation, but that this practice might need to be reviewed with the enlargement of the committee's membership. The leader of the British delegation, a middle-ranking Foreign Office official with unusually broad linguistic skills, replied that he was perfectly happy to continue to use French, or indeed English, German or Italian, if this was what his colleagues found more convenient.)

The Maastricht Treaty of 1992 formalised the status of foreign policy as an EU activity. The concept of a Common Foreign and Security Policy was introduced as one of the three so-called pillars of the institution. But, as with the other new pillar dealing with justice and home affairs, the structure remained intergovernmental. The Council of Ministers was the dominant body involved, and decision making was by unanimity. Common positions could thus only be achieved if everyone was in agreement, and in their absence individual member states remained free to act on their own.

The Treaty of Amsterdam signed in 1997 created the post of high representative for the EU's Common Foreign and Security Policy, a post designed to give it a name and a face to the outside world (Javier Solana, the Spanish former secretary general of NATO, was the first incumbent) and introduced some flexibility into decision making. Whereas common strategies had to be agreed by unanimity there was provision for majority voting, under certain conditions, in their implementation, as well as for the practice of constructive abstention whereby a member state could decline to support an EU policy but not prevent it from going ahead.

Under the Lisbon Treaty of 2007 an EU External Action Service was created and the high representative post was combined with that of a vice president of the European Commission. This officeholder was also given the responsibility of chairing meetings of EU foreign ministers when they discussed foreign policy.

Despite these changes the EU's Common Foreign and Security Policy remained essentially intergovernmental in character. It comes into play on issues where everyone agrees, but does not stop individual member states from acting on their own when they judge it necessary. The European Parliament has no formal role in the policy's development or execution – merely the right to be informed about what decisions are taken.

The EU's achievements in the foreign policy field have so far been pretty modest. It has issued many declarations and produced innumerable strategies for relations with its neighbours. It is a major provider of development aid and has for years propped up the Palestinian economy. But it has never replicated at the political level the clout it has in the foreign trade field. On all the big international issues of recent years – the invasion of Iraq or the bombing of Libya, for example – opinion within the EU has been divided and the individual member states have made their own decisions.

Perhaps the EU's most significant foreign policy achievement has been, unsurprisingly, in the area where politics and trade overlap, namely the imposition of sanctions. In the contexts of both Iran and Russia the EU has been the vehicle for the effective use of economic pressure for foreign policy goals.

The EU's involvement in defence is even more recent and tangential. A European defence organisation, the Western European Union (WEU), had existed since the 1940s. But only on paper – it never did anything. Throughout the Cold War it was NATO which provided for the security of Europe and was the only forum for European defence co-operation.

Things began to change in the 1990s. The post-Cold War order turned out to be more fragile than many had foreseen, and the civil war in the former Yugoslavia was a reminder that Europe itself was not immune to instability and violence. Defence policy makers began to be interested in various forms of peacekeeping as potential roles for their armed forces. At the same time the United States made clear that though its NATO commitment to defending Europe from external attack remained valid, it expected NATO's European members to take more responsibility for other forms of security challenge in their own neighbourhood.

So in 1992 the governments of the WEU (at the time the only European organisation which existed in the defence field) agreed on a set of generic military missions which they aimed to be able to undertake together. They were known as the 'Petersberg tasks', because the meeting at which they were agreed took place at the Petersberg Hotel outside Bonn. The tasks were all at the low-intensity end of the military spectrum. The WEU was subsequently wound down and its functions taken over by the European Union. In 1999, in the aftermath of the war in Kosovo, EU heads of government agreed in Helsinki that:

> The Union must have the capacity for autonomous action, backed by credible military forces, the means to decide to use them, and the readiness to do so, in order to respond to international crises without prejudice to actions by NATO.

They also rebranded the Common Foreign and Security Policy as the Common Security and Defence Policy and set out some so-called 'Headline Goals' for ensuring that the EU had certain minimum capabilities for the rapid deployment of military forces. These decisions were largely inspired by a declaration issued in St Malo in 1998 between the British prime minister, Tony Blair, and the French president, Jacques Chirac. Other member states had tacitly recognised that an understanding between the two countries with the most significant military capabilities in Europe was essential if the EU was to develop any capabilities of its own in the defence field.

Since 1999 the EU has undertaken 30 or so missions within the framework of its Common Security and Defence Policy. Most of them have been primarily civilian in character and so far no shots have been fired in the EU's name. Some have involved the deployment of military units, notably a peacekeeping mission to the Democratic Republic of Congo and an anti-piracy operation off Somalia.

A continuing source of disagreement has been the question of whether, in order to command and control such missions, the EU should establish its own permanent military headquarters. It has a military committee in Brussels, which operates alongside the political committee responsible for the EU's common foreign policy. But all EU military missions so far have been commanded from a national headquarters. In the case of the anti-piracy operation off Somalia this has been the United Kingdom's Permanent Joint Headquarters at Northwood.

British governments, both under Labour and Conservative leadership, resolutely opposed the creation of any permanent EU body of this kind. In 2011 the governments of the other five big member states – France, Germany, Italy, Poland and Spain – made a joint proposal for one and were supported by Baroness Ashton, the EU's high representative for foreign affairs and security policy. However, the British foreign secretary, William Hague, reiterated his opposition and his colleagues chose not to pursue the project.

* * *

German politicians of almost every persuasion profess support for a fully fledged common foreign policy for the EU – one which, like the Common Agricultural Policy, would subsume those of the individual member states. There would be a single EU Diplomatic Service, a single EU seat on the United Nations Security Council and single EU representation in other international organisations.

Most of them qualify their support for such an outcome as a long-term vision rather than as something to be implemented immediately; they rarely go into any detail about how it would in practice work. Edmund Stoiber's admission in 2002 that such a common foreign policy would mean the disappearance of the German Foreign Ministry (which indeed in logic it would) has never been subsequently repeated. The concept seems to resonate well with German public opinion. Not least because, given that diplomacy is cheap, it would not cost much money.

Yet Germany has done nothing to make this vision a reality. The provisions of the Lisbon Treaty included the creation of a, theoretically at any rate, powerful figure as the EU's high representative for foreign and security policy, with a global network of offices and the ability to bring to bear the full range of the EU's budgetary resources.

However, the two representatives in office since these powers were created have been relegated to the sidelines of European diplomacy. Catherine Ashton, the first incumbent, was involved in the negotiations on Iran's nuclear programme, but only as an accompanying figure to the foreign ministers of France, Germany and the United Kingdom. Her successor, Federica Mogherini, has played virtually no role at all in relation to the crisis in Ukraine: when Angela Merkel and François Hollande met in Minsk with Presidents Putin and Poroshenko she was not invited.

It could be argued that neither Ms Ashton nor Ms Mogherini, though perfectly competent, were heavyweight political figures and simply did not have the clout to impose themselves on the international stage. But it was precisely because of this that they were appointed. Neither France, Britain nor Germany wanted a strong personality in the job.

That France or Britain might be wary of giving an EU figure too much foreign policy power is unsurprising. It was striking, though, that neither in 2009 nor in 2014 when the appointments were made did Germany see it as a priority to bolster the high representative's status. It would have been easy for Angela Merkel, who was chancellor on both occasions, to do so. There are a number of German politicians – former foreign or defence ministers such as Joschka Fischer, Volker Rühe or Frank-Walter Steinmeier, for example – who could have performed the role with distinction and authority. And if Chancellor Merkel had nominated someone of this stature they would certainly have got the job. But she did not, preferring instead a middle-ranking CDU colleague and a middle-ranking Commission portfolio.

In 2012 the then German foreign minister, Guido Westerwelle, convened a group of 11 of his EU colleagues (Britain was not invited to take part) to discuss the scope for enhancing the EU's foreign and security policy. The resulting report revealed more differences among the participants than agreement and it achieved no significant political resonance. Chancellor Merkel conspicuously failed to comment on it.

When it comes to foreign policy, therefore, there is, as in other areas of EU activity, a stark contrast between what German politicians say and what they do.

Still more so when it comes to defence. When the German government was formed in 2013 the coalition agreement included the sentence: 'We strive for a closer network of European forces which can evolve into a parliamentary-controlled European army.' The formulation does not specify how or by whom such parliamentary control should be exerted but the implication is that the European Parliament would be responsible.

In March 2015 the president of the European Commission, Jean-Claude Juncker, suggested in an interview with a German journalist that there was now a need for an EU army in order to impress President Putin and to provide a stimulus for a real EU Common Foreign and Security Policy. The German defence minister, Ursula von der Leyen, immediately supported the proposal. So too did Norbert Röttgen, the chairman of the Bundestag's Committee on Foreign Affairs.

For over a year there was no follow-up. The German government's position seemed to be that though an EU army was a good idea, it was up to someone else to bring it about. Finally, in July 2016, shortly after the UK's referendum, the German government published a White Paper with the title 'German Security Policy and the Future of the Bundeswehr'. It had been trailed in advance and the usual suspects among British Eurosceptics lambasted it even before its publication as advocating the creation of a European army and thus weakening NATO.

The reality turned out to be rather different. Most of the White Paper was analytical and described the security challenges facing Germany in terms very similar to those of the National Security and Defence Review published in the United Kingdom in 2015. NATO was given pride of place and much of the White Paper was concerned with improving NATO's capabilities. The German government recognised that it needed itself to do more and reaffirmed the NATO commitment to defence expenditure of 2 per cent of GDP, without indicating when, if ever, Germany would itself achieve this figure.

As regards the EU, the White Paper noted that 'Germany is striving to achieve the long-term goal of a common European security and defence union.' This was to be done by using all the options created by the Treaty of Lisbon, such as permanent structured co-operation, by developing the network of bilateral and multilateral relations between EU member states, and by initiatives to expand European capabilities in NATO.

It contained one or two concrete ideas. One was the creation of a permanent EU civil–military planning and command-and-control capability. Another was for regular meetings of the Foreign Affairs Council comprised of defence ministers. There were also general aspirations for the better co-ordination of European defence procurement, without any indication of why efforts of this kind would be any more successful in the future than in the past.

Far more significant was what it did not contain. The words 'European army' did not appear. There was no hint of a common EU defence budget and no suggestion that armed forces should be commanded other than on a national basis. The whole ethos was of voluntary co-operation between governments – the basis on which NATO has operated for over six decades without being accused of having supranational ambitions – albeit with a political commitment to co-operate more. The European Commission and the European Parliament were not mentioned. Nor was there any reference to Britain's decision to leave the EU.

The White Paper was generally welcomed in Germany, with most commentators emphasising the government's recognition that the country needed to be ready to take on more responsibility for global security. Predictably, nobody asked what had happened to the European army which Germany's Defence Minister had expressed enthusiasm for only a year before. In this, as in other EU policy areas, German politicians can say things which sound as if they involve some new initiative without being challenged about what it would in practice mean or when it will happen. It is as if, as high priests of the state religion, they are not pressed to reveal their mysteries.

The prospect of an EU army was one of the arguments used by the 'Leave' side during the British referendum campaign. They argued that it would weaken NATO (though they never explained how leaving the EU would stop it happening). But any rational analysis of the German White Paper would conclude that if this was what was meant by an 'EU army', then the EU, far from being a federation, was no more than 28 governments who might or might not choose to co-operate with one another on an ad hoc basis.

It can of course be argued that in failing in the past to push forward the idea of a common EU foreign policy or a European army Germany was simply being realistic. Britain and France were determined to retain their foreign policy freedom of action and their seats on the UN Security Council. Britain was viscerally opposed to, and most Central and Eastern EU members unenthusiastic about, any serious role for the EU in defence. So why should Germany waste time and effort in what would probably turn out to be a fruitless enterprise?

But now that Britain is leaving, the German government will come under pressure to reveal what it really thinks, and what it is really prepared to do, about the EU's role in foreign policy and defence.

No German government could ever expect, and indeed would ever want, to enjoy in these fields the same level of dominance which it now has in the EU's internal governance. This is partly because of a residual hesitation in Germany about exercising international power; also it is because, unlike France and the United Kingdom, Germany is not a permanent member of the UN Security Council.

Reform of the Security Council has been in the air for decades. Its present composition reflects the realities of power in 1945 not those of today. Efforts to reform it have always foundered, however. There is widespread international endorsement of the principle that its permanent membership should be changed, but it has so far been impossible to find agreement about who the new permanent members should be and which, if any, of the existing ones should give up their seats.

Since the 1990s Germany has maintained a claim to permanent membership, while emphasising that in the long run the EU should have its own permanent Security Council seat. There has been, though, no discussion in Germany about how EU membership of the Security Council might work. Who, for example, would represent the EU and how would decisions be taken on how this representative should vote?

As with the notion of a political union, the slogan of 'EU membership of the Security Council' has a comfortable resonance in Germany and politicians do not feel under any obligation to spell out the details of what it might in practice mean. Nor have they done anything to help bring it about.

If the Security Council were to be expanded to include countries like India, Japan and South Africa as permanent members, then Germany would certainly demand to be among their number. This would make it harder for the German government to argue that it did not really want to be a Security Council member in its own right and was only a candidate in the absence of an EU seat. So the current stalemate on the issue suits Germany quite well.

As indeed do the wider structures for the EU's foreign policy activities. A weakly led and consensus-based Common Foreign and Security Policy gives Germany the best of both worlds. There is no risk of the EU developing policies which do not serve German interests or which would pose domestic political difficulties (too tough a line on Russia, for example). And Germany can take initiatives on its own, or with France, which might, as in the case of Ukraine, not always be welcome to all its EU partners.

* * *

Foreign policy does not, on the whole, cost much money. Defence, however, does. The biggest problem in developing EU defence co-operation is financial. With the exception of Britain and France,

213

few EU countries have been willing to spend enough money on their military capabilities. Those EU members who also belong to NATO have endorsed the principle of spending 2 per cent of their GDP on defence (during the Cold War the equivalent guideline was 3 per cent), but few of them are likely to live up to it in the coming years (unless, of course, President Trump delivers on his campaign rhetoric and threatens to withhold American military support from those NATO members who fail to meet the 2 per cent pledge).

Germany spends only around 1.3 per cent. This is still enough to ensure that the Bundeswehr is a well-equipped force, but not enough to give it the all-round capabilities which would enable it to undertake both high-intensity operations in Europe and expeditionary ones elsewhere in the world.

Germany does, however, participate in a more extensive network of collaborative military relationships than any other European country. It has joint military units with six of its nine neighbouring countries. The first of these is a Franco-German brigade, established in 1987. It is a 4,000-strong mechanised formation, based partly in Alsace and partly in Baden-Württemberg. It forms the nucleus of a corps-level unit, the Eurocorps, which was set up in 1992. It was originally a Franco-German enterprise, but was later opened up to participation by other European countries. Belgium, Luxembourg and Spain have since joined as permanent members and Poland is due to do so in 2017. Others have associated member status.

The Eurocorps can be deployed in its own right and is also available to the EU or to NATO. So far it has been involved in NATO operations in Bosnia, Kosovo and Afghanistan. Britain has a liaison officer at its Strasbourg headquarters but has never assigned troops to Eurocorps command.

Germany is also a member of the tri-national German/Polish/Danish corps with its headquarters at Szczecin (Stettin) on the Baltic and a German/Dutch corps based at Münster in Westphalia. The creation of such joint units is, from a German perspective, a concrete way of giving flesh to the concept of a European army.

Control of such joint units remains firmly in the hands of their sponsoring governments. The Bundestag would be required to authorise, on each occasion, their deployment. So for Germany's European partners a key question in considering proposals for more enhanced forms of military co-operation is a simple one. If a crisis comes will the Germans be there on the day?

When it comes to the direct defence of European territory Germany's commitment is not in any doubt. Germany has been a loyal member of NATO since 1954 and there has never been any question mark over the German government's willingness to deploy the Bundeswehr under NATO command in support of its allies. Of course over the years German governments have had particular concerns about certain aspects of NATO doctrine and policy – for example, in respect of the possible use of short-range nuclear missiles. But when it came to the biggest crunch decision that NATO had to face in the days of the Cold War – the deployment of American cruise and Pershing missiles on European territory in response to the Soviet deployment of the SS20 ballistic missile and the Backfire bomber – the German government remained firm.

President Reagan has rightly been given credit for his toughness over the so-called twin-track policy which led to the agreement in 1987 to ban intermediate-range missiles, an agreement which in turn helped precipitate the end of the Cold War and the collapse of the Soviet Union itself. But without the support of the then German chancellor, Helmut Kohl, the policy would not have been possible.

Concerning military decisions and deployments which are only indirectly related to Europe's own security, however, the German track record is mixed. When the Cold War ended Germany's European allies soon became involved in a range of military operations outside NATO's own territory – in Iraq, Bosnia, Kosovo and Afghanistan. For Germany participation in such operations was both legally and politically problematic. The German constitution, as interpreted by the Constitutional Court, precludes German military activity which is not authorised by either the UN or NATO, and German public opinion is uncomfortable with any use of the Bundeswehr other than for the direct defence of Germany itself.

The Red/Green government which was in power from 1998 to 2005 showed political courage in tackling these constraints and facing down opposition, including in its own ranks, to the idea of German troops taking part in activities outside NATO's own borders. As a result the Bundeswehr took part in the NATO bombing campaign in Serbia and in the subsequent peacekeeping operation in Kosovo. It also played a role in the NATO operation in Afghanistan, a role which was, unlike that of the United Kingdom, limited to the support of reconstruction projects in the north of the country.

Gerhard Schröder, the chancellor, and Joschka Fischer, the foreign minister, deserve great personal credit for the leadership they showed in persuading the country to accept an international military role of this kind. Their government had to survive a vote of confidence on the issue in the Bundestag, which they won by a majority of only two. The fact that they subsequently refused to endorse, or participate in, the invasion of Iraq in 2003 was, with hindsight, a further example of good political judgement, even though galling at the time to George W. Bush and Tony Blair.

Under the CDU/FDP coalition of 2002 to 2006 Germany withdrew into its shell. German troops remained in Afghanistan, but the constraints imposed by the German government on how, when and where they could be used became even more rigid, and Germany showed little appetite for any further military adventures.

This became particularly apparent in relation to the civil war in Libya in 2011. Germany was at the time a member of the Security Council and abstained, in the company of Russia and China, on the crucial resolution authorising the use of force to protect the Libyan civilian population. The United States, France and Britain, among others, all voted in favour and the resolution was carried, opening the way for the subsequent NATO-led military campaign of air strikes.

Quite why Germany chose to vote in this way is still something of a mystery. Voting for a resolution in the Security Council does not carry with it any obligation to deploy armed forces. By abstaining Germany conspicuously aligned itself against its three main military allies. Many in Germany felt uncomfortable about this, but the government did not come under any real pressure as a result.

Domestic political considerations may have played a role. At the time both the Green Party and Die Linke were doing well in the polls and the government was running somewhat scared of the public mood. They had not long previously reversed their policy on nuclear energy in the aftermath of the Fukushima accident and had opted for an accelerated run-down of Germany's nuclear plants (a decision which raised doubts about its future ability either to meet its climate change targets or indeed to ensure its electricity supply) and public opinion certainly did not favour war in Libya. All the same, it was viewed in Washington, Paris and London as pretty pusillanimous.

German public attitudes to the use of the Bundeswehr are changing, however. Its deployment in Kosovo was something of a breakthrough: for the first time a German general commanded an operational NATO mission, and for the first time German aircraft fired live missiles at military targets. An important Rubicon was crossed. In Afghanistan too, despite one widely reported incident in which civilian casualties were involved, the German contribution was perceived as a success, not least because the Germans were wise enough to limit their activities to the north of the country and to an achievable mission.

Germany has avoided the kind of risky military commitments, such as Iraq, which so affected the morale and standing of the British armed forces. Its policy over the use of the Bundeswehr has evolved gradually and with the grain of domestic public opinion. There has been no backlash against military exposure abroad of the sort that has occurred in Britain. Most Germans now accept that their security is affected by events outside Europe and that the Bundeswehr has a role to play in the wider world.

There is still a certain squeamishness about the offensive use of force and about casualties, whether inflicted or suffered, but Germany today is a more 'normal' country in security terms. The answer to the question 'Will the Germans be there on the day?' is that if the case for military action is a sound one and their key allies are involved, then they almost certainly will.

Indeed, following the end of the NATO combat mission in Afghanistan there are now more German troops participating in training and support activities there than there are British. Germany is also providing military equipment and training to the Kurdish Peshmerga forces in the fight against ISIS. This reflects the message contained in a thoughtful speech which German President Gauck made at the Munich Security Conference in 2014, that Germany should be willing to take on more responsibility for promoting security in the wider world and should not let its past serve as a reason for looking away. It is likely, therefore, that Germany will, in the coming years, be less diffident about participating in military missions which are not directly linked to the defence of NATO territory. These could include missions carried out by the EU.

So long as the main source of security concern to many members of the EU is the policy of Russia under President Putin, NATO will remain the principal forum for European defence co-operation. For countries like Poland, the Baltic states, Romania and Bulgaria, the Russian annexation of Crimea was a stark reminder of Europe's security realities. EU missions to Mali or Eritrea, were they to be suggested, will be seen as mere sideshows. For the countries of southern Europe, however, instability in the Mediterranean and the wider world is a more direct threat. For them the idea of an EU operation to try to help stabilise the situation in some of the refugees' countries of origin may well look attractive.

Participation in EU operations is voluntary. No member state can be forced into taking part in one if it does not choose to do so. But this in turn means that no member state can, in practice, prevent an operation from going ahead if a significant number of its partners are in favour.

More EU military missions does not mean the 'communitisation' of European defence. Despite their professions of support for the idea of a European army, few German politicians would in practice want the European Commission or the European Parliament to have any serious responsibility for managing a military operation. But many of them like the idea of giving the Parliament some sort of symbolic role in approving the principle of one.

* * *

Germany's track record in foreign policy since the end of the Cold War has been pretty impressive. The reunification of Germany itself was of course due to the skilful way in which Chancellor Kohl handled his dealings with Mikhail Gorbachev and with the emerging political leadership in Poland and the then Czechoslovakia. The rapid expansion of the EU and NATO to include the countries of Central and Eastern Europe was also a project which Germany strongly supported. No German politician would be hubristic enough to put it in these terms, but the shape of Europe today is a product of German leadership.

In the wider world too Germany has, by and large, made the right calls. It was involved in the NATO operations in Bosnia, Kosovo and northern Afghanistan, but absent from Helmand and Iraq. Many people in Britain would wish that our own government had made similar decisions.

The record is not perfect. At the outset of the Yugoslav crisis the German government was too hasty in calling for the independence of Croatia and Slovenia, without thinking about the consequences for Bosnia. On Libya the government of Angela Merkel was unwilling to do what that of Gerhard Schröder had done over Kosovo and Afghanistan: to face down internal party opposition to authorise military action. The spectacle of Germany voting in the UN Security Council against Britain, France and the United States but alongside Russia and China was unedifying to many Germans as well as to the wider world.

The key test of Germany's ability to exercise leadership in the foreign policy field, at least in the eyes of many of its EU partners, is Russia. Germany is critically dependent on Russia for its energy supplies, principally gas, and German companies have invested in Russia on a huge scale. Most notably, Germany and Russia have co-operated in the construction of Nordstream, a pipeline under the Baltic Sea from Vyborg to Sassnitz without having to pass through the territory of any other state.

The decision to build the Baltic pipeline was bitterly criticised in Poland. Ostensibly the Poles were against it on environmental grounds, but the real reason was that it deprived them of potential leverage of the kind which Ukraine had previously employed. In 2006 Ukraine blocked the flow of Russian gas to countries in Central and Eastern Europe because of a dispute with Russia over the price which Ukraine should pay for its own supplies. One of the unspoken incentives for the construction of the Nordstream pipeline was to ensure that the Poles would not be able to do the same in the future.

Gerhard Schröder, when chancellor, was instrumental in negotiating the agreement for the construction of Nordstream; shortly after leaving politics he became the chairman of the company which operates it. When in office Schröder also had a close personal relationship with Vladimir Putin, who arranged for the rules to be bent so that the Schröders could adopt a Russian girl. Subsequently Schröder has been a consistent apologist for Putin, whom he once described publicly as a *lupenreiner Demokrat* (a crystal-clear democrat).

Angela Merkel has fewer illusions about Putin than her predecessor and has been much shrewder in her dealings with him. Nonetheless the two leaders seem to have established a satisfactory working relationship. She is the only international figure with whom he has regular contacts and the only one for whom he seems to have any kind of respect. Language no doubt helps in this: Mrs Merkel speaks decent Russian (she won a prize at school for it) and Putin good German (from his service with the KGB in Dresden). Her avoidance of personal attacks on him also helps.

In substance, however, she has been firm. She brokered the deal at Minsk but has not sought to downplay Russia's responsibility for its subsequent failure. She has, despite Germany's economic interests, insisted on maintaining an EU sanctions regime on Russia which is tougher than many would have predicted.

What she has in common with Schröder in her attitude to Russia is a concern, shared by the German business community, to ensure that Germany can take its own decisions and is not constrained to operate within the framework of too rigid an EU policy. Thus, while the EU foreign policy machinery had produced numbers of concept papers about, and analyses of, the EU/Russia relationship, there was little by way of common action until the Russian invasion of Crimea.

She has also been prepared to annoy the Chinese. In 2007 she received the Dalai Lama in the Federal Chancellery in Berlin (Mrs Thatcher when in office refused to meet him at all), despite official advice that there might be consequences for German/Chinese bilateral relations. The Chinese in response cancelled a minor ministerial meeting, but otherwise things at both the political and commercial level continued much as before. (By contrast, when David Cameron met the Dalai Lama six years later, the Chinese reacted much more sharply. It took two years, and an election victory, before the British Prime Minister was invited to visit Beijing.)

It is not true, therefore, that under Merkel's leadership Germany pursues a mercantilist foreign policy. She does, though, undoubtedly use her office to promote German commercial interests. When she travels to China or to other emerging markets she is usually accompanied by a strong delegation of German business leaders. This is not solely so that she can lobby on their behalf (though she is happy to do this); the reminder to her hosts that so many of the world's leading industrial enterprises have their headquarters in Germany also adds weight to her political message.

The ability to harness economic power to achieve political influence is what has brought Germany leadership in Europe. It is increasingly doing so in the wider world as well. Even without a permanent seat on the Security Council, and even without major interventionist capabilities for its armed forces, Germany's international voice is listened to with attention and respect.

Germany does not lead the EU in the foreign and security field in quite the same way that it does internally, but it is becoming less diffident and more assertive.

In most policy areas it is likely that the EU would under German leadership develop in the same way whether Britain was a member of the EU or not. Foreign and security policy is the one exception. Now that Britain has decided to leave, those who favour a more integrated approach, notably in Germany, will no longer be able to blame British obstructionism for not pursuing further integration. It will be time to put up or shut up.

The conventional view, particularly among British Eurosceptics, is that without Britain the EU's foreign policy will be fatally weakened and its reputation damaged. Who in the world, they argue, will want to pay heed to an organisation from which one of its leading members, also a permanent member of the Security Council, has just walked away?

It is a seductive argument and one not without merit. Most EU countries, including Germany, did indeed see foreign and defence policy as an area where Britain had unique assets from which the EU as a whole could in the past benefit. This does not mean, however, that, now that Britain is leaving, the EU will just give up or carry on as before but with less effect.

There is an alternative scenario, one which was ignored during the British referendum campaign, but which could have consequences far more dramatic for Britain's interests than either immigration or access to the EU's single market. It is the possibility that, freed from the veto which Britain used to have, the EU may develop in the way that German politicians have long advocated, that it would become a single foreign policy actor in its own right and would acquire its own autonomous defence capabilities.

This would mean, in 20 years' time, an EU seat on the UN Security Council, EU embassies replacing, not just complementing, national embassies, a single EU voice on the world stage and a collective military entity (however organised) called an EU army. It could even mean the EU joining NATO in its own right.

This for Britain would be the nightmare scenario. Living along-side an economic superpower will present its own challenges. Living next to a political and military one, in the way that Canada lives next to the United States, would mean a fundamental change to Britain's position in the world. It is unlikely that when Boris Johnson mentioned Canada as an illustration of how Britain might negotiate a trade agreement with the EU he had this sort of relationship in mind.

Will it happen? Is this what German politicians will push for now that Britain is out of the way?

It is not wholly inconceivable. There will no doubt be calls from the usual suspects (particularly in the Commission and the Parliament) for a major initiative of this kind. In the acrimonious atmosphere generated by the UK's departure, some in the EU, and not just in its institutions, will relish the chance to show that the Eurosceptics in Britain were wrong. Far from the EU's foreign and security policy being fatally undermined by Britain's departure, it will, they will claim, be reborn and revitalised.

But it is unlikely. Germany's track record so far does not suggest a disposition to convert its rhetoric about European foreign and defence policy into reality. And other member states too will have misgivings about the loss of nation statehood which handing over control of these areas to the EU would involve.

This does not mean that things will just remain the same once Britain has gone. Developing a more co-ordinated foreign policy for the EU does not require any change to the treaties. The EU already has all the powers it needs in order to play a more political role in the world. The question is whether it has the will to do so.

Germany and France will be the two key players in determining this. They will not necessarily make the same calls in an EU without Britain as they did when Britain was a member. For both countries Britain's withdrawal offers opportunities as well as disappointment. A more concerted EU foreign policy will not inevitably mean hand-ing over power to the EU institutions. No French government is likely to want to do this. Nor, on the basis of her attitude so far, would Angela Merkel see this as the best way forward.

What France and Germany may do is to try to reintroduce into the foreign policy field the concept of Franco-German leadership which they practised for many decades in other areas of EU business. In other words, they would consult together and formulate joint positions and then seek endorsement for them from the other member states.

On internal EU issues implementation takes place through the normal legislative or administrative process, involving the Commission and the European Parliament. But foreign policy does not usually require legislation – except when it comes to sanctions – and this makes it easier for one or two countries to act, either explicitly or implicitly, in the EU's name.

Franco-German leadership of this kind would not necessarily deprive the EU's high representative of a role. But the role would be a supporting one, rather than one of policy initiative, of the kind that Baroness Ashton played in the negotiations about Iran's nuclear programme. A development along these lines would probably satisfy German yearnings for more EU integration in foreign policy and defence. It could also have implications for the representation of the EU in the Security Council.

At present the EU is represented as an observer at meetings of the UN General Assembly and its subsidiary bodies and is a member in its own right of some of the specialised agencies such as the Food and Agriculture Organisation. Any EU state which sits on the Security Council, whether as a permanent or a non-permanent member, is under an obligation to take account of common EU foreign policy positions and to request that when appropriate the EU high representative can address the Council in the same way that representatives of other organisations such as the Arab League do. But that is all.

Now that Britain is leaving the EU, things could change. With Britain gone France could offer to represent the EU formally in the Security Council and to speak wherever possible there in the

EU's name. It is conceivable that there could be a delegation headed by a French ambassador but including representatives of the EU's External Action Service which in all but name would allow the EU to speak and vote in the Council in its own right. This would not require any amendment to the EU treaties or to the rules of the Security Council itself.

From a French point of view such an arrangement would have two advantages. It would allow France to act as the EU's spokesperson on a key platform of the international stage, and this would give France itself extra clout and influence. It would not, however, bind France into an exclusive EU foreign policy which would deprive the French president of the ability to defend France's own vital international interests.

It would also suit Germany. It could be characterised as a stepping stone to the long-professed German goal of a single EU Security Council seat. And it would allow for a de facto division of pre-eminence between France and Germany in the foreign policy field. France could take the lead on the EU's behalf on those major issues of international peace and security which come up in the Security Council. Germany could do so on those issues, such as relations with Russia, which do not.

Other member states might be suspicious of such a development but would not necessarily seek actively to prevent it. Franco-German leadership of EU foreign policy would still allow the high representative to play a role, and there would be plenty of positions as special emissaries and the like for nationals of other member states to undertake.

In any case, they may have little choice. The precedent of Ukraine suggests that Germany is not wedded to the idea that its foreign policy in Europe can only be conducted through the formal institutional machinery of the EU. If other member states cavil too much at the idea of Germany and France acting in the EU's name or on its behalf, they may have to face the prospect that the two countries will simply do it anyway.

Britain's departure may therefore be a catalyst for more concerted EU foreign policy making, rather than the cause of its collapse. There will no doubt still be a tendency to focus too much attention on words and not enough on action. And there will be tensions between the member states on certain issues: about how tough a line to take on Russia, for example, or about whether to recognise a Palestinian state.

For Germany it will be an opportunity to exercise further leadership, albeit in partnership with France. A Franco-German-led EU foreign policy is not a foregone conclusion now that Britain is leaving. But it is at least on the cards.

* * *

Also on the cards is something called, however misleadingly, an EU army. In the foreign policy field Britain was a brake on the EU's ambitions, but did not seek to thwart them completely. In the case of defence Britain pretty much vetoed anything that was more than symbolic. Not only did Britain prevent the creation of a permanent military headquarters for the EU, it contributed only minimally to those EU operations which were authorised.

How far, without Britain, will the EU really be willing to go? Britain was not alone in having misgivings about the development of an autonomous EU defence capability. Following the initial rejection by the Danish electorate of the Maastricht Treaty of 1992 Denmark was granted, among other things, an opt-out from any form of military planning or co-operation within the EU. For most of the 21 members of the EU who are also members of NATO, it is that organisation which they regard as the primary vehicle for co-operation with their European partners.

More importantly, the current financial pressures on the budgets of all EU members mean that there is no appetite for increases in defence spending. So there will be no new resources available for any EU defence initiatives that may be proposed.

This does not mean that the issue of EU defence capabilities will vanish now that Britain will no longer be a member. It may not have the saliency of the euro or immigration but it will not disappear completely from the agenda. Some in Europe, particularly in the Parliament and the Commission, will keep pressing for action – without, if past precedent is anything to go by, ever specifying what form the action should take.

France and Germany will decide, and although it will probably not feature among their early priorities, at some point in the next 20 years there will almost certainly be some sort of joint initiative on their part. It will most likely take the form of a rebranding of the Eurocorps as an EU military formation and an invitation to all other EU countries to commit capabilities to it. Several have of course already done so. A rebranded Eurocorps could be characterised as automatically available for EU military missions and thus as some sort of nucleus of an EU army. It would not need any financing from the EU budget or any involvement of the European Commission or Parliament.

Nor would it add anything to the totality of European military capabilities. But for those who hanker after more EU visibility in the field of defence, as many Germans do, it would have a certain symbolic value. Its military capability would be limited, but not insignificant. The fact that Britain will leave the EU does not mean that the other member states are incapable of putting together the kind of force package which would be needed to conduct the sort of low-intensity operations that the EU might contemplate.

There are likely to be more EU missions with a military component over the coming years. The lesson of the refugee crisis is that instability anywhere near Europe's borders can rapidly have a direct impact on Europe itself. So there will be calls for EU preventative diplomacy to try to head off crises.

The experience of Iraq and Syria will give many governments pause before they embark on any form of military intervention. But the French operation in Mali (like the earlier British one in Sierra Leone) shows that it can sometimes work. The initial emphasis of EU action will no doubt be to train up local military capabilities in the countries of concern – in Central and North Africa, for example. Training missions can, however, sometimes morph into combat support.

It is quite possible therefore that in 20 years' time the EU will have a number of operations under way designed to help promote stability on the other side of the Mediterranean and that these will include military units wearing some kind of EU insignia. There will also almost certainly by then be an EU permanent military headquarters. With Britain no longer present to object, a sensible case for one can be made. Even training missions need some forum for organisation and co-ordination, and a small command-and-control centre will not necessarily cost a lot of money. From outside the EU Britain will not be able to stop it and will probably in the end send liaison officers to join it.

For Germany, a joint military unit wearing an EU badge would not be that different from the plethora of multinational formations in which the Bundeswehr already participates. It would also, as with NATO or the UN, offer a legal framework which would make it easier for the Bundestag to approve a prospective operation.

* * *

Developments of these kinds in the EU's foreign and defence policies would not mark any dramatic step change. Nor would they imply any challenge to the supremacy of NATO as the vehicle for the projection of hard power or the instrument of Europe's direct defence.

Of course much will also depend on the policies of President Trump: on whether he actively encourages the Europeans to develop autonomous defence capabilities and on how he handles relations with Russia. But if this is indeed how Germany seeks to shape the direction of the EU's foreign and defence activities over the coming years it will not necessarily say so in advance. Successive German governments have talked up the case for an EU foreign policy or some form of EU army. They will be reluctant to acknowledge that when it came to it their ambitions were so modest – still less that this would mark the limit of what the EU could realistically achieve.

Limited though it might be, an agenda of this kind would mark progress of a sort. As with Germany's EU policy more generally, it would not involve the German taxpayer subsidising others. It would fit in well with Germany's traditional approach to how the EU should evolve: direction of travel is more important than the identification of a destination.

⛫ EIGHT ⛫

The Shape of Things to Come

In one of the television debates held in the run-up to the European elections in 2014 Nick Clegg, the leader of the Liberal Democrats, was asked what the EU would look like in ten years' time. He replied that he suspected 'it will be quite similar to what it is now'. He later, according to his friends as reported in the *Mail on Sunday*, regretted the remark because it made him sound oblivious to the need for reform; the need for EU reform is something which every politician in Europe is now expected to advocate.

Reform can, of course, mean different things to different people. For some it denotes the repatriation of powers to the member states. For others it is a relaxation of the regime of budgetary austerity. The withdrawal of the United Kingdom and the rise of populist or Eurosceptic movements more widely has given rise to much soul searching within the EU. So far, however, there is little agreement on what direction of change is needed.

This is particularly true in Germany. Angela Merkel herself is not much interested in the institutional aspects of EU reform. She is happy with the system as it is. She has never suggested that the structures or decision-taking arrangements of the EU need any fundamental change. As regards its policies she has said in the past that it should focus on improving Europe's competitiveness and interfere somewhat less in the internal affairs of its member states when there is no compelling reason to do so. She has often quoted the statistic that Europe accounts for 8 per cent of the world's population, 25 per cent of its gross national product and 50 per cent of its expenditure on social security.

An EU agenda of the kind previously favoured by mainstream British Conservatives – more free trade and less regulation – ought therefore to appeal to her. It does, but only up to a point. She has shown no enthusiasm for creating a genuine internal market in services, and she has little sympathy for the view that the EU should avoid legislating in the social field and should leave it to individual member states to decide how they want to organise their labour markets.

In both these areas German national interest points in a protectionist direction. Germany does not want to face competition from architects, plumbers, insurance salesmen or funeral directors from other member states. And it wants to limit the ability of firms in other member states to offer lower prices based on lower labour costs. Angela Merkel, like her predecessors, bases her policies on Germany's national interest, rather than on any preconceived ideological doctrine.

Her coalition partners, the Social Democrats, are similarly attuned to Germany's national interest but they are also more imbued with ambitions for the EU's institutional future. Heavily influenced by Martin Schulz on EU policy, they have become avowed partisans of a federal Europe, albeit without explaining what this would mean. Even the Social Democrats, however, baulk at the idea that German taxpayers' money should be used for wider European policies. So, while they favour a federal Europe, they do not favour a big federal budget.

Both the main political parties in Germany support the concept, enshrined in the original Treaty of Rome, of an ever-closer union between the peoples of Europe. Angela Merkel declared, in the aftermath of the EU summit on 27 June 2014, that there could be different speeds for member countries to pursue this goal; she was happy, in the context of Britain's renegotiation, to accept that not all member states should be forced to sign up to it.

Neither she, nor any other mainstream German politician, has so far been prepared to acknowledge that the process of European integration might be reaching any kind of natural end point.

Even following the shock of British withdrawal the assumption in all public debate in Germany is that the EU needs to continue to move forward, that in some areas at least 'more Europe' is required. The loss of the United Kingdom, the success of AfD domestically, and of Eurosceptic parties more widely, has certainly caused a degree of reflection. There is more concern now about the impact of 'more Europe' on public opinion. There is less talk about integration for its own sake. But no German politician has advocated that the EU should stand still.

* * *

What might a German-led Europe look like in 20 years' time?

It is a question which, at one level, it is futile to try to answer. So much depends on the events about which Harold Macmillan so wearily complained: on trends in the global economy and on developments in the domestic politics of member states. Could anyone in 1980 have predicted an EU of over 20 member states by the early 2000s? Could anyone in 1990 have foreseen the euro crisis of 2010? Did anyone reckon with Britain leaving? Or with Donald Trump?

Yet not to attempt to address the question carries its own risks for policy makers. For too long the EU has been content to proceed on a day-by-day basis, taking decisions which, with hindsight, had long-term consequences without thinking at the time of what those consequences might be.

The decision in 1979 to replace an assembly of national parliamentarians with a directly elected parliament is one such case. So too were the decisions to enlarge the scope of majority voting in the Single European Act of 1986 and to proceed in 2007 with the Treaty of Lisbon despite the rejection by referenda in France and the Netherlands of the Constitutional Treaty whose terms it replicated. In each of these cases the political momentum of the day prevailed. Nobody sought to analyse what the impact of the changes might be in 10 or 20 years' time. Even had they done so, they might have failed to make an accurate prediction. For many in Europe the way things have turned out is precisely what they would have hoped for.

But not of course in the case of Britain. The EU was never an organisation into which Britain comfortably fitted. Even before the decision to leave, Britain was no more than a semi-detached member: not in the euro, not in the Schengen zone, with only a limited involvement in the EU's Justice and Home Affairs policies and opposed to the mainstream EU view about the legitimacy of the European Parliament.

Britain now has to negotiate a new, essentially trading, relationship with the EU from the outside. Whatever form this relationship may eventually take, our interests will be affected by how the EU develops. So it is worth thinking about the direction in which Germany is going to lead it.

* * *

There are two key questions about the EU's future: who will be in it, and what it will do.

The EU in 2017 had 28 members, the most recent one, Croatia, having joined in 2013. Negotiations are underway with a number of other applicants, but it is unlikely that any of them will conclude for another five years or so. Thereafter it is quite probable that one or all of the remaining West Balkan countries – Serbia, Montenegro, Macedonia, Albania and Kosovo – may join. Whether they do will depend partly on their economic performance and partly on the resolution of particular political issues: the status of Kosovo, for example, and the name of Macedonia. But there are no fundamental reasons why they should not be considered to be viable candidates. Nor would their accession, if it happens, change the underlying nature of the EU itself.

The same would be true in the event that an independent Scotland applied for membership. There would be political complications. Spain would be reluctant to agree because of fears that it would encourage Catalan secession. There would also be huge difficulties, both of timing and of substance, in co-ordinating Scotland's accession with the United Kingdom's exit. Hypothetically, though, if Scotland were to join, it would not change the EU itself.

In all cases there would naturally have to be changes in the decision-making and voting arrangements. The prospect of up to half a dozen new members, all small and mostly poor, might prompt a rethink about the current system. Will it still be thought necessary, for instance, for each member state to have its own commissioner (already with 28 there are not enough portfolios to go round)? Will states with tiny populations continue to be so grossly over-represented in the European Parliament and in the Council's voting arrangements by comparison with the larger ones?

These are issues which, though politically contentious, are capable of resolution without calling the EU's overall homogeneity into question. Much more intractable would be the consequences of the accession of the two large European countries which aspire to membership, namely Turkey and Ukraine. In both these cases it is Germany who will decide whether they join the EU or not.

Turkey has been an associate member of the EU since 1963. It applied for full membership in 1987 and negotiations began in 2005. By opening such negotiations the other member states have accepted that Turkey is a European country entitled to be considered for membership. But the negotiations have been protracted from the start, and there is little likelihood that they will be concluded any time in the foreseeable future.

The principal reasons for this are fears in Germany about Turkish immigration. No German government can afford politically to entertain the idea that 80 million Turks would have the right to move to Germany to join the 3 million or so of their compatriots who are already resident there. However long the transition period might be for such an entitlement to come into force, the logic of EU membership is that one day the right to free movement will apply. Having declined to give Britain any dispensation from the free movement rules, Germany could hardly claim such a right for itself.

By comparison with their British counterparts, German governments have, over the years, been honest about their misgivings over the prospect of Turkish EU membership. They have been persuaded, somewhat reluctantly, that it would be a strategic mistake to say 'never', but they have consistently made clear that the opening of negotiations does not mean that their success is guaranteed.

The United Kingdom's position was, by contrast, one of pure hypocrisy. Successive British governments argued vigorously in favour of Turkey's accession, on the grounds of Turkey's key strategic position and its importance as a NATO ally. However, they were never prepared to discuss the consequences for the EU of adding to its population such a vast number of people from such a poor country with such a different set of social and cultural traditions. Even in 2014/2015, when it was arguing for stricter controls on immigration within the EU, the British government, and most British politicians, still purported to favour Turkish membership.

I once attended an Anglo-German conference at which the issue was discussed. A former British foreign secretary spoke eloquently about Turkey's strategic importance, its vital role in NATO, its pivotal position in the Middle East. Surely, he argued, the case for anchoring Turkey in the EU was overwhelming. Why was Germany dragging its feet? The other British participants nodded sagely. None of them seemed interested in the question of whether giving 80 million Muslims the right of free movement into the United Kingdom was a good idea or would be acceptable to British public opinion.

So long as Turkish membership was at best only a long-term prospect the British government could get away with its disingenuity. But at the height of the referendum campaign the issue suddenly raised its head. Prominent campaigners for 'Leave', many of whom had previously supported Turkish membership, alleged that it was now about to happen and would add to the immigration burden. David Cameron and others responded by saying that it was not remotely on the cards and would not happen for 100 years. Unsurprisingly the Turks, who had seen Britain as their best friend in the EU, were outraged.

Until the summer of 2015 the negotiations between Turkey and the EU seemed to be in limbo. Though they drifted on, they were making poor progress. Turkey itself was becoming more authoritarian. It already had, on some accounts, the highest number of imprisoned journalists in the world. Its judiciary was weak and its civil society under pressure. Its President, and the majority party which he leads, seemed to be moving towards a more doctrinaire form of Islam. Its policy on Syria was idiosyncratic.

Then came the refugee crisis. Turkey was the principal transit route for those fleeing the war in Syria, and these genuine asylum seekers were joined by thousands more from Afghanistan, Pakistan and elsewhere in the Middle East. Turkish middlemen and smugglers arranged their short passage across the Mediterranean into Greece; from there they flooded into the rest of Europe.

It became apparent that without Turkish help it would be impossible to control the flow; the Turkish government made clear that any such help would be linked to the broader issue of Turkey's relationship with the EU. Hence the deal brokered by Angela Merkel involving measures in Turkey to limit the refugee trade in return for visa-free travel for Turkish citizens in the Schengen zone and the acceleration of the negotiations about Turkey's EU membership.

The situation in Turkey could change over the next 20 years. It is possible that when President Erdoğan leaves the scene secularism will return and a more liberal style of democracy will flourish (though on past form a military takeover is just as likely). But the problem of potential immigration will remain, whatever Turkey's internal political circumstances.

For Germany, free movement is one of the key principles of the EU on which little or no compromise is possible. So for any German government Turkish accession to the EU is likely to be, to say the least, problematic. Therefore the most that Germany is likely to be willing to offer is a special relationship involving some, but not all, of the rights of full membership.

Whether such a status would be acceptable to Turkey is doubtful. But given the importance of the issue to Germany, and the fact that even among other member states enthusiasm for Turkey is limited and declining, it seems improbable that Turkey will join the EU any time soon.

Immigration is also a factor in German thinking about Ukraine. Here though it is the Russian dimension which is the more dominant. Until the events of 2013 and 2014 most Germans would probably have seen Ukraine as historically part of Europe and as a potential EU member, even if on a distant time scale. Much of western Ukraine was once part of the Austro-Hungarian Empire and Lviv, the principal city of western Ukraine, was, under its German name of Lemberg, historically and culturally part of the German-speaking world.

During World War II, when Ukraine was occupied by the Wehrmacht, many Ukrainians collaborated with the Nazis. There were Ukrainian SS battalions who fought against the Red Army and Ukrainians were among the most cruel and ruthless guards in the concentration and extermination camps. The Nazis did not give Ukraine the sort of autonomous status which they granted to Slovakia and Croatia but they certainly tried to exploit the hatred which many Ukrainians felt for the leadership of the Soviet Union.

After the war Ukraine was part of the Soviet Union, but, along with Belarus, had a seat at the United Nations as a notionally independent state. When the Soviet Union collapsed and Ukraine asserted this independence, many in Germany saw it as a country which one day could become a credible candidate for EU membership. There were hopes that it would gradually lose its Soviet past and espouse the values of liberal democracy in the way that Poland, its western neighbour, was rapidly doing.

Things did not work out that way. For 20 years after independence Ukraine was mired in corruption and criminality. There were elections, but the leaders whom these elections threw up were hardly paragons of democratic virtue. Above all, there was a continuing, and seemingly unbridgeable, political divide between the western and eastern parts of the country: between those who wanted a closer association with the EU and NATO and those who still thought of themselves as linked umbilically to Russia.

Viktor Yanukovych, the president elected in 2010, tried at first to ride two horses. He came to power in an election that was generally regarded as reasonably free and fair not because he was personally popular, but because he was seen as an alternative to the corrupt, incompetent and chaotic regime which had followed the so-called 'Orange Revolution' of 2004 when Yanukovych had been the losing candidate.

Yanukovych drew most of his original support from the Russian-speaking eastern part of the country and had good relations with the Russian leadership. He quickly struck a deal with Russia to obtain badly needed gas supplies in return for a long extension of the Russian lease of military bases in the Crimea. Having, as he perhaps thought, secured his flank in that respect, he then signed an association agreement with the EU giving Ukraine preferential access to the EU market and providing for co-operation in a wide range of other fields.

He had misjudged the Russian reaction. President Putin made clear to him that if the agreement came into force Ukraine would be excluded from trade with Russia and with the Eurasian trading bloc that the Russians were trying to create and that gas supplies would be cut off. Yanukovych panicked and cancelled the EU agreement. The result was a popular uprising which caused Yanukovych to flee the country, provoked Russia into the military occupation and annexation of Crimea, and which generated a civil war.

The German government tried its best to mediate in the early stages of the Ukrainian crisis. Its foreign minister, Frank-Walter Steinmeier, was active, along with his French and Polish counterparts, in seeking a formula which would have allowed for a peaceful and gradual transition in Kiev at the time of the demonstrations there against President Yanukovych. Chancellor Merkel was assiduous in keeping channels open to President Putin in the months that followed.

When in the winter of 2014/15 the crisis descended into full-scale war, Merkel became centrally involved in the search for a political solution. Together with President Hollande, she brokered in Minsk in February 2015 a ceasefire following all-night talks between the two of them and Presidents Poroshenko and Putin.

She was careful, in presenting the agreement publicly, to say that it offered 'a glimmer of hope, no more no less'. There was no hint of triumphalism about her own role and no reference to German leadership. But she certainly showed a deftness of touch in her approach. On the one hand she firmly opposed the idea of providing arms to the Ukrainian government, even though President Obama had made clear that he had not ruled out this option. On the other hand she consistently made clear to President Putin that if the terms of the ceasefire were not respected, and he continued to provide military support to the separatists, then further and tougher sanctions would follow.

Angela Merkel is more hard-nosed about Russia and about President Putin than any previous German chancellor. However, even she will be reluctant to do anything which might constitute a permanent breach in the relationship between Russia and the EU. She will therefore be conscious of the risks which Ukrainian accession to the EU, or any preliminary steps in that direction, might pose.

The experience of Cyprus has shown the dangers to the EU of accepting as a member a state whose government does not control all the territory to which it claims sovereignty. At least in the case of Cyprus there was an established ceasefire and a potentially viable political process. In Ukraine there is so far neither.

So neither Merkel nor her successors are likely to want to rush into any commitments about Ukrainian membership of the EU. Even if Ukraine's governance and economic performance improve, of which there is currently little sign, the political constraints will loom large in German thinking. It may be that, as with Turkey, negotiations about Ukrainian membership will begin in the next 20 years, but they are unlikely to reach any outcome.

There are other countries which aspire to EU membership, for example Moldova, which clearly is part of Europe, and Georgia, whose geographical Europeanness is questionable. Both of them also have unresolved territorial disputes with Russia or with Russian-supported breakaway proxy states. Both are politically and economically fragile.

From a German perspective Moldova is a potential candidate for EU membership if the issue of the status of Transdnestria could be resolved. There is no sense of urgency about the issue, nor is it clear, following the election of President Dodon in 2016, that Moldova wants to join.

Hence the likelihood is that, as far as membership is concerned, the EU in 20 years' time will indeed look pretty similar to what it is today – minus the United Kingdom. Perhaps a little larger as a result of the accession of a few more small countries, but without any big new players.

* * *

Numbers are not everything. A subsidiary question to that of who will be in the EU is whether all its members will have the same status.

The EU is already a remarkably flexible organisation. It has a certain number of key policies to which everyone subscribes – the single market and free movement, for example. But others – the common currency, border controls, justice and defence – are only undertaken by a limited number of member states. At the moment this flexibility has developed on an ad hoc basis. As certain policies have been introduced, individual member states either have chosen not to take part or have been judged as not ready for the constraints involved.

What is not yet clear is whether this will continue to be the case in future, or whether there will be some more formal type of differentiation.

Until recently there was a shared concept of such differentiation between the traditional EU federalists and British Eurosceptics. It was shared not because they both favoured the same goals, but because a certain course of development would have enabled them both to secure their separate sets of objectives.

Under this approach a core group of EU countries, centred round the eurozone, would continue the process of further integration, transferring more and more competences to the European level until at some point the EU took on most of the attributes of a federal state.

In addition there would be an outer periphery of EU members who would retain their independence but would remain part of the EU's single market and would perhaps participate in certain other EU policies where the benefits of common action were palpable and the concerns about loss of sovereignty less acute.

Those on the periphery would, according to this model, not try to prevent the members of the core group from integrating further in whatever areas they chose. Those in the core group would respect the rights of the peripherals to equality in decision making in those areas which were common to all. The two groups of countries, the 'Ins' and the 'Outs', the integrationists and the independents, would happily co-exist within a single framework, but with differing ambitions.

It was a seductive recipe which seemed to cater for the interests of everyone. Michael Howard, when leader of the UK Conservative Party, actively encouraged it. It also formed the basis of the approach of his successor, David Cameron, to the EU. The exact details of how such a dual EU might function were never spelled out by its proponents. Would, for example, the institutions of the EU – the Commission, the Parliament and the Court – have differing memberships or differing roles depending on which group of countries was involved? Although such questions remained unanswered, the model seemed for a time as if it might be a feasible way ahead.

It even appeared to offer some scope for the United Kingdom to exercise a form of leadership within the EU. Just as Germany would lead the core group centred on the eurozone, so too, some wishful thinkers among the British commentariat dreamed, the United Kingdom would be the natural leader of the Outs. And if, as many British Eurosceptics thought likely, the euro came sooner or later to grief, then Britain would be able, with the sotto voce cry of 'We told you so', to help restore the EU to something like its original form – a predominantly economic community.

Even before Britain decided to leave, the experience of the Fiscal Treaty showed that the EU was not going to divide neatly into two classes of membership. There will indeed be a core group centred on the euro which will meet separately and may on occasion adopt rules or obligations which will apply only to those countries which use the single currency. But there is no coherent grouping of Outs with common political aims.

With the exception of the United Kingdom and Denmark, all the EU's member states are legally obliged to join the euro at some stage. And even if in most cases early membership is not – for either economic or political reasons – in prospect, none of them is interested in a special status which excludes the possibility of joining the euro. Not even the Danes see themselves as permanent Outs. In 2014 the Danish prime minister, Helle Thorning-Schmidt, said in a BBC television interview that she believed that sooner or later Denmark would indeed join.

All of them (with the exception of the Czechs, who initially refused to sign, but did so later after a change of government) became parties to the Fiscal Treaty. And none of them showed any interest in institutional arrangements based on two classes of EU membership. Still less did they see Britain as exercising any leadership or representative role on their behalf.

The countries not in the eurozone do indeed share a common concern about decision making. They all see the risk that the eurozone, when it meets separately, may take decisions or adopt positions which it would then seek to impose as a bloc on the wider EU membership. Britain had particular worries about such a possibility in the banking sector; others too see a potential problem.

Hence the decision in December 2012 to introduce a special system of decision making for the European Banking Authority. In order for the Authority to take action, separate majorities of both eurozone and non-eurozone countries will be required. It was also one of the key issues in the negotiations about Britain's future membership of the EU which culminated in the agreement of 19 February 2016. That agreement included specific provisions to ensure that the interests of countries not in the euro were safeguarded when the eurozone took its own decisions.

But there are no fields in which all the non-eurozone countries share a common interest. They are not in any sense a homogeneous group. Some, like Sweden and Denmark, share Britain's commitment to free trade and budgetary discipline. Others, like Poland, Bulgaria and Romania, are in favour of a bigger EU budget and more EU support for agriculture. None of them is antipathetic to EU social legislation. None of them has reservations about the Schengen Agreement.

So now that Britain is going, the notion of a formalised two-speed EU is not going to appeal to anyone. This does not mean that there will not, in the future, be more examples of flexibility or of opt-outs, but they will continue to be negotiated on a case-by-case basis. No EU head of government has shown any interest in a special status within the EU.

David Cameron's renegotiation showed that it would not be possible to enmesh a change to the status of the United Kingdom within a wider recasting of the whole structure of the EU. There simply was not the appetite for it elsewhere and Britain did not have the political weight to force the issue.

The EU will continue for some time to be divided between those countries who are in the eurozone and those who are not. Denmark has a permanent opt-out, Sweden and Poland, who are theoretically obliged to join one day, are not going to wish to do so any time soon, and countries like Romania and Bulgaria are simply not economically ready for it.

Whether there will continue to be separate meetings for eurozone countries remains to be seen. The eurozone will dominate the EU both economically and politically – so much so that there will be little point in pretending that it is a separate entity. The likelihood is that the EU will meet as a single body with different voting arrangements depending on the nature of the item on the agenda.

*   *   *

German views will be decisive in determining who will be in the EU in 20 years' time. They will also be decisive in determining what the EU will do.

The starting point for any examination of this aspect of the EU's future must be the euro. This will be the central preoccupation of any future German government, just as it is of the current one. The survival of the euro as a strong and stable currency is of existential importance for Germany. So Germany's main aim in its European policy will be to consolidate the regime of stability for the euro which was initiated by the 2013 Fiscal Treaty. By contrast with this fundamental requirement anything else on the European agenda is of secondary importance.

German insistence on strict adherence to the terms of the Fiscal Treaty will continue. Germany will also seek to add to the disciplines already in place more EU supervision of eurozone countries' budgetary policies and, if possible, of other policies relevant to the competitiveness of their economies. Any future disbursements from the EU's Stability Mechanism should, in the German view, be heavily dependent on the acceptance by recipients of more intrusive surveillance by the Commission of the way they manage their economic affairs.

The majority of eurozone governments support this approach. Some, like Finland and the Netherlands, because they would be likely to be net contributors to the Stability Mechanism rather than beneficiaries from it; others, like Spain and Ireland, because having been through the pain themselves they would not want others to be given a softer ride.

Not everyone supports it. France and Italy, at least under socialist administrations, argue for a different approach. Although they accept the Fiscal Treaty, to which they are of course signatories, they claim they need more time to implement its provisions and more flexibility in interpreting its requirements.

Hence the concern on the part of the German government at the appointment in 2014 of Pierre Moscovici as the member of the Commission responsible for economic and financial affairs. Before his appointment Moscovici had been for two years the finance minister in the French government, a period in which it became clear that France was not, as agreed with the Commission, going to reduce its deficit to 3 per cent of GDP by 2015. The prospect of a senior representative of one of the euro 'sinners' being responsible for the monitoring of the Fiscal Treaty gave rise to negative comment in Berlin. Both Wolfgang Schäuble, the finance minister, and Sigmar Gabriel, the economics minister, criticised the choice on the grounds that it sent the wrong signal to have someone from a struggling country in charge of such a key portfolio. There was some relief that Moscovici's freedom of manoeuvre would be circumscribed by the appointment of the former Finnish prime minister, Jyrki Katainen, as vice president of the Commission with broader responsibilities which included the field of economic policy.

So long as France and Italy have difficulties in meeting their Fiscal Treaty targets German worries over the euro will continue. It seems unlikely, though, that over the long term this will give rise to any change in the EU's policy. At the margins there will be arguments over the speed of adjustment required in particular countries, and no doubt there will be calls for certain types of public expenditure to be discounted in the calculation of a deficit. Judgements may be made by the Commission or by the European Central Bank of which German fiscal hawks will disapprove. From time to time the European Central Bank may take measures, such as its recourse in the summer of 2014 to a form of quantitative easing, which will be criticised by monetary purists. Overall, however, the management of the euro is likely for the next 20 years to proceed broadly along the lines which Germany has prescribed.

This is not just because of the power which Germany exercises within the EU. It is also because the German prescription reflects both EU law and EU culture. The rules of budgetary discipline are clearly enshrined in the Fiscal Treaty; both the European Commission and the European Central Bank, who are responsible for monitoring and implementing the euro's rules, are historically committed to doing so in a rigorous fashion.

Greece posed a particular challenge. Despite the settlement reached in 2015, it is still unclear whether Greece will stay in the euro and if so on what terms. The problems which Greece faces are inherited from the past, from a time when there was no external control over budgets or deficits, no proper supervision of banks and no verification of national statistics.

Under the regime of the Fiscal Treaty all this has, in principle at any rate, changed. Banks are better capitalised and supervised. Governments are obliged to open their books and, most importantly, are committed to living within their means. There is a stability mechanism in place to deal with banks or governments which face problems. The transition to this happy state of German-inspired rectitude has been difficult and has taken longer than originally envisaged. But, with the exception of Greece, every member state of the euro is on the right path. Once the goal is reached – i.e. when everyone's debts and deficits are within the prescribed limits – then it is, again in principle, just a matter of maintaining cruising speed.

So could nothing ever go wrong again? If it did, how would a German-led EU respond?

Nothing in Europe is impossible. Politics and personalities change. Sudden crises can take hold. Now that the legal regime is in place, though, eurozone countries who are unable or unwilling to comply with it face an uncomfortable choice. They are liable to sanctions of up to 1 per cent of their GDP if they fail to meet their targets and even, in the last resort, of expulsion from the euro altogether. In the latter case they would find it impossible to borrow money on the market at anything other than a cripplingly high rate.

Would the Commission in such circumstances really have the nerve to enforce the letter of the law?

In the case of a small country they probably would. Losing a member state like Greece or Portugal in this way would be damaging to the euro's prestige, but probably not to its market credibility. Germany would regret such a development, but would almost certainly go along with it if this is what the Commission proposed.

France, Spain or Italy would be a different case. France is already falling behind in its deficit-reduction programme. The Commission has done nothing about it. When challenged as to why France was allowed to get away with ignoring the rules, the Commission's president, Jean-Claude Juncker, simply shrugged and said, 'Because it's France.' Things might, however, be different if a major country consistently flouted the rules and as a result got into such difficulties that it needed a bail-out.

How Germany would react in such a situation would depend on the circumstances of the crisis and on the extent to which specifically German interests, such as the exposure of German banks, were involved. In 1992 the German government was prepared to accept the departure of the United Kingdom and Italy from the European Exchange Rate Mechanism because it was unwilling to make any financial sacrifice in order to ease the pressure on their currencies. The consequences were politically unwelcome, but did not involve damage to Germany's own economic interests.

In 2011 Germany did agree to bail-outs for Greece, Portugal and Ireland in order to keep them in the euro. This was because the alternative – a default or a debt restructuring – would have carried economic penalties for Germany itself. The three countries had borrowed recklessly, but it was German (and to a lesser extent French) banks which had equally recklessly lent them the money. Many of these banks were the small to medium-sized regional *Landesbanken*, in some cases partly in public ownership.

The German government's political priority was to ensure that these banks did not have to take a financial hit. So, rather than allowing the three countries to be relieved of any part of their debt, and thus to have the opportunity to pursue economic policies not so critically constrained by the need to repay it, Germany chose to support the option of a bail-out mechanism linked to a severe austerity programme.

Whether this was a wise choice is disputed. Even in Germany some commentators argued that it was short-sighted of the German government to privilege its banks in this way and that they should have been required to take at least a bit of a haircut (to use the jargon) as the price for their irresponsibility. Instead the government saw the national interest as safeguarding the banks from any loss.

In theory the EU is now protected from a recurrence of the banking crisis of 2008. New supervisory rules are in place and tough requirements have been imposed on banks' liquidity and reserves as well as on certain aspects of their behaviour. Taken together with the provisions of the Fiscal Treaty on member states' debts and deficits, these rules ought to ensure that irresponsible lending and borrowing are avoided or at any rate are identified in time for corrective action to be taken.

Of course the existence of rules and commitments is no guarantee that they will be obeyed or honoured. Within a year or two of the introduction of the euro several of its members, including Germany, were in breach of the 3 per cent deficit limit which was supposed to apply to its member states' budgets. And in 2014 France, having previously undertaken to reduce its deficit to 3 per cent by 2015, announced that it would be unable to do so until at least a year later. The Commission, and Germany, expressed mild disappointment but did not protest too much.

Overlooking a small slippage in a timetable is not the same as accepting a fundamental change of policy. Where France or Italy are concerned, Germany will show more understanding of political difficulties than it would in the case of Portugal or Greece. What it will not do, however, is to rewrite the Fiscal Treaty on their behalf – not least because German public opinion would not allow it.

Germany may not always be governed by a CDU or CDU-led administration. The SPD has recovered in the past from a seemingly permanent decline in popular support and may well do so again. The taboo on co-operation with Die Linke may not last for ever. The personal dominance of Angela Merkel in German politics tends to obscure the fact that for the last ten years the overall political balance in Germany has been more left- than right-inclined.

The rise of the AfD means that no German government can ignore the realities of German public opinion. The worries which the AfD's voters have about the euro and about the intrusiveness of EU legislation are shared more widely among the German electorate. They are not going to disappear, whatever happens to the AfD itself.

Germany is not in future going to agree to debt write-offs or to bail-outs for countries who are unable or unwilling to live within the Fiscal Treaty's constraints. Some form of debt relief for Greece – probably an extension of repayment times, rather than a write-off – may well be required in the short term to cope with the debt burden which the country has inherited from the past. But no German government is likely to be willing thereafter to grant bail-outs or debt relief to another eurozone member which flouts the rules and falls on hard times. It will also view with extreme scepticism calls for forms of credit sharing, such as eurobonds, which would leave Germany indirectly liable for the borrowing of others.

Above all, Germany will not extend in any meaningful way the size of the EU's budget. The mantra of no transfer union will continue, and ideas for new EU funds to help member states cope with unemployment or infrastructure investment will be given the shortest of shrifts.

The EU's overall financial envelope for the period from 2014 until 2020 is established at a level which involved virtually no change in real terms from the one which preceded it. The British prime minister, David Cameron, made clear during the discussions in 2013 that he would not in any circumstances agree to an increase; since unanimity is required to raise the EU's revenues, he could not be outvoted. To the dismay of the European Parliament, he was strongly supported by Angela Merkel as well. In the past the position of a German government in such a situation would have been to shelter behind Britain and the other budgetary hawks but to urge the need for some kind of compromise. On this occasion things were different. Angela Merkel made it clear that she supported the British position (as did the Dutch, Swedish and Finnish governments) and that, as far as Germany was concerned, the EU would have to live within its existing means.

The German approach in the run-up to 2020 is unlikely to be any different. Without the UK Germany will, on the basis of the present budgetary arrangements, be an even bigger net contributor than it is now. The pressure from public opinion will be to reduce this contribution, not to add to it. There will be arguments about whether the shortfall caused by Britain's departure should be made up by compensatory additional payments from other member states or whether the overall size of the whole budget should be reduced. Whatever the Commission or the Parliament may demand, there seems little chance of Germany agreeing to any increase.

So the likelihood is that in 20 years' time the size of the EU's budget will in real terms be pretty similar to what it is today. It currently represents around 1 per cent of the EU's GDP. By contrast the federal budget of the United States is around 20 per cent.

Even 1 per cent of GDP represents a lot of money – around 140 billion euros. It allows for significant financial interventions in certain policy areas (the EU is the biggest single provider of development aid in the world). But it is far removed from the critical mass required of a body with pretensions to becoming any kind of superstate.

The limited size of the EU's budget will also constrain its content. The policy areas which dominate the spending of individual member states – social security, health care, education or defence, for example – will not feature in it at all or only marginally. Agriculture is likely to remain the biggest single item of expenditure – not because of its intrinsic importance, but because it will remain the only significant spending policy to be conducted exclusively, or at least mainly, at European level.

This is not to say that there will be no change at all to the ways in which the EU spends its money. There is a strong intellectual case, for example, for adjusting its regional fund in such a way that only the poorer member states benefit from it. There is scope for a shift of priorities in expenditure on research and on infrastructure projects. Even agriculture may one day be subject to serious reform. But the budget is not going to become an instrument with major macroeconomic impact.

It will still no doubt generate political controversy. The European Parliament, the majority of whose members link the importance of their institution to the amount of money it spends, will continue to argue for more of everything. The arguments between the net contributors and the net beneficiaries will resume every five years when it is time to negotiate the next financial framework.

Even so, a reasonable hypothesis would be one of little significant change: a budget of around 1 per cent of EU GDP; a hodge-podge of expenditure areas with little in common with each other; agriculture the biggest single item; Germany the biggest net contributor and Italy a constant complainant.

* * *

Germany may be firmly opposed to a bigger EU budget, but it does want the EU to have more power in relation to national budgets within the eurozone. Finance Minister Wolfgang Schäuble has argued that the Commission should be given the power to enforce the application of the Fiscal Treaty in the way that it has the power to enforce competition law. This would mean (presumably) that a national budget which the Commission did not approve could not legally enter into force.

Such a change would require an amendment to one of the existing EU treaties: either the EU Treaty itself or the Fiscal Treaty (assuming that after the United Kingdom's withdrawal they are still separate). There does not seem to be much appetite among Germany's partners for this. Already there are rumbles of political discontent when an elected government is obliged to submit its budget to the Commission for comment. In 2012, before the Fiscal Treaty had entered into force, the Belgian minister for social affairs, Laurette Onkelinx, asked, 'Who is this Olli Rehn?' when her country's budget received critical comments from the Commission. She demanded to know why the unelected Commissioner for Economic Affairs should have the right to pass judgement on the decision of a national government responsible to a national parliament.

This is precisely the logic of a single currency. A year later, when Pierre Moscovici, the French finance minister, visited the Commission's headquarters to submit his country's draft budget for the following year, Olli Rehn commented, 'this is the real spirit of governance at the European level.'

Logical though it may be, the idea of giving the Commission yet more rights to tell national governments and parliaments what they can and cannot do when drawing up their budgets does not exactly resonate with public opinion. Amendment of the EU Treaty would in some member states require a referendum.

Whether the same constitutional requirement would apply to an amendment of the Fiscal Treaty is less clear, but there would be massive political pressure for one in countries such as France and the Netherlands (both of whose electorates rejected the Constitutional Treaty in referenda in 2005). Few governments would want to take the risk either of ignoring public opinion or submitting to it. The experience of the British referendum has had a chilling effect.

So perhaps the EU in 20 years' time will still be limited to the powers which it already has.

Whether these powers will be enough to preserve the euro is of course another matter. At the technical level they could. If every member of the eurozone maintains the discipline which the Fiscal Treaty prescribes, and if this discipline is enforced, then there is no reason why the euro should not maintain its position as a strong and credible currency of the kind that the Deutschmark used to be.

The social cost will continue to be huge. Countries whose economies are not as competitive as Germany's will be continually forced to deflate and to cut back on their borrowing and their public expenditure. Unemployment in Greece, Spain and Portugal will be high. France and Italy will face big political challenges. The uncertainty caused by Britain's withdrawal will make things even worse.

But there is no sign that the German government sees any need for a rethink. There has been talk among German politicians about the need to relaunch the EU now that Britain is leaving, but no precision about what such a relaunch might involve. There has certainly been no hint of readiness to look at changes to the current policy on the euro. Many serious economists predict that unless such changes occur the euro will be doomed to collapse (this is, for example, the view of Lord King, the former governor of the Bank of England). They may be wrong, as economists often are, but the German government simply refuses to address the issue.

Germany does not offer any comfort to those in other member states who are suffering the consequences of the policies which it has insisted on. It implies that it is up to their national governments to put their houses in order; Germany does not accept any responsibility. Of course Germany too has its public opinion and this does not give its government much room for manoeuvre. Still, there is something disingenuous about its position. Rejecting any element of common financial responsibility would be natural if Germany favoured a loose EU confederation of nation states. It is hard to reconcile it with advocacy of a political union.

* * *

Even if the EU does not acquire any new powers, there is still plenty it can do within those that are already there. Many of these, in areas such as the internal market, social and environment policy, directly affect the day-to-day lives of its citizens. The way that the EU has legislated in these fields has been a major factor in the decrease in its popular support. The view expressed by David Cameron that it is too interfering is widely, even if not universally, shared. Even in Germany the slogan that the EU should do less but do it better finds a ready echo.

But not in the European Commission or the European Parliament, though. Some commissioners and some EU parliamentarians occasionally make speeches in which they acknowledge that the EU has over-legislated, but they rarely identify specific directives which ought to be repealed. There has been only one case in recent years (a proposed directive on how olive oil should be served in restaurants) where the Commission has withdrawn a legislative proposal as a result of a public outcry that it was unnecessary.

The Commission has not been wholly oblivious to criticism about its over-fondness for regulation. In 2007 José Manuel Barroso, its then president, commissioned a task force under the chairmanship of Edmund Stoiber, the former minister president of Bavaria and a long-time critic of excessive EU activism, to examine ways in which the economic burden of EU laws could be reduced, particularly for small and medium-sized enterprises. Stoiber laboured away for seven years. He made a number of recommendations of a general kind about the nature of regulation and he noted that in many cases it was the way that member states transposed EU law domestically that caused problems. When he retired from the post in 2014 he claimed that there had been a breakthrough in thinking in the EU.

What Stoiber did not do, however, was identify any areas where EU regulation was not needed at all. He did not challenge, or indeed investigate, the economic consequences of social measures such as the Working Time Directive. Nor did he examine the behaviour of the European Court of Justice, whose rulings have often interpreted EU laws in a more far-reaching way than was anticipated at the time of their enactment.

And one of the key recommendations of Stoiber's task force was rejected by the Commission. He had proposed that each piece of draft legislation should, before it was approved by the Commission, be subjected to an economic impact assessment conducted by an independent and impartial body. This idea was championed by the British Prime Minister as well, but Jean-Claude Juncker firmly rejected it, arguing that the Commission was capable of conducting such assessments itself.

Perhaps it is, but it doesn't. The Commission is supposed to provide such an assessment for every piece of legislation, but it has consistently failed to do so. It never tries, for example, to examine the consequences for employment or for the viability of small and medium-sized enterprises of measures such as maternity or paternity leave or holiday entitlements. Nor does it ever offer a judgement on whether a measure to harmonise standards within the EU will have consequences for the competitiveness of EU firms in the wider world.

The reason why the Commission is unwilling to submit its proposals to independent examination is obvious. An impartial body would be likely in many instances to draw attention to the costs of Commission proposals on economic operators: not only overall but in individual member states.

The Commission is adept at drawing public attention to the benefits of its proposals when it comes to the liberalisation of markets. It is much less keen on discussing the price that has to be paid for imposing higher social or environmental standards. Allowing an outside committee or organisation to do so would be a significant impediment to the Commission's freedom of manoeuvre. There are no signs that the Juncker Commission will be any more open-minded in this respect than its predecessors.

What Juncker did do, however, was appoint the former Dutch foreign minister, Frans Timmermans, as a vice president of the Commission with responsibility for better regulation. This was hailed in some quarters as a sign that things had changed. Timmermans's first act in his new job was to demand from all his fellow commissioners a list of draft directives which had not yet been adopted and which could be withdrawn.

This review was reflected in the new Commission's work programme for 2015. The Commission emphasised what it called the principle of discontinuity, i.e. the need for an incoming Commission to review all the legislative proposals still on the table and to take its own view of whether or not to proceed with them. On this basis the Commission identified 80 proposals which it proposed to withdraw.

At first sight the number seems impressive. But in most cases the reason for withdrawing the proposed law was either that it had become redundant as a result of other legislation or because it was clear that there was no chance of its adoption because of opposition from member states. In some cases the Commission indicated that after withdrawing a proposal it would submit a different one aimed at achieving the same result. There were no cases in which the Commission concluded that the issue concerned was not one which needed to be dealt with at the European level or that the economic burden of implementing a proposed law was excessive. The Commission has so far given no indication that it is considering the repeal of any directive which is already in force.

That said, the tone of the Commission's initial work programme marked a change from what had gone before. It acknowledged that European citizens want less EU interference in their daily lives and that the EU should therefore concentrate on the big social and economic issues such as fighting unemployment and improving competitiveness. It also promised more transparency about what it is up to. There were no grandiose commitments and no lofty ideals: nothing much indeed for Eurosceptics to find fault with.

It may be that following Britain's departure the Commission will be more cautious about proposing new legislation which is likely to be controversial. It may be too that the Commission will be more focused on measures which will stimulate economic growth rather than on ones which impose economic costs. What seems unlikely is that there will be any fundamental rethink of what the EU is for.

Not even Frans Timmermans has called for this. The Commission of Jean-Claude Juncker has a declared ambition of wanting to regulate better in the future. Yet it has not shown any disposition to repatriate powers to the member states or to give up its authority in any particular area. Its 28 members have retained all the portfolios of previous commissioners. Not one of them, either in hearings before the European Parliament or in other public fora, has suggested that his or her powers should be reduced.

So a reasonable hypothesis is that in 20 years' time all the regulations and directives currently in force will remain in force. The key question is how many new ones will have been added.

* * *

From a German perspective the prime candidate for new EU legislation within the existing treaty framework is tax harmonisation. Successive German governments have argued that the EU needs a harmonised base and a minimum level for corporation tax. They also sometimes suggest that harmonised VAT rates would be desirable.

There is a case for the harmonisation of the structure of corporation tax on the grounds of efficiency. It would be easier for companies operating across the EU if they could have only one set of rules for submitting their tax returns, rather than having to use 28 separate templates. But it is striking that the business community in Germany, while acknowledging that such a change would be convenient, has never made it a particular priority.

This suggests that the real concern behind the German enthusiasm for corporation tax harmonisation relates to the rates of such tax, not to its structure. What Germany objects to is the ability of countries like Ireland and Luxembourg to attract business investment by offering low, or zero, rates of corporation tax to companies who locate their corporate headquarters or production and distribution facilities in their countries.

It is not an unreasonable concern. In 2015 the British government agreed, as part of new arrangements for the devolution of power, to grant Northern Ireland the right to set its own level of corporation tax, following years of complaint from politicians there that the lower level of corporation tax in the Irish Republic was threatening the North's economic competitiveness.

The problem is that under the current EU Treaty tax issues are decided by unanimity. This means that legislation can only be adopted if all member states perceive it as being in their interest to do so. They rarely do. Ireland, the Netherlands and Luxembourg, for example, have consistently refused to alter the low rates of corporation tax which they apply. The United Kingdom, which on an objective analysis might have benefited from some greater uniformity of practice in this area, was resolutely opposed to any EU measure in the field of direct taxation at all.

With Britain gone, the opponents of tax harmonisation will be more exposed, but they are unlikely to soften their position. It would of course be open to Germany to seek to use the so-called enhanced co-operation procedure in this area. This would mean that a limited group of member states would be authorised to introduce within an EU framework a measure which would apply only to themselves.

There is a precedent for this in the form of the Financial Transactions Tax, albeit not, from Germany's point of view, a very encouraging one. The idea of a tax on transactions between financial institutions has been around for some time. Originally, under the nickname of the Tobin tax, it was conceived as a means of increasing, on a global scale, resources for international development. In the wake of the banking crisis it was instead seen in many quarters as a means of punishing the banks and/or forcing them to compensate for the financial support which many of them had received from governments.

If applied on a genuinely global scale such a tax has many attractions. But discussions in the G8 and G20 groups of countries rapidly showed that this was not going to be possible. The United States in particular was implacably hostile to the idea.

However, in part under French and German pressure, the Commission in 2011 proposed the introduction of such a tax within the EU. Opinion in the Council was split; the United Kingdom – the country with the largest banking sector in Europe – refused to countenance a measure which would put institutions based in Britain at a competitive disadvantage compared to those elsewhere in the world. So in 2013 the Commission proposed that the tax be introduced through the mechanism of enhanced co-operation. Of the EU's then 27 members 11 agreed to go ahead on this basis. The drawbacks of such a procedure soon became apparent. Banks in the prospective participating countries expressed worries about the potential loss of business to financial centres elsewhere in the EU, particularly London.

It is still unclear whether, and if so on what terms, the Financial Transactions Tax will come into force (its introduction has been delayed several times). But it is widely regarded as something of a half-baked mess.

Harmonising corporation tax on such a basis would be even more problematic. There would be no incentive for the countries in which the rates are currently low to take part; the result would be to accentuate the differences within the EU as a whole. Understandably, Germany has never shown any interest in the idea.

Germany's best chance in recent times of securing change in this area was in the context of the Irish bail-out in 2010. Germany tried initially to insist that as a condition for receiving financial support from the EU Ireland should agree to increase its rate of corporation tax. The Irish government refused and Germany, which received no support from elsewhere for its demand, eventually dropped the idea.

It is hard to see, therefore, how Germany's goal of harmonising rates of corporation tax, and perhaps of other forms of taxation, is going to be achieved. There is currently just too much opposition to it. If it were combined with some wider political project involving a substantially larger EU budget and far-reaching resource transfers, then it might stand a chance. Germany has so far shown no signs of wanting to go down this road.

Following Britain's withdrawal, the prospects for some lesser form of corporation tax harmonisation are greater. But the most that looks achievable is agreement on a common tax base and on a (probably very low) minimum level – the sort of harmonisation which currently applies to VAT. This might eliminate the worst excesses of the regime currently applied by Luxembourg, but it would still allow each member state the freedom of action to set its own rate.

Fiscal union, like political union, is a phrase which trips easily from the lips of German politicians. They are rarely challenged as to what in practice it would mean. If what is intended is an EU in which most taxation is set centrally at rates and with structures which are common to all its participants, then, on the basis of current political realities, in 20 years' time there will be no fiscal union.

* * *

New legislation does not necessarily mean new burdens or new costs. Many of the existing directives and regulations are vehicles for opening markets, removing protectionist barriers or establishing conditions under which cross-border trade can flourish. Common standards are often ridiculed for being unnecessarily prescriptive, but it is the existence of common standards which allows goods or services from one EU member state to be sold in another.

It is natural therefore that, as new types of product become available, the Commission should, as part of its responsibility for the single market, seek to ensure that they can be traded freely and fairly. This may mean new forms of harmonisation or the application of competition law to new areas. The Commission's track record in recent years in regulating new forms of commerce is on the whole encouraging. It has, for example, pushed for the liberalisation of rules on telecommunications, while at the same time pressing the companies involved to renounce practices which were unreasonably disadvantageous to consumers. The Commission's role in lowering roaming charges for mobile phones used outside their countries of registration is just the sort of thing which public opinion wants to see it doing.

One area where the Commission will be likely to intervene more in the future is the digital economy. As more goods and services are bought online, and as more products of a digital nature appear on the market, there will be a need for common rules about how such trade operates. Ensuring an effective single market and free and fair competition in the digital field will be a significant challenge.

The commissioner initially responsible for dealing with it was a German. Günther Oettinger was appointed to the Commission in 2010. He was a middle-ranking CDU politician who had previously served for five years as minister president in Baden-Württemberg. Oettinger's portfolio in his first five years at the Commission was energy. He was generally considered to have performed competently, even if without any great flair. His main concern was to try to reduce EU member states' dependence on Russia for gas supplies, but he achieved only limited success. His main project, the Nabucco pipeline from Turkey to Austria, now seems unlikely to come to fruition.

Oettinger was reappointed to the Commission in 2014 and took the new portfolio of the digital economy. There was some surprise in Germany both at his reappointment and at his portfolio, but it probably suited Angela Merkel to have someone in Brussels who did not have too high a political profile. Oettinger did not indicate, other than in very general terms, what his priorities would be or how he envisaged achieving them and in 2016 he was moved to another position in the Commission. In supporting his appointment to the new portfolio in 2014, though, Angela Merkel probably had in mind both the opportunities and the risks which the growth of the digital economy poses for Germany.

Germany is home not only to SAP, the world's biggest provider of computer software for businesses, but also to a growing number of small entrepreneurs and start-ups. They will all stand to profit from a liberalisation of the rules for digital commerce.

The wider mood in Germany will be more cautious. The consumer protection lobby is strong, and its notion of consumer protection is not based on freedom of choice but on the imposition of stringent conditions. Any new form of commerce, whether it is longer opening hours for shops, factory outlets or the provision of car insurance online, is greeted with a degree of suspicion.

Hence the instinct of German politicians will be to try to control and regulate digital trade. This will of course be difficult, given the nature of the trade itself, but it would be unwise to assume that Oettinger's succesor will set out to break down all the barriers.

It would also be unwise to expect rapid progress in the wider provision of services. Similar suspicion applies in Germany to the provision of cross-border services. Germany does not welcome Polish plumbers – or indeed plumbers from anywhere except Germany itself. It will accept them if they are resident in Germany, have acquired the relevant German qualifications and pay German taxes and social security contributions. It will resist firmly any suggestions that a plumber from over the border in, say, Zgorzelec should be able to walk across the Neisse river bridge and ply his trade in the German town of Görlitz.

Germany is not alone in the EU in its opposition to freedom of services. In 2004 Frits Bolkestein, the then commissioner for the internal market, proposed a directive which would have limited to some degree the ability of member states to impose restrictive practices in the services field. It was greeted with a chorus of opposition from unions, interest groups, the liberal professions and governments in many member states. In Berlin 40,000 people demonstrated against it, mostly bussed in by the trade unions.

Bolkestein was accused of wanting to encourage social dumping, by allowing companies from countries with lower social security entitlements and lower contribution rates to compete with those where the benefits and the charges were higher. No one in the debates in the European Council or the European Parliament had the courage to point out that this is precisely the logic of a single market.

Eventually the proposal was emasculated to the point where it involved little change from what had gone before. It was adopted in 2006. The experience of trying, unsuccessfully, to defend it left scars on Bolkestein and his colleagues. The Commission will think more than twice before taking such a political risk again.

A further constraint on the Commission, at any rate in the short term, will be its commitment to securing the coming into force of the Transatlantic Trade and Investment Partnership. This agreement, known under its abbreviation TTIP, is an ambitious attempt to remove trade barriers between Europe and the United States. The incentive for it came about following the failure, or at least the temporary failure, of the global trade negotiations initiated under the aegis of the World Trade Organisation in Doha in 2001.

The TTIP, if achieved, would cover around 46 per cent of the world's GDP and would, according to its proponents, result in a substantial boost to the economies of both the United States and the EU. It focuses not on the traditional issues of tariffs and quotas, since these have already largely disappeared, but on other forms of trade barriers such as regulation and legal incompatibility.

The Commission was given a unanimous mandate by the Council of Ministers to negotiate such a deal (along with a parallel one with Canada) and all EU governments are therefore committed to the principle of one. But several aspects of it are politically controversial. Its opponents allege that it will encourage the role of the private sector in areas (such as health care) where governments may not wish to allow competition from private firms; that it will lower social and environmental standards; and that its provisions for dispute resolution will give excessive powers to autonomous tribunals rather than to national courts.

The treaty with Canada was signed in November 2016 following a last-minute wobble when the regional parliament of Wallonia in Belgium expressed objections. These were eventually overcome, but the experience showed how sensitive some of the issues involved in modern international trade agreements have become.

President Trump's antipathy to the Asia Pacific Trade Agreement may mean that he will suspend negotiation of the transatlantic one as well. Even under a less protectionist US president it would have been challenging for the Commission to complete the negotiations and secure the ratification of the treaty (which requires the assent of both the European Parliament and 27 national parliaments) within the next few years. Many of the sensitivities involved are similar to those which arise in the context of the liberalisation of services within the EU itself. The Commission may be reluctant to fight simultaneously on two fronts.

German governments, like British ones, have over the years supported the principle of free trade, and Angela Merkel has been unwavering in her endorsement of TTIP. Her coalition partners, the Social Democrats, have been more ambivalent. They are influenced by the German trade union movement which, somewhat to the surprise of many commentators, has come out in opposition to it.

This left the then SPD party chairman, Sigmar Gabriel, in something of a dilemma. He was, as economics minister, responsible for articulating the government's policy and, in due course, for piloting any ratification bill through the Bundestag. He knew, though, that within his party the mood was, to say the least, cautious. He therefore identified a number of red lines, relating to the use of independent arbitration procedures, which he claimed must not be crossed if Germany was to endorse the eventual deal.

Whatever the misgivings of the trade unions and others about TTIP, Germany will continue to favour an open international trading system. The principle of it is ingrained in the thinking of so much of the country's business community. But, as the trade agenda moves away from the traditional issues of tariffs on goods and into the realms of services and regulatory issues, German enthusiasm may cool a little.

Facing competition from other countries' industrial products has never been a problem for German manufacturers. They have been able to rely on improvements in quality and technical innovation to meet the challenge and they have generally succeeded. It may, however, no longer be so self-evident that Germany's interests are best served by allowing foreign companies to bid for contracts in transport, health care or insurance. This does not mean that Germany will abandon free trade. Rather, pushing further forward with it may no longer be seen as quite so vital for the German economy.

*　*　*

Of course the EU is not just about budgets and markets. Much of the rest of its agenda – social affairs, environmental issues, immigration, crime and justice, for example – is what its critics have in mind when they accuse it of being too interfering, and is what, according to public opinion surveys, most alienates its citizens.

Germany has no interest in rolling back the so-called *acquis communautaire* in any of these areas. All the legislation which is currently in force suits Germany quite well. Not surprising, since much of it was designed to replicate previously existing German practice.

Neither is there much enthusiasm in Germany for major new advances. There are no calls for new forms of social protection or social entitlement to be enshrined at the European level. Nor, other than from the Green Party, is there support for proposals for tougher environmental standards. This is partly because most German politicians now recognise that maintaining the competitiveness of German firms is more important than imposing new burdens on them. But it is partly also because the more that Europe legislates in these fields, the greater the risk of demands that the EU budget should pick up some of the bill for the costs.

So far this has not been an issue which German governments have had to take seriously. The EU has enacted all its social and environmental legislation hitherto on the basis that it is for individual enterprises or individual governments to take the responsibility for implementing it.

This might change in the future. In 2014 an article in *Trésor-Economics*, a research periodical published by the French Ministry of Finance, advocated the introduction of a eurozone unemployment insurance scheme designed to offer support from the EU's budget to countries suffering from cyclical shocks on their labour markets. The idea has not, yet, been taken up by the French government, but the prospect of such a scheme would send shivers up the spines of most German economic policy makers. It would be the thin end of a potentially very expensive wedge. If a principle were ever to be established that the EU budget should bear the financial brunt of paying for the consequences of EU social or environmental legislation, then the EU would have become a form of transfer union, something to which the vast majority of German politicians are fundamentally opposed.

So Germany will probably not be pushing for more EU action in these fields. This does not mean that nothing will happen. The European Parliament, which in recent times has been complaining about the paucity of new EU legislation, will no doubt continue to agitate for 'more Europe', and the individual commissioners responsible for social and environmental affairs will no doubt come under pressure from their officials, whose jobs depend on it, to put forward new proposals. But if Germany is cautious about anything which might have cost implications, then the Commission as a whole may well choose not to chance its arm too much.

* * *

There is one field in which change in the EU in the next 20 years is certain. This is in relation to immigration and the operation of the internal border regime. The change started in 2015 and it is driven by events over which the EU has little or no control. The combination of the Schengen Agreement and the Dublin Regulation is no longer viable. If migrants arrive in massive numbers on the EU's periphery, it is unrealistic in practice to suppose that they will all be kept there and registered. If they move on, it is unrealistic politically to allow them to choose for themselves where they settle – in particular because so many of them will choose to stay in Germany.

This dilemma became apparent in the summer of 2015. By the end of that year the Schengen regime was in semi-meltdown, with controls back in operation on many internal EU borders and fences going up on many external ones. Immigration had become a toxic political issue in several EU countries, including Germany, where in the public debate calls for humanitarian generosity had been superseded by talk of expulsion and enhanced coastguard operations.

The problem itself looks pretty intractable and it is hard to predict how a German-led EU will seek to tackle it and with what prospect of success. Since Germany's own direct interests are involved, though, this is the one area where the German government may be prepared to spend serious amounts of new money on EU programmes.

As a result there may be EU-funded holding centres for refugees in Turkey and North Africa as well as in Greece and Italy and an EU-funded coastguard force with rules of engagement which permit it to turn boats back. There will also be political pressure, accompanied by threats of reduced funding from EU aid programmes, on countries such as Albania, Algeria and Morocco to take back asylum seekers whose claims have been rejected.

What is less easy to foresee is whether Germany will continue to insist on some legally binding formula for the redistribution across the Schengen area of refugees already in Europe who cannot be returned to their countries of origin, or whether Schengen can ever be restored to its status quo ante, i.e. without any controls of any kind on its internal frontiers.

However things turn out, there will be profound changes in Germany itself. The arrival of a million immigrants in 2015 cannot now be reversed. Whatever German politicians say about the need for them to return to their home countries when conditions there improve, it is a fantasy to suppose that more than a fraction of them will do so.

Germany in 20 years' time may well be a multi-ethnic, though probably not multicultural, society with as many racially diverse faces visible in its big cities as in Britain or France. This will pose a challenge for the country's social and economic cohesion. In the past the Germans have shown themselves more capable of meeting this sort of challenge than any other nation in Europe. There is no reason why they cannot do so again.

*   *   *

On present trends a German-led Europe in 20 years' time will be characterised both by what it does and by what it does not do.

There will be more discipline within the eurozone and probably more eurozone members. There will be tighter rules for eurozone banks, and some collective arrangement for guaranteeing their solvency. There will be more common, and commonly funded, action to safeguard the EU's external borders against illegal immigration. There will be a bit more co-operation in foreign policy led by France and Germany. There will be a few more low-intensity military operations carried out in the EU's name, and there will be an EU permanent military headquarters. The Franco-German Eurocorps may rebrand itself as an EU military formation.

There will not, though, be any major new transfers of power to the centre, and there will not be any EU responsibility for the policy areas which involve big spending – social security, health care, defence, education.

In its institutional form the EU will continue to look like Germany. But the distribution of power within it will be radically different. It will not have the attributes of a federal state. It may choose to call itself a political union; this will be an issue of terminology rather than of substance.

If this is indeed how the EU evolves, it will mean the end of many dreams. If despite the euro and immigration crises of 2015 and despite the withdrawal of the United Kingdom the EU does not fundamentally change its character, then probably it is never going to. Such an EU will suit Germany well. The country's political class, or at any rate parts of it, will no doubt continue to bloviate occasionally about the need for more Europe. They will not do anything to bring it about, though, and they will be aware that the public mood is not with them.

What will be clear is that Germany's leadership of the EU is geared principally to the defence of German national interests. Germany exercises power in order to protect the German economy and to enable it to play an influential role in the wider world. Beyond that there is no underlying vision or purpose.

For the poorer members of the EU this German-led Europe will be a cold place: no resource transfers, no common credit, just budgetary rigour. But they have nowhere else to go. For France too it will be a disappointment. Even if, on occasions, a façade of Franco-German leadership is maintained it will be clear where, on internal EU issues, the real power lies. But France will be at least an equal player on the EU's foreign policy.

It will be a disappointment too for British Eurosceptics. Having conjured up the demon of an all-powerful European superstate, they will be deprived of the opportunity to say 'We told you so' to the British public.

And as for the British public itself? In 20 years' time many of them will have forgotten that Britain was ever a member of the EU. Those who voted to leave will see nothing in the development of the EU itself to make them regret their choice. Others, looking back on the referendum and the years of introspection about Europe, may wonder what all the fuss was about.

Index

271

Index